Write, If You LIVE to Get There

Ceep on diggin and live in hope!

Mary Jo Sonntag

Write, If You LIVE to Get There

Tracing Westward Expansion through 120 Years of Family Letters

Compiled and Edited By

Mary K. Sonntag
&
Mary Jo Sonntag

WORD ASSOCIATION PUBLISHERS
www.wordassociation.com
1.800.827.7903

All inquiries should be addressed to: maryjosonntag@verizon.net

Printed in the United States of America.

ISBN: 978-1-59571-898-3
Library of Congress Control Number: 2013911923

Designed and published by

Word Association Publishers
205 Fifth Avenue
Tarentum, Pennsylvania 15084

www.wordassociation.com
1.800.827.7903

Contents

Acknowledgements

I would like to thank those family members who, over the past 75 years, have provided source material on the Phillips family.

I am grateful to my Aunt Rebecca McConahy's genealogical research to establish her mother's credentials for membership in the Daughters of 1812 and the Daughters of the American Revolution (DAR). She contacted her cousin, Joseph Fields, Relief Phillips Field's son, a Presbyterian minister who had written a family history.

During the span of years between the 1930s and the 1960s Harriet Davis Gibson wrote to Rebecca McConahy, Myrtle McConahy Keefer, and me about her travels to meet family members in New England and Utah. Her reflections added a great deal to our understanding of the family's movements around the country. She was the great-granddaughter of Wells Davis, the granddaughter of Amos Davis and the daughter of George and Harriet Andrews Davis.

Paula C. Alger, of Derry, New Hampshire, provided extensive information on the Davis line. I found her by answering a 1998 ad in *Yankee Magazine* seeking information about Wells Davis. Paula's husband is a descendant of Martha Jane Davis, child of Wells and Abigail Dodge Davis.

My mother, Myrtle McConahy, did enough research on the family to gain admission to the Daughters of the American Revolution (DAR) and the Daughters of American Colonists (DAC). The ancestral records of Moses Chase, in his Majesty's service, provided her entry to the DAC, and that of her great grandfather, Elisha Phillips, to the DAR. Supposedly, she was going to join the Mayflower Society on the basis of her colonist ancestor, John Alden, but I can't verify this.

I want to extend my heartfelt thanks to Holly Van Dine for her invaluable help organizing this material and helping tell the story.

Last but not least, I am indebted to my daughter Mary Jo Sonntag for her hard work and persistence in pursuing this project, including prodding me to keep at it.

Mary K. Sonntag
January 2013

Prologue

Discovering Family Treasures
by Mary K. Sonntag

My mother, Myrtle McConahy Keefer, died in 1962. As her only child, I inherited a white wooden chest filled with family memorabilia—fragile old letters, deeds to property, and jewelry. I tucked away my mother's old chest (an inheritance from her mother, Mary Phillips McConahy) while I raised my family.

Then, in 1992 my daughter, Mary Jo, had a business trip to Sacramento. She said she would like to explore the Placerville, California area—the center of the Phillips family history. I told her to look for the Phillips plot in Union Cemetery. She found not only the plot but also the grave of my Great Uncle Dan Phillips. When Mary Jo returned home we agreed that the two of us had to return to Placerville. That inspired me to pull out the white wooden chest.

I spent the next year going through the hundreds of letters written by members of the Phillips family and their friends, starting in 1842 and continuing through the turn of the century. Most of the letters were from Great Uncle Dan Phillips and the family of Joseph Wells Davis Phillips, my grandmother's oldest brother.

Happily for us, this family kept in close touch as they migrated from Vermont and Pennsylvania to Illinois, Colorado, Kansas and California, leaving detailed, personal accounts of everyday life in American during the late19th and early 20th centuries. They wrote about health and disease, births and deaths, the difficulties of making a living, the price of crops—central issues of any age. They were people I liked. They showed considerable curiosity and courage, they worked hard and took big risks to improve their lives, and they stayed in touch with one another.

In May 1993, Mary Jo and I headed off to Northern California. Our trip followed a trail of places mentioned by Great Uncle Dan in his letters, as well as locations my mother and grandmother had visited in 1907 -1908. It was pouring rain on Memorial Day when we visited the giant Sequoias in Calaveras State Park. The ranger laughed when he took our money. We had the place to ourselves and hiked around under umbrellas calling it quits in the Visitor's Center. While wandering in the gift shop, Mary Jo casually picked up a book.

"Mother," she said, "isn't this your mother's cousin?"

And there it was: the story of Sierra Nevada [Vade] Phillips. She is the subject of one whole chapter in *Women of The Sierra* by Anne Seagraves. This was exciting to us because it meant some family members must have supplied the author with information about Vade. We took note of Evelyn Myers name as a potential contact. Later, when we visited Great Uncle Dan's grave in Placerville, we noticed fresh flowers near the family obelisk, so we knew there must be active family in the area. We contacted the cemetery manager, and he said to come back after the Memorial Day holiday.

So, on we went to another cemetery in Donner Pass where, amazingly, according to family letters, Vade had successfully persuaded a small family group to vacation one winter. With the help of a caretaker, we located the two unmarked graves in the old section where Ida Meloche, Vade's sister, and her son, John Meloche (who was raised by Vade after Ida died), were buried. It was a beautiful spot, on top of a mountain, with scenic mountains all around.

Later that day we arrived at Meeks Bay where, in the summer of 1908, my mother and grandmother helped the Murphy family run the resort. The owner introduced us to Carol Van Etten, an author writing a history of the resort called *Meeks Bay Memories*. She had not been able to find much information about the resort prior to 1920, so we came to her rescue with our letters and photos.

While I talked to Carol, Mary Jo called the El Dorado Historical Museum. Its director, Denis O'Rourke-Witcher, asked if we had any idea how important the Phillips family was in El Dorado County history. We were beginning to get the idea! He suggested we drive to Placerville on Route 50 and visit Phillips Station below Echo Summit, where there is a historical marker, a family cemetery and several original cabins. We were thrilled, of course. A mudslide delayed us a bit that day, but as we waited for the road to be cleared, a beautiful rainbow appeared. Mary Jo said it was a sign our ancestors were smiling down on us.

Denis and his staff asked if we had talked to Sally, but I had no idea who "Sally" was. My mother had corresponded for years with Alice Bryson, Vade's youngest daughter, and I knew that she had three daughters, Betty, Jane, and one other whose name I didn't know. Shirley Pont, a museum volunteer, said that "Sally" was actually Evelyn Myers (the woman mentioned in the book we found at Sequoia!) who was Alice's youngest daughter. Shirley gave me Sally's phone number.

"Do you remember a woman from Western Pennsylvania who corresponded with your mother for many years -- Myrtle McConahy Keefer?" I asked Sally/Evelyn. "I'm her daughter. I'm down at the El Dorado Historical Museum and I'd like to meet you."

Sally said, "I'll be there in ten minutes."

We had a wonderful meeting that lasted hours past closing time. The museum was being remodeled, so we sat together in the back room amid the sounds of saws and hammers. We talked about our mothers and other relatives, and who of the family was still in the area. We looked at pictures and examined books containing articles about the Phillips family. We told Sally about finding Ida's grave (her family had searched for years and not found it), as well as our meeting with Carol Van Etten at Meeks Bay (Sally later contacted her and contributed information to the book).

Sally said they still owned 107 acres at Phillips Station and were working hard to keep it in the family. Of the original 160 acres, some had been appropriated for Route 50, some more taken for a ski resort in the 1930's, and in the depression years, even more was sold for housing. The U.S. Forest Service has the right of eminent domain over the land even though the family owns the land and has cabins there. The property's prized possession is the 20-acre meadow that holds the source of the American River. Mary Jo and I were flying home the next day, so my time with Sally was short. But we never quit talking. I learned that Vade's granddaughter, Louise Sickles Day (87 years old and still living in Marin County), had established a trust fund in honor of the five women who had worked their whole lives to save Phillips Station. The Phillips heirs will be able to maintain the Phillips' property in perpetuity.

Sally and I parted reluctantly but with pleasure at our meeting, and we promised to keep in touch.

Final Meetings 1995

In June 1995 Mary Jo and I visited Sally again. In the intervening years since our first meeting, I had transcribed some seventy-five letters, most of them exchanges between the families in Western Pennsylvania and Northern California dated between 1842 and 1962. I had also begun a correspondence with Louise Sickles Day. Louise had worked on Phillips family stories and sent me a wealth of information before she died in November 1994. I looked forward to sharing the information with Sally.

Much had happened in Sally's life since our last visit. She had spent the past year in treatment for colon cancer. And sadly, her son, Rodney, had died of a heart attack while at a lawyer's convention in Monterey. He was only 45 years old.

When we pulled into the driveway of Sally's house, Mary Jo said, "I've been here before! In 1992, I walked past this house to enter that old pioneer cemetery."

She told Sally.

Sally said, "That's funny. When I spot people in that cemetery, I often go out and help them find graves."

Wouldn't that have been something if Sally had gone out to help Mary Jo back in 1992? We might have had the pleasure of each other's company for a bit more time.

Sally and Wally took us over Johnson Pass to Grass Lake where, in about 1859, Joseph Wells Davis (JWD) took his cattle to graze. We stopped at Phillips Station to follow the meadow back to the source of the American River. We talked about where various buildings were when Phillips Station was a resort, and how it had changed over time. Such a beautiful spot!

Sally made arrangements for us to meet with Shirley Pont from the El Dorado Historical Museum and their historian. We plied them with questions about the family and shared our old letters and pictures. We also met Sally's sister Jane who was recuperating from an illness in the hospital. She was excited to meet us and so pleased to have copies of the letters. Six years older than Sally, Jane had memories of Great Uncle Dan from the early 1930s. She kept saying that her mother was smiling down on us. It was a pleasure to meet her even under rather difficult circumstances.

Sally seemed so healthy and in great spirits when we were there, but Jane later wrote that Sally was terminally ill. She died December 31, 1995. Jane wrote several more letters, but then the letters stopped and we learned that Jane had died September 3, 1996.

It's too bad we were all so old when we met, but I'm glad we did, however briefly. These Phillips descendants were such welcoming people. They weren't strangers at all.

Saddened by the deaths of Louise, Sally, and Jane, as well as a decline in my husband's health, things Californian were once more put aside.

Back to Work

After my husband's death, I sold our house and moved to an apartment, and in 2003 Mary Jo and I started organizing our ancestors' history. I transcribed many more letters, and Mary Jo diligently typed them, carefully preserving the phonetic spelling and lack of punctuation. Sometimes the penmanship was excellent, sometimes it was quite difficult to decipher. In the end, we transcribed more than 200 letters. The result of our work is this book which we hope will be of interest to historians, other family archivists, and educators and students in women's studies programs. The entrepreneurial nature of our ancestors speaks volumes about the enterprising nature of early American women and men.

This has been a monumental task. But, through it, we have grown to know the writers and to admire them for their fortitude. Let the letters tell their stories.

The Patriarch
Revolutionary War Soldier Elisha Phillips
1755 - 1842

Rebecca McConahy (1874-1939) (our aunt and great aunt, respectively) was perhaps the first in the family to delve into the stories of our ancestors. We were lucky enough to find the written records of her research in the white wooden chest filled with family memorabilia. We think she wrote this around 1937, and since Elisha Phillips is the patriarch of the family, his background provides a fitting beginning to our exploration. In Rebecca's words…

Elisha Phillips was born February 16, 1755, in Gloucester, Rhode Island, and from there he moved to Pomfret, Connecticut, from which place he enlisted in the Revolutionary War in 1775, and served as a patriot in the army at various times from then until 1779. On December 10, 1776 he married Mary Meachem, who was born January 13, 1756, and died August 9, 1835, to whom the following children were born: Druzilla, Stephen, Asa, Michael, Joseph Meachem, Mary (Polly), Elisha, Elijah, Laura, Phoebe, and Sophia.

Elisha Phillips later moved to Vershire, Orange County, Vermont, as in his application for pension, he gives that as his address. His pension was allowed August 28, 1832. In 1837 he came to Pennsylvania with his son-in-law, Elijah Pangburn, and located in Beaver County, where his sons,

Stephen Phillips and Joseph Meachem Phillips were living. He died June 12, 1839, and was buried on the farm of his son, Joseph M. Phillips, on a knoll overlooking the Beaver River, which knoll lies between the P. & L. E. R. R. and the Baltimore & Ohio R. R., near East Moravia, now West Pittsburgh, Pa., at which place the Daughters of the American Revolution placed a stone at his grave in 1931.

The following is the military history of Elisha Phillips as shown in the Revolutionary War Record, Section V.L.M., S.F. 21423, Department of the Interior, Bureau of Pensions, Washington, D.C.:

Date of Enlistment	Length of Service	Rank	Captain	Colonel	State
1775	8 months	Pat.	Lyon	Huntington	Conn.
Summer 1776	2 months	Pat.	Kibby	Chapman	Conn.
1777	3 months	Pat.	Granger	Pease	Conn.
1778	3 months	Pat.	Lovejoy	Enos	Conn.
Fall 1779	3 months	Pat.	Felt		Conn.

The bodies of Elisha Phillips and his son Joseph Phillips were moved to an honored veteran plot on Valor Ridge in Castle View Burial Park, New Castle, PA. Lydia Davis is not shown on the burial list at Castle View Burial Park.

Isolated Graves Mark Last Resting Place of Soldier of 1775 and Son

Where the Beaver River winds around in a double "S" curve, in Taylor Township, just east of the P. & L.E. railroad bridge there is a peculiarly shaped hill. Like some blunt nosed promontory it sticks out to the riverbank and drops almost sheer to the water.

On the top of this odd shaped hill lie the remains of two soldiers of the United States, one Elisha Phillips, a soldier of the Revolution, the other Joseph Phillips, his son, a soldier of the War of 1812.

One might pass the spot for years without ever knowing the existence of the graves. Giant sycamore trees stand as waterfront sentinels down the hill from the graves, while in the immediate vicinity are a few oaks, and a dense matting of underbrush. To get to the graves from a highway means a hike for a quarter of a mile through weeds and burrs, and underbrush that traps the legs and seems to be attempting to hold you back.
(1931)

Marked by D.A.R.

Once on the top of the hill, the stone markers on the graves can be found. Both the stones were placed there some time ago by the D.A.R. Not another marker is on the hill, although some shallow depressions look as though bodies might have been removed a long time ago.

Just why the old soldiers were buried in this desolate spot is not known even to the man who now owns the hill and the property surrounding it, Joseph Isabella. He believes it was once an old graveyard. Residents in Taylor Township have a legend that it was once an Indian cemetery but this story seems to have little basis.

It might have been the burying ground on a private farm for about three hundred yards away are some gnarled old apple trees that might be the last remnants of a farmstead.

If there once were any homes or buildings close by, the day is long since gone. Wind swept and rain drenched, the last resting spots of the two old heroes are alone in their splendid location. Below them the murmur of the Beaver as it lazies down to meet the Ohio. Above them only the cry of the birds. The only touch of modernity is the railroad about 100 yards away.

Connecticut Yankee

…Should vandals ever steal the markers or the D.A.R. targets marking the graves, the burial places of the two men would soon be lost for the underbrush grows fast.

The paths of glory may lead but to the grave, but the graves certainly should be some place where a grateful people could pay proper reverence.
(1931)

Early Heroes Are Reinterred
Remains of Elisha and Joseph Phillips Removed from Old Cemetery

No more will the remains of Elisha and Joseph Phillips lie in a forgotten spot in Lawrence County. On Tuesday afternoon the remains of the two heroes, father and son, were interred in Castle View Burial Park, inside the old fortress on Valor Ridge.

For years their remains laid in lonely graves in what was once an old cemetery south of West Pittsburgh on a hill overlooking the Beaver River. Their descendants recently petitioned to have their remains removed to Castle View and this was done. A short service was held at the graveside with Rev. J. M. Cottrell offering prayers.

Elisha Phillips was born in 1755 and served with a Connecticut regiment in the Revolution. His son Joseph was born in 1788 and served in the War of 1812.

The remains of the two men were remarkably well preserved. One of the leg bones of Elisha Phillips showed that the leg had been broken, and that nature had apparently healed it up without much assistance from man.
(1936)

Where We Pick
Up the Story

The earliest of all the letters we found in the family chest were written between 1842 and 1858 and center on the lives of my great grandmother, Lydia Davis Phillips, and her nine children.

In 1837, Lydia and her husband, Joseph Meachem Phillips, and their five children (JWD, Charles, Lydia, Relief, and Amoret) traveled by oxen team from a farm in Vermont to East Moravia, Pennsylvania (now West Pittsburgh) in what was then Beaver County. They were headed for property near Joseph's brother, Stephen Phillips, who owned 101 acres along the Ohio River and who, among other activities, operated a boatyard. Joseph and Lydia's new farm was located above the Beaver River (near an area called Hardscrabble because canal boats had difficulty getting over the riffles on the river).

I some times think I shall see some of my friends in Vermont but as our lives are uncertain we know not what a day may bring forth.

—Lydia Davis Phillips, 1844

Freedom Boatyard was once Famous, as told by Rebecca McConahy

Once famous along the Ohio River for the 108 splendid riverboats and barges constructed there, the old Freedom boatyard was the first industrial enterprise in the valley community whose 100th anniversary was observed August 21, 1902.

Succeeding Stephen Phillips (brother of Joseph Meachem Phillips) and Jonathan Betz, who had engaged in the boat building industry at Phillipsburg, now Monaca, Stephen Phillips and John Graham purchased 101 acres of land along the Ohio River at Freedom from General Abner Lacock, and established a boatyard there in 1832. The land purchased for $2,000 was intended as a site for a town. In the ensuing four days fourteen houses were erected at the site. The boatyard occupied three acres of land, which, with buildings thereon was valued at $638 for taxation purposes.

Stephen Phillips, son of Elisha Phillips and Mary Meachem Phillips was born Friday, November 26, 1779. He probably came to Western Pennsylvania in 1813 and settled at Phillipsburg, now Monaca, where he engaged in the boat building business. Later he moved across the Ohio River and continued in the boat building business. He was drowned off the steamer Poe on the Ohio River at Wheeling, West Virginia on his passage home from Portsmouth, Ohio on November 17, 1855. His body was never recovered. He was married to Rhoda Parsons, who was born Friday, October 25, 1782, and died at Freedom, PA, March 1, 1861.

Lydia and Joseph's children included Amoret Phillips, the daughter of Joseph's first wife Relief Childs, who died in 1820. Amoret married John

Henry, of Mt. Jackson, Pennsylvania in 1840. That same year Lydia's seventh child, Alden Church, was born and Daniel Davis arrived a year later. Lydia and Joseph welcomed their ninth and last child, Mary, on February 13, 1846. Mary was my grandmother and owner of the family memorabilia chest.

Lydia seemed to have a very generous and caring nature. This remembrance from Rebecca McConahy speaks volumes:

> A mother left a six-week-old baby boy at the home of Mrs. Lydia Davis Phillips near East Moravia about May 1st, 1852. The mother stated that she was hunting for work and would come back for the baby when she found a job. She never came back. Lydia Davis Phillips raised the baby as her own son. He was known among his schoolmates as Willard Phillips.
>
> The baby's birth name was Willard Martin and his mother was Mary Moulton. He was born in Freedom, PA on Monday, March 22, 1852. Willard drowned on March 6, 1867 while skating on the pond at the Tindall schoolhouse where he attended school, aged 14 years, 11 months, 11 days.

[Note: Rebecca wondered if Mary Moulton was a descendant of Druzella Phillips Moulton. Druzella was the eldest daughter of Elisha Phillips and Mary Meachem and the sister of Joseph Wells Phillips.]

In 1846, Lydia and Joseph's oldest boy, Joseph Wells Davis, known as JWD, left home first for Illinois and then the western frontier. He married Mehitable Jane Ball, and together they followed the Gold Rush migration to California in 1851, acquiring property and raising two daughters, Sierra Nevada (b.1854) and Ida (b.1858). The turn-of-the-century correspondence centering on Sierra (known as Vade) forms the middle section of this collection.

After her husband's death in 1849, Lydia stayed on the farm with the children, some of whom were still school age. The Methodist Church was an important part of all their lives.

Lydia's second son Charles Carroll married Elizabeth Lutton in 1854 and moved to a home near his mother in East Moravia. Soon the other children started to move away:

Lydia Maria [mah-RYE-uh] married James Henry Pollack and moved to Illinois. Amoret and Henry moved to Arcola, Illinois, where their family grew to nine children.

JWD, reached California early in the1850s, but moved back east in 1857 because Mehitable Jane was so homesick. The siren call of California beckoned, however, and the family returned in 1858. Their epic trip through the Panama Canal is remembered by Louisa Sickles Day in 1994 and is included in the chapter, Leaving Moravia.

In 1870, Lydia Davis Phillips was buried on the farm joining her father-in-law, Elisha and her husband, Joseph. She was to have been moved to Castle View Burial Park along with Elisha and Joseph, however, the cemetery has no record of her grave. She must be alone on the farm.

Phillips Family Chronology
1755 - 1998

Elisha Phillips (1755- 1839) was born in Gloucester, Rhode Island, and from there he moved to Pomfret, Connecticut. On December 10, 1776 he married **Mary Meachem**, who was born January 13, 1756, and died August 9, 1835.

Children: Druzilla, Stephen, Asa, Michael, Joseph Meachem, Mary (Polly), Elisha, Elijah, Laura, Phoebe, Sophia

Elisha Phillips later moved to Vershire, Orange County, Vermont. In 1837 he left for Pennsylvania with his son-in-law, Elijah Pangburn (who was married to Elisha's daughter, Laura Phillips), and located in Beaver County, where his sons, Stephen Phillips and Joseph Meachem Phillips were living.

Joseph Meachem Phillips (1788-1849) married his first wife, **Relief Childs**, May 13, 1798. Relief Childs died July 8, 1820, leaving to survive her one daughter, Amoret Phillips. In 1825, Joseph Meachem Phillips married **Lydia Davis**, daughter of Wells Davis and Mary "Polly" Kelly, of West Fairlee, Orange County, Vermont.

Children: **1826:** Mary died in infancy, **1827:** Joseph Wells Davis Phillips, **1829:** Charles Carroll Phillips, **1831:** Lydia Maria [mah-RYE-uh] Phillips, **1833:** Relief, **1835:** Henry, died at 11 months, **1837:** Alden Church Phillips **1839:** Daniel Davis Phillips, **1846:** Mary Louisa Phillips

****

1837   Family moved by oxen team to Western Pennsylvania and settled on a farm near East Moravia, now West Pittsburgh. Amoret Phillips (born 1819) was part of this family.

Amoret Phillips married John Henry in Mt. Jackson, PA. They had nine children.

1849   Joseph Meachem Phillips died and was buried on the family farm in East Moravia.

1850   Lydia Maria Phillips married James Harvey Pollock.

1851   Joseph Wells Davis Phillips (JWD) married Mehitable Jane Ball in Quincy, Illinois, took passage on the ship *Northern Light* to San Francisco, CA, and settled in Nevada City. Esther, who was Mehitable Jane's daughter from her first marriage, was with them.

Children: **1854:** Sierra Nevada "Vade" Phillips, **1858:** Ida May Phillips Meloche (buried with her son John in unmarked graves at the cemetery in Truckee in the old section, plots 45-5 and 45-7)

1854   Charles Carroll Phillips married Elizabeth Lutton.

Children: **1855:** Relief, **1857:** Joseph, **1859:** Audley, **1861:** William, **1863:** Bessie, **1866:** Mary, **1870:** Charles, **1872:** George, **1876:** Evra

1857 Amoret and John Henry moved their family to Arcola, Illinois.

JWD and Mehitable Jane moved back east.

1858 JWD and Mehitable Jane returned to California and began renting the property at Phillips Station as a way station.

1862 JWD and family purchased 160 acres at Phillips Station from A. E. Clark for $2,000.

1863 Lydia Maria Pollock and family moved to Illinois and settled at Foosland. She and her husband had eight children – seven sons and one daughter.

Children: **1851:** David Wells Pollock, **1853:** Joseph Phillips Pollock, **1855:** Samuel Pollock, **1858:** Robert Martin Pollock, **1860:** Charles Pollock, **1863:** Milton DeWitt Pollock, **1866:** Grant Pollock, **1869:** Emma Pollock

1865 Relief Phillips married Cyrus Fields on October 26 and lived in Little Beaver Township, Lawrence County, PA, not far from Enon Valley.

Children: **1866:** Ira Phillips Fields, **1868:** Mary Lydia Fields, **1872:** Joseph Cyrus Fields

1867 Charles Carroll Phillips and his family moved to Illinois.

1868 Phillips family farm in East Moravia was sold. Pending their move to Illinois, Lydia and Mary lived with Relief and Cyrus Fields. Lydia Davis Phillips, her son Daniel, and daughter, Mary moved to Ashkum, Illinois. Daniel was living in Illinois where his Uncle Amos Davis lived.

Alden Church Phillips joined JWD's family in California.

1869   Alden Church Phillips died in California from internal injuries inflicted when a dog spooked the horse he was riding.

1870   Mary Phillips returns to the home of Relief Fields in Western Pennsylvania near Enon Valley from Illinois with her mother Lydia, who was ill. Lydia died here. Daniel remained in Illinois.

Phillips Station was leased to John Sweeney.

1871   After visiting relatives in Vermont, Mary Phillips returned to Western Pennsylvania.

1872   Mary Phillips married Joseph Hennon McConahy on June 11.

Children: **1873:** Lydia Mabel, **1874:** Rebecca, **1876:** William Charles, **1879:** Relief, **1883:** Wells, **1886:** Mary Myrtle

1872   After living in Illinois and Kansas near or with various relatives, Daniel joined JWD in California.

1873   Phillips Station burns for the first time.

1874   Charles Carroll Phillips went to Kansas and later to Victor, Colorado where he mined gold.

1876   Phillips Station burns for the second time.

1879   Mehitable Jane Clark was born at Glenbrook, NE. She was known as Hetty or Hettie.

1881   Relief Fields died near Enon Valley, PA.

1886   Vade Clark bought Rubicon Springs resort.

Lotus post office established.

1889   JWD Phillips died at his home near Johnstown, CA.

1895   Robert and Milton Pollock graduated from medical school.

Samuel Pollock graduated from dental school.

Joseph Hennon McConahy died at home in Ellwood City, PA.

Amoret Phillips Henry died in Arcola, Illinois.

1898   Vade Phillips Clark married James Bryson.

1899   Charles Carroll Phillips died in Victor, Colorado.

Alice Bryson was born (Vade's daughter).
James Harvey Pollock died in Foosland, IL.

1900   Wells McConahy worked his way across the country and disappeared in California. It is not known what happened to him.

Vade sold Rubicon Springs Resort to Daniel Abbott.

1901   Vade operated the Inn at Tahoe City.

Hettie Clark (Vade's daughter) married Frank Sickles.

1902   Wells Sickles was born.

Relief McConahy married S. A. (Bert) Hartung of Beaver Falls, PA.

1903   Lydia Maria Pollock died in Foosland, Illinois.

Jurgens post office established.

Esther Doss (Vade's half-sister) died in Petaluma, CA.

John Meloche (Ida Phillips' son, raised by Vade) died of tuberculosis.

1904   Vade leased Rubicon Springs from Daniel Abbott and ran the resort until 1908.

Charles Hartung was born.

1905   Lydia McConahy married Ralph Brown and moved to Swissvale, PA.

Myrtle McConahy contracted typhoid fever.

Louise Sickles was born.

1906 Mehitable Jane Phillips died in Sparks, Nevada.

Myrtle McConahy and her mother, Mary Phillips McConahy, went to California and stopped in Colorado on the way to visit the Pollock's in Rocky River.
Late summer, Vade, Myrtle McConahy, Mary Phillips McConahy, and Dan Phillips stayed at Rubicon Springs.

Myrtle lived at Meeks Bay and Phillips Station but did not work there. Her mother, Mary, worked there.

1907
-08 Winter: the family (Vade, Myrtle McConahy, Mary Phillips McConahy, Dan Phillips) stayed at the ranch at Garden Valley.

1908 Summer at Meeks Bay.

Myrtle in Denver where she worked at the Denver Dry Goods to earn money for her return to Pennsylvania. She stayed with Elizabeth Lutton (Charles Phillips' wife).

Florence Hartung was born.
Vade returned to Phillips Station and rebuilt the resort.

Mary Phillips McConahy returned to Western Pennsylvania in the fall because her daughter Lydia was ill.

Ralph Cowell of Moana Villa purchased Rubicon Springs Hotel.

1909 October – Mary Phillips McConahy returned to California with Lydia and her son, Cecil. They stayed at Sea Bright, Santa Cruz, and Galt.

Myrtle returned to Western Pennsylvania.

1910 Mary Phillips McConahy and Lydia at Galt.

1912 Phillips Station burned again.
Myrtle McConahy married Norman Keefer and moved to New Castle, PA.

Mary Phillips McConahy returned from Denver to Western Pennsylvania for Myrtle's wedding.

"Vade" post office named after its postmaster, Mrs. Vade Bryson.

Lydia at Bakersfield with her husband Ralph and son Cecil.

1914 Ralph Brown died in Bakersfield, CA.

Lydia at Bakersfield, CA until 1916 when she returned to Western Pennsylvania.

Jurgens post office dissolved.

1916 Grace Hartung was born.

1918 Lydia McConahy Brown married D.D. Dowds of Beaver Falls.

1919 Alice Bryson married Henry Lyon and had a daughter Betty.

1920 Mary Norma Keefer was born (Myrtle McConahy Keefer's daughter).

1921 Vade died May 28.

Mehitable Jane (Hettie) Clark Sickles and Alice Elaine Bryson Lyon inherited Phillips Station.

Mehitable (Hettie) J. Clark Sickles appointed postmaster Sept. 24.

Jane Lyon was born (Alice Bryson Lyon's daughter).

Mary Phillips McConahy and daughter Rebecca visited her family in California.

D. D. Dowds died.

1927 Evelyn "Sally" Elaine Lyon was born (Alice Bryson Lyon's daughter).

1928 Elizabeth Lutton died in Denver Colorado.

1929 Phillips Station closed. Cottages were converted into summer housekeeping cabins.

1930 Rubicon Springs sold to Sierra Power Company.

1932 Mary Phillips McConahy died in Ellwood City, PA.

1933 Daniel Phillips died in Placerville, CA.

Myrtle McConahy Keefer corresponded with Vade's youngest daughter, Alice Bryson Lyon, until Myrtle's death in 1962.

1935 James Bryson died at Visalia, CA.

1939 Rebecca McConahy died.

1942 William Charles McConahy died.

1943 Lydia Mabel McConahy Brown Dowds died.

William Charles McConahy died.

1945 Relief McConahy Hartung died.

1950s The Highway Department bought the 20 acres on the north side of Route 50 expecting to turn it into four lanes. This did not happen.

1952 Heavy snows collapsed the buildings at Phillips Station.

1953 Heavy snows collapsed the hotel at Rubicon Springs.

1961 Vade post office was closed.

1962 Myrtle McConahy Keefer died in New Castle, PA.

1983 Alice Elaine Bryson Lyon died at Echo Summit, CA

1994 Evelyn "Sally" Elaine Lyon Myers' son Rodney Lumley died.

Louise Sickles Day died.

1996 Evelyn "Sally" Elaine Myers died.

1998 Jane Brunello died.

The Early
Lydia Davis Phillips
Letters
1842 - 1858

Lydia Davis Phillips to her half-sister Mary Davis Prescott. Mary was the daughter of Wells Davis and his second wife, Abigail Dodge.

To: Mrs. Pomeroy Prescott
               West Fairlee
               Orange County
               Vermont

Mailed: Moravia PA
               January 13, 1842

Moravia
January 11, 1842

Dear and Respected Sister

     We received your kind letter dated September 22[1841] last evening. Also one from brother Michael Joseph Phillips. We were very much pleased to hear from our friends in Vermont but they were so long a coming we want to hear from you again as you wrote Father and Mothers health was very poor. My health has been very good this year past. Mr. Phillips health has not been so good. Altho it appears better now than it has been this summer and fall. He is not able to do much hard work now. He has worked very hard since we came to this place. The rest of our family is well at present and I hope that these imperfect lines will find you and the rest of our friends enjoying good health and smiles of our blessed Saviour. Which is the greatest blessing we can enjoy in this world. I think I can say I find peace in believing. Altho at times I have doubted and fears on account of my short coming in duty. But we have great encouragement to be faithful in the cause of Christ. Is there none but the willing and obedient shall eat the good of the land. I think that Mr. Phillips enjoys that religion that will stand by in the trying hour of Death. Oh could I know my kind Father and all my Dear friends had an interest in the Saviour of sinners. What joy it would be to my Soul. There seems to be quite an Awakening in this place at this time. There has been quite a number cherist a hope for themselves of late. We have preaching most every Sabbath of some kind and frequently evening meetings. Also there seems to be quite a stir in the caus of temperance about us now which is very much kneded. Amoret and her family was well the last we heard from them. She has another son about three months old. We have a school this winter and send all our children but the youngest. Mary Baird came here this fall and her sister Alvira. Her sister Caroline came two years ago and was married this fall to George Smith. Mary is teaching school and has eight dollars a month.

Brother Stephen P buried his son Stephen this fall. He died in the triumph of faith left a wife and two children. Concerning Daniel and Amos I can not tell you anything about them as we have not heard from them sins Ephriam wrote to us last winter.

Last summer was very dry and crops light. Wheat is one dollar per bushel corn forty cts butter 10. This winter has been warm but little snow yet.

I will now draw this scrawl to a close hoping our friends will pardon us for not wrightin oftener as it is not because we have forgotten them or because we do not wish to hear from them for we often think of wrightin to them but put it off until a more favorable opportunity which seldom comes and time steals every minute unperceived by us. Give my love to all enquiring friends. Tell Grumony [?] I often think of him and the meetings we used to attend. Wright to us soon be shure and direct all your letters to Moravia Beaver County Penn. If directed to Shanango it is so long a coming it gets to be an old one before we get them. The letters you and Pomeray wrote soon after you were married we did not receive until the winter after Daniel and Ephriam were here to see us. Tell Relief and William Aunt Lydia often thinks of them and tries to pray for them. Tell them to pray for themselves.

Good by to Father and Mother Brothers and Sisters
I remain your unworthy sister
Lydia Phillips

Lydia Davis Phillips to her father, Wells Davis. Lydia is talking about Wells' second wife, Abigail Dodge, who raised Lydia. Lydia's birth mother was Mary "Polly" Kelly.

To: Mr. Wells Davis
            West Fairlee
            Orange County
            Vermont

Mailed: Irish Ripple, Pennsylvania
            May 7
            Moravia, May the 5 1844

Dear and Respected Father

    With a heart full of love and affection for you I retire for a few moments to converse with you by way of writing. I received a letter from sister Mary last fall that informed me that your companion and my Mother was no more. That she had paid the great debt of Nature which we must all do sooner or later. It was a great consolation to me that she appeared redy and willing to go and my great desire is that you and I may be prepared to meet her in heaven I often think of the many pleasant hours are gone with many of our dear friends Into Eternity never to be realized by us any more may these repeated warnings suitable affect our hearts and may it lead us to put our trust in the Saviour of sinners there is no other name given under heaven whereby we can be saved only in and through Christ who has died in it all may come and partake of the waters of life freely without money and without price Oh come to Christ if you have not don it before by way of prayer and supplication and let our requests be known to him who Careth for you. Be not ashamed to own Christ before a wicked and gainsaving world. But seak an interest in him at the loss of all earthly things and you will be safe you will have a friend to go to when all others fail you

It is a general time of health in this place although it has been sickly this Spring with the Scarlet Fever and measles and there has been a number of deaths by the numb palsy [paralysis and uncontrolled movement] and there was one of our neibors last fall was stabbed in his heart at his own store and died almost instantly. His wife having died four weeks previously and left a family of six children dependent on the world for support the cause was debt the perpetrators are now in jail awaiting their trials. We enjoy a comfortable degree of health and have don for this year past with some exceptions Alden had the fever Ague last summer but got well and Maria had a spell of quinsy [tonsillitis with pus] last winter our friends have all been well as for us I know Amoret has three sons. Relief is now with her.

The Winter past has been very warm but little snow Delay not in wrightin as we have don but wright soon as you get this wright all the news you can let me know where Daniel and Amos is and where Alice lives where Relief and William Huse are and how you all get along in this world

Give my love to all enquiring friends I some times think I shall see some of my friends in Vermont but as our lives are uncertain we know not what a day may bring forth may we be prepared to meet in heaven if we never meet on earth I hope our friends will come and see us. Tell Daniel we wer much disappointed when we heard that he had gone to Vermont and did not call to see us

Good by to all
I remain your affectionate Daughter

Mr. Phillips sends his respects to you and says tell them to wright we want to hear from our friends the children all sends their love to you and say they mean to go to Vermont before long and I now says to my friends one and all pray for us and pray for ourselves that we may all be faithful to the end of life that we may receive a Crown at the right hand of God and meet to part no more forever.

Excerpts from letters to Myrtle McConahy Keefer from Harriett Davis Gibson (Granddaughter of Amos Davis)

Mormon Connections

Lydia's father, Wells Davis, and his first wife, Mary "Polly" Kelly had a son, Daniel, born in 1808 in Amesbury, Essex County, Massachusetts. Daniel became a Mormon on April 3, 1845 at the age of 37, joining the Mormon westward migration of 1847. Daniel was adopted by Herber Chase Kimball, a prominent leader of the Latter Day Saints in Navoo, Illinois and later in Utah. Kimball married Vilatte, widow of Joseph Smith and raised her children. It was the custom of prominent men to adopt others into their families and Kimball adopted Daniel because he was single and "so alone." Daniel spent two years in England as a missionary, returning to the Kimball household about 1856. Kimball gave him the management of the Kimball Mill in Bountiful, Utah, and left Daniel the land south of Bountiful when he died. Daniel married Charlotte Anne Murray in 1859 and had four children – two boys and two girls. He had seven grandchildren when he died. He helped to build the old church at Bountiful, and he and his wife are buried in the cemetery nearby.

Wells Davis and his second wife, Abigail Dodge, had a son Amos Davis. Amos was born in Vermont and went to Navoo, Illinois on horseback where he became a businessman and owned a store. His name is mentioned in many land histories. He married my grandmother Harriett Louise Andrews. She was born in Bennington, VT. When gold was discovered in California, Amos and Harriett went west. To reach California, they drove a team of oxen over 2500 miles. Think how that wagon was made, pulled by three teams of oxen and one team of bulls. They had a store in the gold region. Amos and Harriet had four children: Ethan Cuber, George Edmund, Richard Herbert, and Chloe. Harriett became a Mormon and abandoned the family. After a long period of time, Harriet reappeared and asked to be reinstated as Amos' wife. This was not possible. Amos had married his second wife Jane Isenberger in 1866. They had four children: Amos, Jacob Wells, Mary Jane, and Guy. Grandmother Harriet became homeless and died when my father was 8; grandfather Amos died when he was 14. Maybe all our people were wanderers.

Sept 12/58 G. S. L. City Deserett

Brothers And Sisters.

It is through the
Goodness And merces of God I am Privel
-eg to write A few lines to you at this
time to Let you know that I am Well
And am Rejoicing in the Principles of the
Everlasting, of our Lord And Saviour
Jesus Christ Which he has Restore to the
Earth in this our day through his servo
-nt Joseph Smith Who Was An Apostle
And Prophet of God. And if you Was there
you Would take the testimony of your friend
And Brother And you Would believe in the
Lord Jesus Christ And Repent of your sins And
be Baptized for the Remision of your sins
And that you Riceive of the Spirit of God that
you my have A Knowledge for your self.
And not always be Grouping about in the
Dark And Seeking And never able to Come
To A Knowledge of the truth.
Yes I say be Baptized by one having been
Endowed With Power from on hig And if
you Will do this the Eyes of your under
-standing Will be opened And your minds Will
be Enlightened so that you will not follow
your Blind Guids Which can not See
And by keeping the commandments of God you
Will have the Spirit of Eternal Light And
truth Abiding With you.

Sept 12/58, Great Salt Lake City

A letter from Daniel Davis, Lydia Davis' brother and a Mormon missionary, to his family in the east.

[Ed.note: underscore lines indicate words that were indecipherable.]

Sept 12/58
Great Salt Lake City

Brothers and Sister,

It is through the Goodness and merces of God I am privileged to write a few lines to you at this time to let you know that I am well and rejoicing in the Principles of Everlasting Gospel of our Lord And Savior Jesus Christ which he has restored to the Earth in this our Day through his servant Joseph Smith who was an apostle and Prophet of God. And if you was wise you would take the testimony of your friend and Brother and you would believe in the Lord Jesus Christ and Repent of your sins and be baptized for the Remision of your sins and that you receive of the Spirit of God that you may have knowledge for yourselves. And not always be groping about in the dark and seeking and never able to come to a knowledge of the truth.

Yes, I say be baptized by one having been endowed with Power from on high. And if you will do this the eyes of your understanding will be opened and your mind will be Enlightened so that you will not follow your Blind guide which can not see any by keeping the commandments of God you will have the Spirit of Eternal Light and truth abiding with you.

I know that Lord has Prophets on the Earth in this Day. I know that this is the Dispention [?] of the fullness of time and the God of __ has got up his kingdom here on Earth. And it is no more to be thrown down by wicked man and Devils and the priests of Baal which preach in this day for hire and divine for money. I know the Church of Christ is organized with Apostles and Prophets and Pastors and Teachers for the perfecting of the Saints and I know that the Lord has commune with his servant Brigham and the Apostles of the Church of Christ have the Revalation of Christ. There are things that I know but you know them not because you are in the Dark. The light has come but you wont' come to the light therefore you can't see. I know that the Lord is with the Latter Day Saints as he was with the farmer and has provided for their wants and they have all got the Gifts and Blessings of the Gospel as they are rewarded in the New Testament. These are things that I know it is not that I suppose or think so or believe to or that I have found it out by my learning or some learned one has told me but I came to this knowledge by hering the Gospel preach. And believing it and obeying and having the __ once of Baptism administered by one having authority by the laying on of hands for the Gift of the Holy Spirit in the like manner you may receive and don't procrastinate the time for the Lord is about to scourge the inhabitants of the Earth for they are killing his Prophets and Apostles. And those whom he sent unto them with the Everlasting Gospel and they have rejected it. Therefore he will come out of his hiding place and take vengeance on them that obey not his Gospel.

In the Spring of 1855 I was called by Revelation to go to England and preach the Gospel and Baptise for the reminion of sins and I went in obedience to will of the Lord to fill the Holy commandment and the Lord was with me. And blest and prospere me and I was an instrument in the hands of the Lord in causing many to rejoice in the truth. Preaching faith repentance and baptism and the laying on of hands for the receptions of the Holy Gost and in testifying of living Prophets and Apostles. And after laboring this two and a half years I was called home.

And circumstances being such I could not come to see you neither going or returning but think not hard of me because I did not. I was gone from home three years and two months and in that space of time I traveled over thirty thousand miles. And many days I preached three times a day and walked ten to fifteen miles. I say the Lord was with me and blest me with health and strength and with his Peace and Holy Spirit that not withstanding I was evil spoken of and was stoned. I did rejoice in the truth and still do.

Dr. Herber Kimball and family was all well the last I heard from them. This is a good time of health among many Saints and plenty of everything as pertains to the comforts of Life and the favor of heaven. The Words of the Prophet Joseph Smith are being fulfilled here in their place for the saints are increasing here in the valleys of the mountains. And they are slaying the wicked and they will do it to righteousness.

I remain your friend and brother,
Daniel Davis

Joseph H. McConahy in Lexington, KY to his mother, Mary Hennon McConahy, in Pennsylvania. Joseph will marry Mary Phillips.

Lexington, Ky.
April 18, 1859

Dear Mother,

Having written some lines to you some time ago and having not yet received any tidings I now with pleasure seat myself again to hold sweet communion with one that I love honor and respect above all things. I hope therefore you will chose not to treat me with silent contempt which is not the part of friend to friend much less of Mother to son.

I wrote to Mary in February concerning Willi's coming here but she did not think it worthwhile to write to let me know whether or not he intended to come as he did not make his appearance I suppose you have concluded not to send him.

I am engaged in teaching near Lexington. I left my other school simply because I had this offer of a better school which I accepted as a matter of course. I like my present situation much the best.

As to my health high living and inactivity have greatly impaired it. So much close confinement is injuring me materially but it is not worthwhile to pine as my school will be out in two months.

I have some serious notions of choosing for better or worse a living loving companion to share my joys and sorrows through this vale of tears. If I conclude I will not go home in July if no I expect to see you in a short time.

The farmers have all their spring crops in except corn and most of them have finished that. On last Monday the thermometer stood at 80 degrees above zero that is what they used to call pretty warm in Penn.

Times are good and women in the market and other things in proportion. Wm Carden and I are sixteen miles apart but we manage to see one another once in two or three weeks. I suppose Charley elevated so much with his two babies that he will not continue to speak to common man.

Tell Father that I would be highly pleased to hear from him as he has not written to me for a long time.

Give my love to all inquiring friends and write as soon as you receive this as I am anxious to hear from you. Direct to Lexington Fayette County Ky.

Yours affectionately,
J. H. McConahy

Lexington, Ky.
June 4, 1859

Beloved Mother,

Your kind epistle came to hand and was eagerly perused and I hope duly appreciated. I am not yet so far gone but that I have time to pause ere I make the leap to see where I will lite.

And as you expressed a desire to see me before I close the contract for life your request shall be granted. You say that all that glitters is not gold yet pure gold always glitters. I suppose that you wish me to marry a lady in the North where beauty does not glitter as brightly or knowledge penetrate so deeply if so we will consider the matter when we meet.

I had supposed that the means of my success would have been received exultingly but it seems that frowns and long faces were the order of the day. Yet I am willing to take direction in things of such vast importance as to a description of the lady I will let you judge for yourself when you see her lest I should flatter her and give a false representation of her.

I may be home in two weeks probably not till Christmas. My school will be out the tenth of this month. I have made arrangements to visit the Mammoth Cave in company with some ladies and gents if I can get off honorably. I will come home if out I will not come home till Christmas. Cowden expects to start for home in about two weeks.

My health is improving some. I feel better at the present time than I have in the past few months. I have quit the use of tobacco in any shape and live on cornbread and sweet milk. No coffee or tea and very little meat. I think in a short time I will be perfectly well.

Strawberries and cherries are about done. Corn has high harvest in about two weeks and others things in proportion. If I could live without teaching school I would quit the business as it does not agree with me.

I would like very much to see all of you and hope that you will not think that I have forgotten you or remain passive as to coming to see you as I will have but a short vacation in my school. I will not have time to go home and to the cave too and I am very anxious to see this great natural curiosity and may not have another opportunity soon. It is a strong inducement for me to visit it at the present time.

Give my love to all and write soon and tell the girls to write.

I am your most affectionate son.
J. H. McConahy

Family Names

The name "Relief" is quite common as a girl's name in the Phillips family. Supposedly it originated in early New England as a name given to a baby girl born in a blockhouse settlement besieged by Indians. Those inside were facing starvation when relief arrived in spite of Indian fire and cupidity. Two baby girls were born at that time; one was named Relief.

The name "Wells" was originally a surname. Lydia Davis Phillips was the daughter of Wells Davis, who was the son of Ephriam Davis and Martha Chase. Martha Chase was the daughter of Lt. Wells Chase, who was a Minuteman in the Revolutionary War and fought at Lexington, Concord, and Bunker Hill. He was the son of Moses Chase and Elizabeth Wells. Moses Chase came to this country from England as a colonist and served in his Majesty's army. He settled in Massachusetts.

Notes
Phillips Chronology
1825 - 1859

1825   Joseph Meachem Phillips married his second wife Lydia Davis at West Fairlee, Orange County, Vermont.

Children: **1826:** Mary died in infancy, **1827:** Joseph Wells Davis Phillips, **1829:** Charles Carroll Phillips, **1831:** Lydia Maria Phillips, **1833:** Relief, **1835:** Henry, died at 11 months

1837   Family moved by oxen team to Western Pennsylvania and settled on a farm near East Moravia, now West Pittsburgh. Amoret Phillips (born 1819) was part of this family. Amoret was Joseph's daughter to his first wife Relief Childs who died in 1820.

Additional children: **1837:** Alden Church Phillips, **1839:** Daniel Davis Phillips, **1846:** Mary Louisa Phillips

1837   Amoret Phillips married John Henry in Mt. Jackson, PA. They had nine children.

1849 Joseph Meachem Phillips died and was buried on the family farm in East Moravia.

1850 Lydia Maria Phillips married James Harvey Pollock.

1851 Joseph Wells Davis Phillips (JWD) married Mehitable Jane Ball in Quincy, Illinois, took passage on the ship Northern Light to San Francisco, CA, and settled in Nevada City. Esther, who was Mehitable Jane's daughter from her first marriage, was with them.

Children: **1844:** Esther (Mehitable Jane's daughter), **1854:** Sierra Nevada ("Vade") Phillips, **1858:** Ida May Phillips

1854 Charles Carroll Phillips married Elizabeth Lutton.

Children: **1855:** Relief Phillips, **1857:** Joseph Wells Phillips,, **1859:** Audley Phillips, **1861:** William Phillips, **1863:** Bessie Phillips, **1866:** Mary Phillips, **1870:** Charles Alden Phillips, **1872:** George Phillips, **1876:** Evra Phillips

1857 Amoret and John Henry moved their family to Arcola, Illinois.

JWD and Mehitable Jane moved back east.

1858 Ida May Phillips Meloche was born. She is buried with her son John in unmarked graves at the cemetery in Truckee in the old section, plots 45-5 and 45-7.

JWD began renting the property at Phillips Station as a way station.

Children of Lydia Davis and Joseph M. Phillips

Mary Phillips, an infant (b) January 26, 1826 (d) died in infancy

Joseph Wells Davis Phillips (b) Orange County, VT, February 9, 1827 (m) Mehitable Jane Ball
(d) Placerville, CA, January 13, 1889

> Children: Esther (Mehitable Jane's daughter) (b) 1844
> Sierra Nevada Phillips (b) 1854
> Ida May Phillips (b) 1858

Charles Carroll Phillips (b) Orange County, VT, July 30, 1829 (m) Elizabeth Lutton
(d) Victor, CO, April 1, 1899

> Children: Relief Phillips (b) 1855, Joseph Wells Phillips (b)
> 1857, Audley Phillips (b) 1859, William Phillips
> (b) 1861, Bessie Phillips (b) 1863, Mary Phillips
> (Mollie) (b) 1866, Charles Alden Phillips (b) 1870,
> George Phillips (b) 1872, Evra Phillips (b) 1876

Lydia Maria Phillips (b) Verhsire, Orange County, VT, June 15, 1831 (m) J. Harvey Pollock
(d) Foosland, IL, April 4, 1903

> Children: David Wells Pollock (b) 1851, Joseph Phillips
> Pollock (b) 1853, Samuel Pollock (b) 1855, Robert
> Martin Pollock (b) 1858, Charles Pollock (b) 1860,

Milton DeWitt Pollock (b) 1863, Grant Pollock (b) 1866, Emma Pollock (b) 1869

Relief Phillips (Fields) (b) Orange County, VT, March 10, 1833 (m) Cyrus P. Fields, October 26, 1865 (d) Near Enon Valley, PA, January 21, 1881

Children: Ira Phillips Fields (b) 1866, Mary Lydia Fields (b) 1868, Joseph Cyrus Fields (b) 1872

Henry Phillips (b) VT, April. 1, 1835 (d) March 26, 1836

Alden Church Phillips (b) Near East Moravia, PA, August 26, 1837 (d) Near Lake Tahoe, CA, September 5, 1869

Daniel Davis Phillips (b) Near East Moravia, PA, July 24, 1839 (d) Placerville, CA, February 2, 1933

Mary Phillips (b) Near East Moravia, PA, February 13, 1846 (m) Joseph H. McConahy, June 11, 1872 (d) Ellwood City, PA, May 7, 1932

Children: Lydia Mable McConahy (b) April 2, 1873, (d) May 4, 1943; Rebecca McConahy (b) January 29, 1874, (d) September 8, 1939; William Charles McConahy (b) October 11, 1876, (d) March 13, 1943; Relief McConahy (b) June 23, 1879, (d) May 8, 1945; Wells Phillips McConahy (b) July 1, 1883, disappeared in California 1900. He was never found. Mary Myrtle McConahy (b) June 25, 1886, (d) March 24, 1962

Leaving Moravia

1860 - 1869

Lydia and Joseph's seven children reflect the general 19th century migration from the east to points west. Joseph Wells Davis (JWD), the oldest son, left first in 1850, ending up in the Sierra Mountains in California. The charming story of his journey to San Francisco with his new wife, Mehitable, their subsequent trip home to the east and final return to the west is told by Louise Sickles Day. JWD opened a hotel for silver prospectors, farmed, and raised goats and cattle. JWD's brother, Alden joined him in California in 1868.

During that same time, Lydia Maria and James Harvey Pollock married and moved to Illinois with their seven children. They farmed at first, then acquired a store and went on to produce their eighth child, Emma, their only girl. Illinois also attracted Charles, his wife and their six children.

In 1868, another brother, Dan, 29 years old, joined his

The first thing that come was them great big worms
and very near eat up the potatoes
And when they left, the bugs came
they eat what they wanted
and left the rest for us
They kept Leif and me in the potato patch
all day finding worms.
You bet we smashed the livers out of them.

—Kate Morton, friend,
in Kansas, 1868

Uncle Amos Davis in Hancock County Illinois, and urged his mother to join them there, where "land can be bought for $7 up to $40." He was searching for property to satisfy a U.S. government land warrant issued to Lydia Davis Phillips for her husband's [Joseph] service in the War of 1812. Before settling in Illinois, Dan and his brother Charles visited Kansas to give it a look. Dan fell ill and returned to Illinois. ("...Kansas haint much of a place as people say it is," says friend Kate Morton in her 1868 letter to Mary Phillips.)

In 1868 Mary Phillips was 22 years old and corresponding with several suitors as well as many friends who had left Moravia, Pennsylvania.

Although the Civil War was approaching and some of those friends were in the military, the war's effect on the family members isn't discussed much in these letters.

After the East Moravia, PA farm was sold in 1868, Lydia and Mary lived with Relief and Cyrus Fields on their farm in Enon Valley, Pennsylvania. Later that year, Lydia and Mary departed for Illinois to claim Lydia's new land and to be near her brother and sister, Charles Phillips and Lydia Maria Pollock. Eventually Lydia bought a farm in Ashkum, Illinois. Daniel did the farming. Mary taught school, although she had trouble collecting her wages.

1870 was a tough year for the family. Lydia Davis Phillips became ill almost as soon as she arrived in Illinois, and returned, with Mary, to Relief Fields' farm in Pennsylvania. She died a week later, at the age of 65, and was buried on the old Phillips farm beside Joseph and his father, Elisha. (In 1936 the graves of Elisha and Joseph were moved to Castle View Burial Park in New Castle, PA. (There is no record showing that Lydia's grave was also moved, so she is probably alone now on the knoll above the Beaver River.)

And in California, JWD tells of Alden's death as a result of injuries received in an accident with a horse. Alden was 32 years old and had lived in California for a year. After Alden's and Lydia's deaths, JWD notes, "This was my year for hard luck." He was plagued by a number of smaller disasters, when some of his buildings and fences were burned in wildfires, and "a good cow got drowned." A year later he mentions that he is 45 years old, "on the shady side of life."

The letters that follow chart the westward migration of the Phillips clan.

The Letters

To Mary Phillips from D. W. A. Freeman, her boyfriend. Freeman was a soldier in the Civil War, stationed at Camp Curtin, which was near Harrisburg, Pennsylvania. The camp was named after the governor of Pennsylvania during the Civil War.

(Ed. note: The family has buttons from Freeman's civil war uniform and another letter which has faded and is unreadable.)

Camp Curtin
January 22nd, 1862

Friend Mollie,

I received yours day before yesterday but as I was on guard yesterday I had not time to write. I was sorry to hear that you had the sore throat fore I know how it goes. Well I am well and so is the company in general and getting along fine. J. W. Blanchard gave us an oyster supper last Saturday night we had it in the quarters we had a table sat through the quarter and after supper we had some toasts from difernt ones in the co and we made the old house sing with cheers then we cleared away the table and pitched in to dansing I eat the oysters both raw and cooked it snowed yesterday and I think we will go out a rabbit hunting if we can get out Tell NC she must have been hard up I have not written to her yet nor do I feel like writing to her Now diner is ready and I must stop

I would have liked to have been at that roast where was it? I hope you will be able to go to school soon I can not think of much to write I would like to I'll write you again but suppose not fere a while I do not know when we will leave here or get paged ether I am tyard of writing Camp Curtain we had a change in our family Dad and OS left us and we took in Richy and Wat I must close write soon

Your most affectionate friend
D. W. A. Freeman

Leaflet of Memory sent to May Phillips by D. W. A. Freeman in 1863.

A Leaflet of Memory
A leaf from the hours, the happy hours
When first we saw the light of love,
When all the earth was full of flowers,
And all the sky was blue above.
Still memory's sun in genial flight
Gilds all their charms in golden light.

The next three letters are to Mary Phillips from a friend, who used to live in Wampum, Pennsylvania.

July 23, 1862

Dear Friend,

It is with pleasure that I seat myself in form to answer your kind and welcome letter that came to hand yesterday which afforded me great pleasure.

Indeed it is a busy time with me   I am farming this year and I have had a good time of it for every thing has been in a flood of water for 3 weeks   Small grain is very near all lost I would go to war but I am to much of a coward if I got shot it would be in the back I guess Though probably I may go yet   I cannot write as long a letter as you did.

Tell Charles & Daniel to be very careful of their paper and ink and not waste any of it.

You said your letter would not be worth anything I thought it was a good one I would like to get one like it every week

I was down to St. Louis the other day to see my Brother he has been sick in the hospital he has gone to Richmond now There is plenty of sickness in St. Louis and all over Missouri They are fighting there Now I live 20 miles from St. Louis.

Mary you must excuse me for not writing much this time. You spoke about my coming out there very likely that I may give a blister and stumble around that way I should like to see you all very much indeed.

I has rather see you Mary than to here from you. But time and luck may bring things around yet. You must write soon and often. So I must close give my love to all and keep some for yourself

From your affectionate friend
C. A. Armstrong

Highland, Madison County, Ill
November 23, 1862

Dear friend Mary

I once more seat myself in order to answer your kind and welcome letter that came to hand some time since. It was not your request Mary to answer your last letter but I thought I would bother you once more anyhow and I would like to bother you a great many more times if it should be congenial with your feelings

I have no news Mary I am well and the rest of the folks in general and I hope these few lines Mary find you enjoying the same Blessings of God there can't be much sickness here for there is no one here to get sick but women and they are scarce The men have all gone to war only a few like me such as they won't have in the Army tell Charles he had better stay at home what has Charles done with his cattle and horses

I must close as it is getting late give my love to all From you affectionate friend and well wisher

C. A. Armstrong
Please write as soon as you receive
Miss Mary L Phillips

Highland Madison Co., Ill
April 28, 1863

Well Mary I read your kind and warm letter yesterday & I am trying to answer it today I had been looking for a letter from you for a long time had given it up & at last yesterday to my surprise I read which gave me much satisfaction indeed I wish I could write you as good a letter as you did me but I cannot so you must say it is well done considering who done it

The folks are all well at present except myself & I am doing better I have been laid up all winter with the bleeding at the lungs but I am able to make about a ½ hand at work though I am well of the Rheumatism Mary why did you not ask me to some of your raisings I think you are quite selfish sort of people you wrote about the stock which I was very ___to here if you had written more I would like to know all about them I was surprised to hear that Charles was gone to California although I knew he wanted to go & thought that he would get to I would like to go very much myself & I do not know but I shall when I get able but a person cannot tell what they will do until this war is settled Sometimes I think I will have to go & settle it myself but so far have not wanted any hand in it though there is pretty warm times in this state at present there is a great deal of bitter feeling among the people there is a fair prospect of having to fight here at home though I think Dave Freeman & myself could settle this war if they let us alone thought that is enough about the war I had rather talk about something good to eat – Well Mary they have all gone to church & left me here alone to keep house & I think they will get wet for it looks like rain

I heard from Amos' folks the other day they were all well I may go back up there next spring thought I do not know how is Daniel a getting with his rheumatism & how is his broken legs a getting along – Well Mary I guess I will have to close

Give my love to all & keep a good share for yourself

Yours respectfully
With true esteem
Write soon & often

& do not delay &
study hard at school &
don't let your mind go astray
Why should we at our lot _____
Or grieve at our distress
We are prone to yield to wickedness
And suffer Great distress

C. A. Armstrong

This is a letter to Mary Phillips from Rachel Lutton, who was from Moravia.

Shaws Flat
Tulome County, California
August 13th, 1865

Miss Mary

    I was very glad to hear from you I have neglected writing to you I supose you will expect me to give you a good one but I will not promise how good it will be I will do the best I can and that is nothing only I want to see you very much I often think of our childish ways but they are past never to return on this side of time

    I do not know what to write to make my letter interesting but I will tell you how I am getting a long in my studies Well they are Aritmetic Grammar/Spelling is altogether different from what it is at home when you half to give two definitions. I went to the circus the other night it was very good.

    Mother is washing away she gets 29 cents a piece I wished you could come to this country Vade goes to school she learns very fast Pa started for Placerville he has gone to see if he can get on a place probably he will keep a store I have just got my new linen dress done Alden got $10.00 in a pan full of dirt the other day I am very sorry Mr. Grisby had so many misfortunes with their children but such is the case sometimes I must write a few lines to Rachel. Give my love to grandfather and all the rest of the folks.

Write as soon as you get this Mary

Mary,

    I thought I would write you a few lines to inform you of my good state of health Don't you remember the last day of school what a time we had I wish you and Mary were here there is not one little girl that thinks alike they are all of the time a quarling I want you to write to me often. I am tired of writing I would write more but is time for me to stop

So good By
Write soon
Rachel Lutton

A token of friendship and love presented by Mehitable Jane Phillips to her mother-in-law, Lydia Davis Phillips, March 9, 1866.

A Blessing

May the blessing of God await thee; may the sun of glory shine around thy bed; and may the gates of plenty, honor, and happiness be ever open to thee; may no sorrow distress thy days; may no grief disturb thy nights; pray the pillow of peace kiss thy cheek; and the pleasures of imagination attend thy dreams; and when length of years make thee tired of earthly joys, and the curtain of death gently closes around thy last sleep of human existence, pray the angels of God attend thy bed, and take care that the expiring lamp of life shall not receive one rude blast to hasten on its extinction.

Joseph McConahy at Phillips Station to his mother, Mary Hennon McConahy in Moravia, Pennsylvania.

Phillips Station,
November 13, 1865

Dear Mother,

After a long and continued silence on both sides I again communicate the stylus to inform you that I am still alive but not so robust as usual. Since my arrival in this country my constitution is completely busted and there seems to be no hope of recovery whilst confined to these mountains. Physicians tell me that my disease is Catarrh in the head and that mountain climate is injurious and that there is danger of it injuring the lungs and bringing on quick consumption. I have suffered considerably last spring and summer. I went down on the seacoast about two months ago and have just returned. I gained fifteen pounds whilst below and feel much improved but expect to dwindle down to the old low point. If I remain in here among the mountains my days will soon run out. My moral nature has been severely tried since in this country. I have never been inside a church or heard a sermon since I left old Pennsylvania and I sometimes despair of ever getting back there again. What is gold worth to a man who had no health to enjoy it?

I am becoming somewhat embarrassed in my mining speculations as my expenses exceed my income by about one half. I have in my possession about ten thousand dollars worth of property and the expense of keeping it is about one hundred dollars per month. I have therefore been compelled to borrow about four hundred dollars in the last year paying at the rate of thirty six (36) per cent per year that is now eating me up as there is scarcely any investment that a man can pay it and come out a winner. I thought of selling out this fall and coming home but the prospect has brightened and promises a good return by holding but another season if I can hold up. I would not sell out before next fall. I expect to teach school in Silver Mountain this winter at seventy-five per month and board myself. My toll road enterprise promises good return but takes heaps of money to build it. We expect good returns from it next summer. I must have some assistance to carry me through this winter and then I am safe. Wells Phillips has assisted with all the money he could spare outside of his business at twenty-four (24) percent per annum. Although that is a large percent, it is one percent cheaper than I could get it outside of him and his finances are in such condition that he stands in need of his money. I could pay him by selling some of my stock at sacrifice which I do not wish to do as I have waited too long and suffered too many hardships not to come out with a good stake. You will think it a little strange when I tell you that I have not had a respectable suit to my back for a period of eighteen months. It has taken every cent that I could raise to keep up my stock. Some portions of the time I have lived on half rations as I wish something worthwhile or nothing (as Robert would say, I have made a lofty strike if I do lose the hammer). Now to the point – I wish Father to borrow me one thousand dollars which he can do at six percent on twelve months time and send to me by express and I will send him my note. There will be no risk as I have property which in short time will be worth ten times that amount. If he will do so, I can save thirty percent and run no risk of losing any of my property. If I thought there was any risk of losing the money, I would not ask it of him, but I feel confident I have been in California long enough to be well positioned with regard to mining speculations. I have good property and mines that prospect well and it surprises everyone that knows my situation how I have got along so well on so little capital as it is an established fact in this country that it takes big capital to make money and I have accumulated good property with little or none for a few hundred dollars is considered no money in Cal. I can always make enough on the greenbacks by selling them here to pay the interest since they are worth only seventy cents in New York and they sell in the mountains here for seventy-five and eighty cents if he sends me the money, send greenbacks and send immediately as I must pay Wells Phillips his money by the first of March 1866.

The prospects of Silver Mountain are better than they ever have been and the chances for making money are good with a little capital. Every claim which has been prospected has proven rich. The time is not far distant when Alpine County will produce more bullion than any county in the State of California.

It seems strange that I get no letters from home. I have not received the scratch of a pen since last June and I have written four since that time. It looks somewhat as if I was cast out of the "Alma Mater" to seek shelter among the grizzly's of the Sierra Nevada's. Rather a cold climate and huge companions for a delicate man. I am getting tired bucking against the human race for the sake of a little money and my constitution will not hold out much longer unless I can have it reorganized and splint it up. Wells has done everything he could to assist me and it would not be human in me not to pay him when he stands in need of it. The probabilities are that now since winter has set in it would take one half or two thirds of my property to pay him where as in six months more the same property would bring five or six thousand dollars. Winter set in day before yesterday with rain and wound up yesterday with about two feet of snow and looks squally today.

Write immediately and let me know how matters stand. Direct to Slippery Ford, Eldorado Co., California in care of J. W. D. Phillips, as there are a family of McConahy's living near. It will be necessary to direct to Wells care or they might get the letter.

Give my love to the family and folks in general.

Your son,
J. McConahy

P.S. You will surely think this a commission. Wells and family send their respects.

J. McConahy

To Mary Phillips from Relief Phillips, daughter of Charles Phillips.

Home,
January the 9th, 1868

Dear Mary,

I received a letter from you about a week or so ago we are all well at present. It is very muddy now. It rained New Year's Day and froze so that every thing was ice. But it thawed yesterday and is very warm today. I have ben a going to school for about 6 weeks there is not many scollars goin they are all French that does go there is 8 girls besides me. There is 15 scollars in all pa was a husking corn today pa says that he will answer grandmother's and Daniel's letters in the course of a week for he wants time to look around.

I received a letter from Kate Morton a few days after you left and they have moved again to Lawrence, Douglas Co., Kansas they went down in a wagon and Mr. Morton had the ague but he was able to work he is working at his trade he gets $2 ½ a pair. Coons has moved up thair Thor was a postoffice order came to manhattan for him and it was sent to him.

I commenced this letter yesterday evening and stopt for to go to bed. It froze last night very hard.

I have 8 patches made for a quilt like yours. Them little chickens that you laughed at is all alive yet. Pa shot nine ducks and they was as fat as butter. The day after you left pa has made a cupboard and a sleigh for Rob Lutton.

We are making all the butter we went on from our cousins and spent my Christmas at Uncle Charles and New Year's at Will Locksom.

Where did you spend yours and what was doing? Well I must close/ my love to all

Good by write soon

Yours as ever
Relief E. Phillips

Slippery Ford - June 28th, '68

Dear Sister Mary

I thought that I couldn't employ my time to a beter advantage than to write you a few lines. I haven't heard from any of you sence I left. With the exception of Charles he wrote to Wells. I wrote to Mother in San Francisco I arrived here May 28th all wright. Found them all in usual health & glad to see me back once more. I have ben quite bissy since I arrived here. The snow was not all out of the road. Teams ware blockaded here. So we done prety good bisniss for awhile. We are doing very well now, if it only continues as good. The Pacific Rail Road is across the mountian and the cars are runing to a place cawled Reno, which is only twenty miles from Virginia City, Nevada. But it does not aper to take all the travel off this road as yet. It is about as good as it was last summer. How it will continue time will tell. We have got a Chinaman cooking. Bunches of snow lais within a few rods of the house. Grass is growing fine now. Where the snow is off there is places where I can stand and get a handfull of snow. I pick flowers with the other. It has been very cold here this Spring or Summer. They wore making hay down at the Bay when I landed & in the Sacramento Valley. The grane was about reddy to eat, there is new wheat & barley in the market now.

Wells and Jane are very much pleased with the potographs. Ida says she is going to keep grandma purse always to remember her. They are all very thankful.

Write soon & let me know how you all are, give my love to all. (How is Milton)

Your Brother
A.C. Phillips

Alden Church Phillips in California to his sister Mary Phillips in Enon Valley, Pennsylvania.

Slippery Ford July 23, 1868

Dear Sister Mary

I once more take my pen in hand to write you a few lines in answer to yours and you need not think strange if I do not write much as I have nothing much to write that you will know anything about. I received your potograph I think it looks very natural. I was to a ball on the fourth at Yanks Station there was about thrity ladyes there we had a gay time Jane Nevada & Ida & two other ladies & one man & my self went a fishing I came back the sam day it was ten miles from here at Falenleaf Lake The rest of them stayed till the next day. I had not time to fish (We have six cows which I had to come back & milk.) I cot one fish one girl cot thirteen Jane one & the rest none If I cood have stayed till the next day I think I cood have cot sum as I was only there two hours

I had not boat after I left they got a boat & had a gay time on the lake Write & let me know when you & Mother intend to go to Kansas if you know I will have to here more from Charles & Daniel before I conclude to go there Wells received one from Charles I have just ben writing to Dan

Wells & I expect or calculate to go on the coast range this next winter to see if we canot git a piece of land there. Wells thinks that I will not be suted if I go to Kansas after living here & I think it would not sute myself   But I will see what Dan has to write in answer to my letter I would like it very much if we cood all live together in one naberhood But we are to much scatered to think of that Wells will not leave this cuntry Giv my love to Mother & Relief & the rest of the family & reserve a share to yourself

Yours truly
A.C. Phillips

Alden Church Phillips in California to his sister Mary Phillips in Enon Valley, Pennsylvania.

Phillips Station
Aug 16th 1868

Dear Sister Mary
I received your letter of July 28th yesterday. I was truly glad to hear from you. Once more I take this first oportunity to write you a few lines, to let you know that I am still alive. Wells & I have been choping wood the last two or three weeks for winter I gess that we have got about nought to last. You wanted to know how I spent the fourth. I went to Lake Taho in the day time & to a Ball at night at Yanks Station as he had just got maried (it was six miles from here) We had a gay time Everybody was there all most in this naberhood. He is a old man upwards of sixty years.

I went fishing one morning to a little lake two miles from here by the name of Tom Audranes lake. I cot 62 fine trout I got back for dinner I went there one day sence but nare a fish did I ceach, as they did not bite. I will give it another trial sum of these days if nothing hapens Wells has cot lots of the river trout but they are quite small to the lake trout. But are fine eating you bet.

As I have said all I can about the fish subject for the presant I will say sum other things. It has been very warm for this regon the last five or six weeks. But there has ben rather a change the last few days sum frost at night but the days are quite warm. I can stand two pare of blankets over me at night, very comfortable. We have got sum hay that we will cut in a week or two. We have got six cows which I milk most of the time Jane helps me sum of the time. Times is very dull here this summer very little travel on the road. You wanted to know what I thot of Mother and things as they have turned out I suppose you know best in regards to them things as I have nothing to say. But hope you may enjoy yourself. If you do go to Kansas I don't want you to sacr all the Injines across here as we have plenty of them here now & they are good beggars. There has been a lot of them camped here the last three weeks hunting & fishing. Would like to have see Mary Lutton very much. If you see her give her my best wishes. A.C.

I received a letter from Charles he wrote that he had the ague. Give my love to Mother & Relief and the rest of the family.

I will now close for the presant as I can think of nothing more to write at presant.

Write soon, the Chinaman is still here cooking.

I remain as ever your Brother,
A. C. Phillips

-- I received your potograph which I have writen a letter in ansr to which I presume you have got ere this. I received the potographs of Mr & Mrs Fields by the last letter. I think they look quite natural. Which I will try and keep.

Letter to Mary Phillips from Kate Morton, an old neighbor from Moravia now living in Kansas. Apparently Mary Phillips wrote to Kate Morton telling her of the family's plans to leave Moravia, Pennsylvania for Illinois. Kate's family is going to leave Kansas and return to Pennsylvania. If the Mortons return to Pennsylvania before the Phillips family leaves for Illinois, they will get to see one another.

August the 20, 1868

Deer Mary,

I received your welcome letter last night and was glad to here from you it found us well and hearty and in hope it will find you and all the rest the same we are going back to PA and Phillips to Illinois. I would have like you had seen Kansas it haint much of a place as people say it is it rained all day yesterday and today but it came too late to do any good here Daniel and pop went down to the office yesterday morning and got a letter for me and Liefy got one from Mary Barge and I got one in it to the peaches is getting ripe the trees is loaded with them the Indians or injun as Moorhead calls them killed about 35 settlers it was about 75 miles from here don't you laugh at my seventy five but I guess the soldiers has run them out if there was nothing to trouble people but them Indians we could live here the first thing that come was them great big worms and very neer eat up the potatoes and when they left the bugs came they eat what they wanted and left the rest for us. They kept Lief and me in the potato patch all day long finding worms you bet we smashed the livers out of them I could read your letter but I don't know wether you can read this I asked clem if he had anything to say to you and he said he had nothing but old Pach is well he picked his mules out last night and got loose and run off and he was out all morning looking after them he found them I wish I was there to go to camp meeting with you Oh Mary we had a hot peach pie it was so good but I had a notion to send you a piece of it there has not been any Indians around here for a long time you never give me your picture I wished you would send me one I cant write much more for there is nothing in Kansas but grasshoppers and Indians I like to write short letter and get long ones I haven't no more to write so I will close hoping to hear from you soon write as soon as you get this if we get to Pennsylvania before you will go to Illinois I will see you

I will remain your friend
Kate Morton

DD Phillips to his Mother Lydia Davis Phillips, who is still in Enon Valley, Pennsylvania. The uncle he refers to is Amos Davis.

Appanoose, Illinois
Nov 9th 1868

Dear Mother,

I again find myself pen in hand to scratch a few lines to you. I received a letter from Charles he is well and likes the place very well is at work at carpenter work. he says that land can be bought for $7 dollars up to 40 dollars here it is from $20 to $75 Now if you have not shipped your bagage I would not you can go by the way of Charles and if it is good land for $7. Seven Dollars an acre and you could rent a small farm we could by forty or eighty acres more than we could here Uncle has rented the house I intend to have and wants you to move in with him for my one fact I don't want to do it nor do I think you would like to So I would advise you to go and see Charles and if you can rent a farm I will come and work it and then we can by a piece of unimproved land and fix it up and have it ourselves and when you come to a stopen place you can have your bagage sent. I want you to be sure and write as soon as you get this and if you go by Charles write from there.

Yours as ever
DD Phillips

This is a letter from Relief Fields in Pennsylvania to her sister, Mary Phillips, who is now in Illinois.

Enon Valley,
December 8, 1868

Dear Sister,

I now seat myself to try and pen you a few lines to let you know a little how we are getting along and that we received your letter in due time and was very glad to hear you had got along safe and well so far on your journey. We are all well at present. For about a week after you left here I had the worst cold I have had since the time we went to the scuching and I took the ague but have got well of my cold now. You wanted to know if we had any cold weather here about the time you left.

It snowed the day you left and the two next days. Sabbath was cold and clear. Monday was warm and most of the snow ran off. The rest of the week was pleasant. Last week it was freeze and thaw snow and blow all of the time. It is snowing now.

Friday, the 9th

I had to stop yesterday to put the children to sleep and just got commenced again. It has stopped snowing but is very cold. We heard somebody going to literary last night with sleighbells. You want to know how the children get along. They do better than we expected them to do. The baby has been very good and stays with Cyrus when I am out without crying. She has another tooth and is growing like a bad weed. Ira goes to bed in his bed by the side of us when we go (if he is not asleep before) and goes to sleep without crying a word.

December 13th

Cold weather yet we butchered the hogs yesterday. The men said it was the coldest day they ever butchered. The beef we killed the next week after you left here. Last Thursday Mrs. Haddes was here to tea. Friday evening Tom Young and Lee Fadders were here. I sent my sock to Mrs. Young and got it stitched. She would not take any money for it. She wanted some eggs and said they were thirty cents per dozen and I gave her a dozen. Have not wore it yet. Have not been any place but to the store and got some flannel for a dress. Do not know when I shall have time to get it made. Wish I had it now.

You do not say how much land Mr. Lutton bought how much it was per acre if it is prarie or timbered watered or dry.

That property belonging to Swagers here in Newport was sold last Friday for six hundred and fifty (or fifty one) dollars to the man that married Old Maid Betsy McGiddiger. I have these two crystal picture frames. They look splendid. You left your belt on the mantle in the room.

I think I had better stop and will end this the first chance I have. I have been thinking I would have some word from Mother before I sent this but have not yet.

If you can read this you can beat me for I think I have stopped twenty five times at least since I commenced this. Ira has spilled my ink. Will not promise to do any better next time.

Will send this to Pollock's address do not know where you are. Good day.

Your affectionate sister
Relief Fields

I had this mailed but will remail it. Most all the snow is gone.

Mary L. Phillips

Saturday 18th Milton just brought a letter from you found us all well. Nancie's brother that was married is on his way home from Tennessee. She would not stay there – she says there is nothing there but mules and Negroes. They are at _____. Tom Young, Lee Fidders and us are invited there tonight.

Slippery Ford
Dec 9, 1868

Dear Sister Relief

I thot that I conot employ myself any beter advantage than to write you a few lines this evining Wells and family have gon to the valley to winter they are seven miles from Petaloma they left here Nov 14th. there is a man here with me his name is John Bell we have a Chinaman who does the cooking there is very little travel on the road now we had nobody tonight sometimes we have six or eight one night we had seventeen sence Wells left here, there has not ben any stormes to amount to any thing this fall two or three snow storms of a few inches, instead of feet as we mostly have

We were buchering today a beef which I shood judge would weigh eight or nine hundred my partner stands by as I wright plaing on the violin so we have some musick there is a great excitement about sum new silver mines that have been struck in the eastern part of the state of Nevada they go by the name of White Pine there is a great rush to them I have got a good ofer to go to start in February or March so as to git there before the Spring rush sets in I think more than likely that I will go it is very cold there in the winter time is one reason I do not like the trip & another reason is the scarsness of water & feed on the way as I will have two mules and a load of provision there will be one man with me we are to go on a prospecteng expedition I canot tell as I will go as yet it will be owing to reports which comes from there it has been some time since I have heard from Mother or Mary have they gone west yet Charles and Daniel got sick of Kansas very soon as the last account I had of them they was in Illinois Dan at A. Davises Charles some other place it looks as if we ware bound to be scatered all over creation or at least all over the United States.

As it is giting late and I have nothing to write will close for the present My love to you all, write soon.

As ever your Brother
A. C. Phillips

Letter from Relief Fields to her Mother, Lydia Davis Phillips, written on the back of Alden Phillips' letter to her dated December 9, 1868. Lydia is in Illinois with Mary.

Enon Valley
Dec 29th 1868

Dear Mother,

I have been thinking and trying to get a chance to write, but there is always something in the way all the time. Cyrus has gone to literary [a debating club] to night. (he has not went many times). I have got the children to bed and have wrote a full sheet to Alden and will try and write a little to you.

New Year's day Mary woked up and I had to stop writing to you and have just commenced again. This afternoon it is almost milking time and shall not try to write much, (I just milk two cows) so if I have a chance to send it to the [post] office in the morning thinking you would like to see what Alden writes will send it to you hopeing you will get it before you leave there if you do leave for some other place.

It rained all of last night and today until an hour or two ago we have been no place, and no person been here but Milton for a few minutes he says Robert Davidson of Wampum was married today to a Miss Tompson acrosst Big Beaver some place and they have a great oyster supper there tonight. Ira [Relief's son] remembers about you yet because he goes to the door and tries to call Mary sometimes. when Cyrus came from the station that day Ira went to wagon and looked so disappointed at your chair for a long time. I set it in your room upstairs. Have you any idea where you will make your home yet.

Wishing you all a happy new year I will close.
Relief Fields

This is a letter from Relief Fields in Pennsylvania to Mary Phillips, who is in Illinois.

Enon Valley,
January 3, 1869

Dear Sister,

This pleasant Sabbath afternoon finds me at home and trying to write a few lines to our Mother and Dan if it will be of any interest to them. It rained Friday and Saturday. The snow has all gone and the sun is shining and it is not freezing up. We are all well. I received a letter from Alden last Tuesday. He is talking of leaving there and going to the eastern part of the state of Nevada. I wrote him an answer that night and took it to the office the next day commenced one to Mother on the blank page of his but did not get it finished and have not got it to the office and not knowing that you might leave there & not get it I thought I would write another letter and keep that until I hear from you. If Mother has not heard from him his would be a greater loss than mine. Mine is so poorly written and blotted I don't know if she can read it.

In your last you want me to write all the news. That will not be much as I have heard nothing that would be of much interest to you.

Mary Ann Scott is going to school this winter. The Literary Club is in a very flourishing condition by what little I can hear from it. Wm Trefor has been going with Ella Russell. Robert Martin is teaching Singing School this winter. He has five if not six for the week at Westhardy and Bethel. They made him one hundred dollars each place do not know what he gets at Enon or at McCauley's Schoolhouse cannot tell where his others are.

Cyrus heard yesterday that they were going to tar and feather Jim Thompson at Newport for keeping bad women and he had to learn. He is at his Father's now and has Mary Sevager there. Some say he is married and some say not. His wife that he did have is married to a man by the name of Warren.

Harriet went the Monday before Christmas to New Castle with Nancy's brother and his wife. They were on their way from Tennessee. They moved there but she did not like it and would not stay. She said there was no society fit to live with.

Harriet went to Darlington by way of Homewood to her Uncle Crawford's and stayed until after Christmas. Found her uncle sick the Dr. says he has consumption – will not live any longer than spring had no signs of it until last fall he sat on the damp ground and husked corn and took a cold which settled in his lungs. Saw her at Enon on Saturday.

I will have to thank Mother and you for the knitting.

Your affectionate sister,
Relief Fields

Moravia,
January 12, 1869

Friend Mollie,

Yours of a very recent date came to hand a short period since was perused with pleasure and was highly entertained with its "better late than never." Thems my sentiments.

Well, old earth has made another circle around old Sol and left me just about where it found me. A___ ain't it whether to advance or recede a lone mile stone by the wayside. There is luck in leisure.

We have had beautiful winter lukewarm all the while with little or no snow until yesterday and last night snow to the amount of 12 inches came down unexpectedly upon us, and at the present writing every thing seems merry as a Christmas bell. I had my first sleigh ride this evening. Lacks without a female companion.

Our social circle has been quite gay so far consisting of social parties, suppers and wedding of the lucky ones. Suppose you would like to know some of the lucky ones. Your old friend John Lutton wed Hannah McKee having wed for better or worse the wedding came off at Anderson McKees and the supper at Lutton's on New Years. The happy pair are enjoying their honeymoon amongst their friends.

Little Bob Davidson of Wampum and Miss Thompson of Brighton were married New Years and gave a ball and supper at Jake McAnlis in Wampum. New Years night thus the ball rolls.

We had a grand Literary at Leonard's School House also at the Hachitracht. John G and Marhead are making a desperate effort to continue the one of government but I think it will fall through.

I have not been to Coleridge since I saw you there. Your old friend Mart Richie makes a raid on the Alsworth farm about once a week his success is evident from the number of visits Mary Lutton Cameron writes us from the inpase ? and is still on hand. She seems considerably under the weather.

I suppose you are so taken with the west and western lads that you will nigh forget those left behind.

Right here I state that my mustache has not grown to a sufficient length to justify a photograph in a short while it will do admirable. My hair has grown quite kinky since you saw me. Ain't it a pity Do you remember that you promised to send me a photograph of your devine self with short hair all frizzled. Don't forget the letter part. Every body so far as I know is well except George _____. Bill Ritter is running the store at Newport in connection with a young man Ralston by name from Allegheny City.

Write soon,
Yours,
J. H. McConahy

Relief Phillips Fields in Enon Valley, Pennsylvania to her mother Lydia Davis Phillips, who is in Illinois.

Enon Station, February 9, 1869

Dear Mother,

As Cyrus is going to the Station this morning to see about shipping your goods. I will write a few lines and put with Aldens. If you had written to me when you first went to Uncles instead of three days before you left you might have had his when there.

We are in usual health I have been troubled with the tooth ache this winter until last Wednesday There was a dentist came along and extracted the two wisdom teeth in my under jaw (I did not know but he would unhinge the whole jaw he was so rough and pull my ears in through my mouth) he did not charge anything for drawing but he filled three and had seventy five cents a piece.

I was very glad to hear that you were well or you would not been able to travel in a wagon this winter hope you will get settled comfortable when you get your things we will do the best we can with them.

Cyrus had a letter from Mr. Martin to know where Dan was his [Mr. Martin's] address is Jefferson Douglas Co., Kansas

I must close

Yours affectionately
Relief Fields

Alden Church Phillips in California to his sister Mary Phillips, who is in Illinois.

Slippery Ford March 29, 1869

Dear Sister Mary

Yours of Feb 12 has come to hand. And I was truly glad to hear from you once more. And hope you have got a good place to live in. I wish it was so that I could be there with you & the rest of the family. If fortune smiles on me I will try to be there sometime. I am perfectly sick of being left up here every winter to see to everything. I wrote a letter to Mother and sent it to Davis'es some time ago. I spoke in that about you moving out here but more than likely you are beter of there, but I thot if you did not know what to do you might come out here. They have got the road broke open again it was a week ago today.

There is some travel on the road. The snow is about four or five feet deep. I have just received a letter from Wells they are in usual health, he writes as if he would start up soon. I will be glad when he gits here. I suppose that I will stay here this summer if nothing hapens more than I know of at present. I would like to have ben with you and Mother on your trip. I think that Davis was charging pretty steep interest. Maby we can make use of Mothers land warant out here. I will see but if she gits a show to sell let it go. Wells intends to take a trip before he comes up to look for land but most of the land here is held by Spanish Grants

March 30th. It snowed about six inches yesterday & last night.

Nothing new from Silver Mountean. Still at work on the mountian tunel. I had some of the rock that they are working on assayed. The result of that assay was fifty six cents in silver & thirteen percent of copper to the ton. So I think likely they are nearing the Ledge, or lead.

I was down to Placerville & got home last week The peach trees are all in full bloom & trees leafing out. The grass is up so that it makes good feed for cattle. And here we are living in snow only fifty miles from there and are likely to for a month or six weeks.

The Chinaman & I are here running the house. John Bell has been here most of the time this winter. He is to work on the road now. We had some gay times riding down hill this winter to see the Chinaman fall & the rest of us made some tall leaps.

Some times. It is very good exercise to keep us from gitting home sick But I had much rather be somewhere somebody loves you, you bet.

We had eleven men to dinner today. & 1 man at night all bound for White Pine There is a big rush for that country this Spring.

March 31st. It is clear & cold today Had six men today for dinner, They begin to give us something to do. The mail carier will be along tonight. I intend to start this with him.

I cannot think of anything more to write at present so I will bid you all goodby. Give my love to all & reserve a portion to yourself.

Yours Truly,
A. C. Phillips

Jane Davis Waterman to her half-sister Lydia Davis Phillips. Lydia Davis Phillips has moved to Illinois. Jane Davis Waterman lives in Vermont. Lydia's brother and Jane's half-brother Daniel is a Mormon missionary.

Pomfret, Vermont,
April 12, 1869

Dear Sister,

In answer to your letter which was thankfully received, we were so glad to hear from you once more I have been thinking a great deal about you this spring I wrote you last year and sent my picture but I do not know whiter you ever got it or not I feel bad to have you any further off although I never expect to see you again in time O may we meet in heaven I wish when you get to Amoret you would have her write to me and write her address I have written to her but yet no answer I wish I could go with you and see Amos do write to me after you see Amos I guess he is a rather rough fellow I wish Relief and Maria would write to me if you go to Kansas do write when your girls get a letter from I wish they would write to me it seems as though a letter never could reach me from Kansas Daniel is way out of the world I wish I could hear from him Pomeroy Prescott has sold his farm and goes to Strafford Bought an eight thousand dollar farm A beautiful place give my love to your dear children how bad they will feel to have you go to Kansas and leave them Dear sister write if you live to get there Your friends in Vermont are all well and seem to be doing well

From your unworthy sister
Jane Waterman

Lydia Maria Pollock in Illinois to her mother Lydia Davis Phillips in Pennsylvania.

Gelta Ill 1869
April 13

Dear Mother

I have been waiting for Daniel to write but he has put off answering it so long and Joseph is going to the [post] office and I must sit down and write some I am up and taking care of the Girl [her new daughter Emma, born March 20, 1869] and feel as well as could be expected. The ground has been covered with snow for 2 mornings but the sun soon took it off. The boys put in the ground some of the onions on last Friday we are planning for wheat I think Davids horseness is not any worse. We have one little calf we had one letter from Relief since you left give me all the news you can from Penna for we will not get much when you have left has Mr. Lutton and family landed if they have you will be ____ and be at home what did you do for a stove when commenced to keep house Nothing more

Write soon
Lydia M. Pollock

A. J. Hughes, an old friend now in Illinois, to Mary Phillips, who is in Illinois.

Douglas Township, Iroquois Co Ill
May 8th, 1869

Remembered friend,

Your letter came to hand in due time and was read with pleasure

You say you had began to think that going to so many weddings I had taken unto myself a companion for life One was not even going to send me word but oh you was mistaken once in your life If you had been along I should have done my best to have you enjoy yourself I do not think it any wonder that I came back or I intended to have some fun if it ever dry up here on this prairie

You must not get so much discouraged with the disagreeable weather The storm was not near as bad on this level county as it was in other parts where it is hilly especially in Peoria County

So you intend to commence teaching school & be a school mom for they will make more money than the farmer this year if it does not come settled weather pretty soon I will write and let you know in time when I am coming but I shall not try to come until the roads are settled so that if all are agreeable we can have a pleasant time

I am glad to har that some of your most intament friends have moved out there you will not then be so lonesome

And I should think it would be very pleasant if you could board with them you must not be so afraid of snakes for I guess there are not very many poison snakes on this prairie   Miss Mary if you have no objection I would be very glad to exchange photographs with you if you do not think me in to much of a hurry Or if you would rather I would wait until we were together in person and then talk the matter over why all right accept my best respects

Yours truly,
A. J. Hughes

Uncle Amos Davis to his niece, Mary Phillips, both in Illinois.

Appanoose, Ill
May 12, 1869

Kind Mary

Recd yours but was not well and told Ethan to write you I was glad that you had such a pleasant journey and found a happy home May you be always prosperous and happy We have been jogging along about as usual The Spring has been cold and backward We have in 100 spring wheat Looked well have planted no corn yet 200 acres planned it rained yesterday and it is raining today Grapes bed fair for a good crop I should like to have you here when they are ripe

I am sorry your Mother could not enjoy herself here But everything may be for the best Say to her we should be glad to hear from her and Daniel or see them at any time This country is improving more this spring than ever before A man down between here and Carthage said there was 34 houses going up in sight

When can you come and see us

Receive this from your uncle

Amos Davis

Slippery Ford, June 8, 1869

Alden Church Phillips in California to his sister, Mary Phillips, who is in Illinois. This is his last letter.

Slippery Ford June 8, 1869

Dear Sister Mary

Yours of May 2nd was received in due time. I had quite a accident happen to me on the 5th of May, but am all right now. I got on a horse to take a little ride but as I rode back to the house the dog came out from under the house. When I had got about halfway of & he scart the horse & I thot my foot would not come out of the stirrup, so I tryed to get back on the horse & in doing so I hurt myself on the horn of the sadle, in the bowels and the ribs. (The horse bucked as hard as he cood) which came very near laing me out. I was in auffle pain for two or three days cood not eat but very little for two weeks as I was very sick at the stomach.

Wells and family got back on the 11th of May. He stayed one week then he started below to git some cows as the Hotel bisniss is about played out and we will have to go to something else. He got back on the 5th of this month. He bot 10 two year old heffers two of them are giving milk. The others will have calfs soon. One has had a calf all ready. he paid $42.50 apiece for them. He also got one yearling bull. We had six cows before three of them are giving milk the others will not come in for a month or two. We have two others the calfs run with them, one of them its bag is spoil so she is not fit to milk the other the calf has run with her ever since last October. So we will not try and brack her at present. We also have seven yearlings & two yoke of oxen. cows are very high and they range from $50 upwards. Hens are worth 75c apiece.

June 9th We have ben visited with a thunder storme but no rain. The Thunder is nothing the like storms you have in Ill. it is very light as a general thing I have no doubt that if you had a velocipede [a child's tricycle] to go to your school it would be a good animal to make quick trips providing you could keep it level. Wells & I are at work at building fence. it goes very ruff with me as I have not dune much work sence last fall except to ride on snow shoes. We donot work very hard we take our time to it.

June 12th I was all righ side up and kicking. I was fishing today. I cot eight trout have got any fish where you live. In regards to Mothers land warent if she will send it out here we will do the best we can with it I think we can lay it so it will increase in value. So she can have someplace of her own when she comes out here. It is bedtime and I will close for the presant. My best wishes to you all.

Yours Truly
A. C. Phillips

JWD Phillips in California to his mother Lydia Davis Phillips in Illinois.

Phillips Station
Sept 19 1869

My Dear Mother,
I wrote to Charles of our great loss in the death of Alden. Persuming you desire to know the particulars of his death I will endeavor to give them.
When he was hurt he suffered greatly for 10 hours or so and did not expect to live after that got better and in a few

days was around as usual without much suffering except for a desangement of the bowels that inclined to frequent stools of loose slimey character. I staid at home about two weeks he changed but little in that time. I went below after our cattle Sent him remedies from Placerville was gone about two weeks. On my return he looked quite well I asked him if he was all right he said I guess so he looked well for some time then I noticed that some days he looked pale and complained of headache I told him he ought to (take) something he said I don't want to take anything So the case stood that way until about the 20th of Aug when he had a chill. (I was absent at the time I was at the Lake building a corrall) I immediately gave him such remedies as are usually given in such cases. broke the chill for a day or two (in the meantime he assisted in milking) after which he had more chills. broke them again for a day or so when he settled into a low fever We continued to administer for fever broke it -- were congratulating ourselves on his recovery when he was taken with a severe pain in the left side and great soreness where he was hurt. Applied poultices which relieved him materially His chills continued but of a lighter type Two days before his death Mr. Williams the man we have here to milk was up to see him remarked to Alden that he must be better for he looked much better than the last time he saw him four days before I certainly thought his recovery more probable than anytime since his side became sore.

The next day about 1 PM he complained of severe pain low down in the bowels at the same time he inclined to vomit gave him some paregoric and applied mustard which seemed to ease him. At supper gave him toast & tea which he threw up and all else that I gave him until 3 AM He complained of cold went and built a fire made some composition tea which he kept down I then noticed that he was failing and that his voice was different. Called up Jane & old Mr Williams &

at 12 past 4 I started for a doctor At 1/2 past 5 he died. he asked for me before he died -- he died very easy never said anything in reference to his death & I asked him no questions. his strength & voice seemed good up to 3 o clock and I was not seriously alarmed He would not consent to have a doctor & would not leave though I repeatedly urged him to go either to the hot springs or to Placerville I supposed at first he died in a congestive chill but the prevailing opinion is that internal mortification took place which I believe and that no human agency could have availed after he commenced having chills

I presume in the last 4 years I have prescribed in a hundred cases of fever of different kinds and have never failed to cure some quite serious. After he was taken with the chills he said he never felt entire relief from the hurt. had I known it I should have urged the use of Remedy for recovery He is buried on the shores of Tahoe Lake about 13 miles from here where I suppose about 15 are buried had no clergyman but our school teacher read appropriate passages of Scripture and prayed Many sympathising friends followed him to his grave for he was universally beloved and respected.

After witnessing it all it seems unreal & that we will see him again but alas such cannot be he has gone to his long home where we shall soon follow. Jane sends her love and sympathy.

We dressed him in his broadcloth (letter torn -- piece missing) had a velvet lined coffin at Genoa

I have but little else to say We feel tolerably well in health but sad at heart. it was a severe stroke to the girls I hope to hear from you shortly and that you are all well

Let us hear from you soon
Yours in sorrow
JWD Phillips

The Phillips Saga
as told by Louise Sickles Day
Great granddaughter of JWD Phillips
and Mehitable Jane (1988)

My Grandparent's Marriage

After John Marshall discovered gold in California in 1848, my grandparents married in December 1851 and sailed on the ship "Northern Light" around Cape Horn, arriving in San Francisco in January 1852. It was a hazardous trip because the ship caught on fire. Everyone on board thought they were goners. They lined up, holding hands, to jump into the water, but finally the fire was extinguished and the ship was able to continue to San Francisco.

> *The following are stories I heard my mother tell. It is now 1988 and as you can see, I am an old lady, and I don't want these tales I to die with me.*
>
> —Louise Sickles Day

They then settled in Nevada City where they had a hotel, the Keystone, and JWD was the superintendent of the United States Mining Co. He was the first one to introduce water pumps in the vicinity for that mining area.

Historical Marker Route 50: Phillips Station

This was the site of "Phillips Station" on Johnson Pass Road that was established in 1860 by JWD Phillips. This area was originally used for cattle grazing, but quickly turned into a busy way station for stage stops, overnight stops for freighters of the Comstock, and later becoming a popular resort. It was JWD Phillips' daughter Sierra Nevada "Vade" Phillips that gave her nickname to the Vade Post Office at Phillips Station. Phillips Station burned in 1873 and was rebuilt. The hotel burned again in 1912, was rebuilt and was destroyed in the heavy snows in the winter of 1951-52.

Return to the East

Following her arrival in Nevada City, Mehitable Jane was continually complaining and wished to return to her dear sisters in the East. She started saying, "Why did we ever come to California? California is "a terrible God-forsaken place anyway! I miss my sisters so much." In 1857, she was once again pregnant. She said she longed to go home to have their baby, but she really intended to move back permanently.

They had a Chinese cook at the hotel. Outside the kitchen door was a big barrel of water where the Chinese cook would brush his teeth, using that water. One day Mehitable Jane observed him vigorously rinsing and spit the water back into the barrel. She was so horrified that she banged the cook on the head saying, "Don't you ever do that again or you can pack your bag." Well, that did it. Mehitable complained so mightily that JWD said to her, "If you are unhappy out here, 'doggone it' we'll go back."

They sold everything and returned east, crossing the Isthmus of Panama this time. That was a very rough trip, and especially with all their belongings along. At the Isthmus mules were hired to make the crossing. Offhand, I don't know how long it would take on mule back and whether they could make it in one day. If not, imagine camping out and unloading all the gear so the mules could eat and rest. Also, imagine them having to camp out. I never heard any tale about that except that it was a rough trip and Mehitable Jane's mule kept cutting up and galloping back with Mehitable Jane hanging on for dear life. It ended that her mule had to be led.

Mehitable Jane joined her sisters and JWD went to Illinois to work in a big general store that the Pollock's owned and ran. Soon Ida Mae was born and Mehitable Jane began to realize that being with her beloved sisters and separated from JWD wasn't all that great. She began to rue the day she ever complained so bitterly to her dear husband and felt very, very sorry about it. But Mehitable Jane was a proud woman and decided she had complained enough. All that time she kept hoping that something would happen to answer her prayers as California began to look very good, especially with her dear husband again. Having complained so much, she didn't say anything to JWD, all the while hoping.

JWD Phillips never wanted to leave California at all. While he was in Illinois, he longed to be in the west. Finally an event happened that solved the problem. One day a tornado came and struck the general store where he was working. JWD and his cousin jumped under the counter for protection. The building couldn't have been anchored too well to the foundation since the whole building went sailing off, leaving the foundation in place and the two men still safely under the counter.

Louise Sickles Day remembers
Mehitable Jane Ball Phillips

Before I continue any more about the history of Phillips Station and the family, I shall relate more about Mehitable Jane Ball Phillips. She was born in Newark, New Jersey in 1816.

George Washington's mothers' maiden name was Martha Ball. George Washington died in 1799. Martha died in 1804 in testate. At the time of Martha's death, Mehetable Jane Ball was 12 years old. Her father was either a cousin, or perhaps a nephew once removed. Whatever relationship it was, Mehetable Jane's father, along with other relatives, paid into a fund to contest for a share of George Washington's considerable estate.

By the time Mehetable Jane and JWD Phillips came west in 1851 the estate was still not settled. Mehetable Jane made payments even after JWD's death in 1884. I have no idea when this estate was settled, but the date could be obtained from the department of historical records in Washington, D.C.

Mehetable Jane had had a previous marriage and one daughter, Esther, from that marriage. This time period was just before the Civil War when the country was drawing up sides of support. For some strange reason, Mehetable Jane did not know which side her husband favored. In due time, she discovered that he favored the south in the matter of slavery. Being of very strong character, Mehetable Jane left him immediately and obtained a divorce. She also took back her maiden name of Ball.

Mehetable Jane was eleven years older than JWD. No doubt she was a robust woman who worked very hard when the mule team traffic was so heavy in those early years. She died one month before I was born, in 1906 at 90 years old.

Following this event, JWD decided then and there to return to California. He wrote to Mehitable Jane saying, "Jane, what do you think of returning to California? I have had enough of Illinois and tornadoes. If you would rather stay with your sisters, that's all right, but as for me, I'm returning west."

Well, Mehitable Jane had never had such good news in her "born days", and soon they were on their way again, crossing the Isthmus of Panama. Once on the Pacific, they caught a steamer for San Francisco. This time they settled in Shaw's Flat, a few miles from Columbia. Again they had a boarding house/hotel.

However, JWD decided to go into the cattle business. For summer pasture all cattlemen drove their cattle to the mountains. JWD rented 160 acres at Grass Lake on the Luther Pass to pasture the cattle there for the summer of 1859. In the fall he returned by the Johnson's Pass road. In what would be a day's drive, they arrived at a beautiful meadow with lush grass for the animals.

Sidelight:

From the Tahoe Tribune, November 13, 1987

In 1860 JWD Phillips settled at Grass Lake. In those days the local Indians were full of tales about Tahoe's severe winters. Hearing these tales, Phillips decided it was best that he move his family back over Echo Summit's dusty road to spend that winter in less rugged country. Upon reaching the area that today is known as Pow Wow, Phillips made an on-the-spot decision that this beautiful meadow, picturesquely set beneath two mountain crags, would be his family's home.

At that time, the Comstock Mines at Virginia City were hauling all the silver and gold bullion over Luther Pass and, of course, JWD observed this heavy travel passing over that pass, then over Johnson's Pass on its way to Sacramento to travel by ship to the mint in San Francisco. He decided then and there to rent the 160 acres at first and then bought the property in September 1862 for $2000 from A. E. Clark. (The land was purchased 13 years before the government survey was made in 1875, a fact that preserved the water rights on the property in the family name for all time.) He built a 2 ½ story way station with five barns to feed the oxen or mules that were hauling the team and the conestogas. The teams were driven over that route both summer and winter. My grandmother, as a small child, remembered the sleigh bells ringing all night long, as they passed Phillips Station. During that era, the way stations were only a few miles apart. It took so many heavy laden wagons to haul the heavy loads of ore and freight going east to the Comstock mine and ore to the west.

Grand Scenery Finest of Camping Grounds, with Pasture for Horses.	**PHILLIPS STATION**
	On the State Road between Placerville and Lake Tahoe
Plenty of Lake and Trout Fishing.	
	Rates $12.oo per week **Address:**
	Mrs. Vade Bryson
No rattlesnakes nor Poisonous vines	Reductions to families Echo P.O., El Dorado Co., Calif.

Letterhead from the Phillips Station Resort

Native Americans

When JWD and Mehitable Jane Phillips first arrived at Phillips, they slept in a little one- room cabin. The first morning after their arrival, JWD awoke very early and quietly got dressed, leaving Mehitable Jane sound asleep in the cabin.

Native American Indians were camped all around the mountainside. Later when Mehitable Jane awoke, there, looking in the two uncurtained windows were Indian heads peering in. Mehitable Jane was very surprised to see all these heads. She quickly threw on something and went outside. With that, the Indians scattered off. Mehitable Jane motioned them to return and very hesitantly they returned. They could see that Mehitable Jane meant them no harm. Mehitable Jane patiently explained that it wasn't polite to peer in windows, at least early in the morning. Of course, she spoke in English, but the Native Americans being very intelligent understood her meaning with head shaking, hand motions and pointing.

From that first day on, our family always had a very good relationship with Native Americans. That was the beginning of years of various loyal Native Americans working for the Phillips family.

(In 1859 Nevada was not yet a state. It was admitted for statehood in 1864. Reservations for Native Americans were established in 1858 for various tribes in the states. In 1917 the Washoe tribe had a reservation established near Carson City. There was another established near Minden, Nevada. From those locations it wouldn't be too far for them to spend summers around Lake Tahoe, Rubicon Springs, and Phillips Station.)

Alice Bryson Lyon remembers
(Vade's daughter to James Bryson.)

There were Indians in the area of the Washoe tribe, a lot of them. They just couldn't stand being closed up all the time. One named Ida went home with a Stockton family, developed diabetes and died, living only a short time after her move. It was Ida who had solicitously 'cumbed' my Aunt Alice's very fine hair and made a papoose dress, complete with doll for her one Christmas. My mother (Vade) would have trusted Ida before anyone else.

Then there was Suzy who washed for Mehitable Jane Phillips. Even I, Louise Sickles Day, remember Suzy so she must have lived to be a very old lady. Suzy was a real actress. She loved to tell tales to the delighted guests. One of Suzy's favorite expressions was 'I so scare' always leaving the "d" off. She was 'so scare' when the white men came in covered wagons. The Indians would go back of the rocks and hide.

I recall that while Suzy loved to be center stage, she felt very comfortable telling all sorts of tales to anyone that would listen. She emoted so much, even as a small child, I wasn't sure how much was actual fact, but you knew Suzy was a real personage. When buying baskets or pine nuts, in making the exchange of money, Suzy was so fast one didn't know what might have happened. She only returned for a few years when I knew her and she enjoyed life to the fullest.

Having been raised with them every summer of my young life, I loved the Native American Indians. Of the various people who had worked at Phillips, there was a couple called Poker Jim and Annie. Annie washed dishes every summer for years. Poker Jim did a few odd jobs such as plucking chickens.

Life at Phillips Station

My grandmother applied for a post office, and through this process it was discovered that there was another Phillips in California. The postmaster, knowing my grandmother well, suggested her nickname of "Vade" for the post office. This post office existed for nearly 50 years. In 1921 Sierra Nevada Phillips Clark Bryson died at the age of 67. At that time my mother, Mehitable Jane Clark Sickles was appointed postmaster.

By 1915 the summer resort business had increased so much that another larger building was erected farther west in a large grove of trees. In those days guests didn't come for a week but stayed all summer. We usually had 150 guests who returned every after year with their families. There were many children and young people who enjoyed the simple pleasures of horseback riding, swimming in a hole in the river, hiking, tennis, dancing in the evening and, of course, always a huge campfire. Husbands would come for two weeks of their vacation and possibly one or two long weekends, before taking their families home.

Sidelight:

Alice Bryson Lyon from the

Tahoe Daily Tribune, February 28, 1975, p. 8D

The demands for supplies at the mines kept the road open in the winter. Teamsters would freight goods on sleighs and "Mother said you could hear them running every hour on the half-hour because of their bells,"

It was during this time that Snowshoe Thompson crossed the Sierra with winter mail for the miners. "He always stopped overnight at the station on his way back from Genoa," Mrs.

Lyon said. "He taught my grandfather to ski using the one long pole as stabilizer and brake, and he was one of our closest friends."

Mrs. Lyon's mother and her sister liked Thompson's visits so much because he and Phillips would don small harnesses with stirrups and give the two girls rides down the side of the mountain and cross the meadow. At that time, the meadow was not as dotted with trees as it is today.

"There was a big pine that was struck by lightening and we used it to make skis," Mrs. Lyon said. "It was called the Snowshoe Thompson tree in his honor."

[Ed. note: From 1856-1876 Snowshoe Thompson braved the winter storms to deliver the mail in the high Sierras on snowshoes. He was the only mail connection between the Sierras and the rest of the country.]

My mother Hettie, a young woman in her twenties, was a waitress in the dining room. Mother had snapshots of two-year-old little Louise, standing in the dining room holding a syrup pitcher over her head pouring the syrup that was cascading down over her face onto a waiting tongue, and, of course, enjoying it immensely.

Uncle Dan always drove the team of the wagon to do the hotel chores. We always bought 40 piglets to raise for slaughtering in the fall. We had a dairy of 20 cows. Milk pans were filled in the milk house. Each day the pans were skimmed for cream for the guests. All the skim milk was hauled by Dan to feed the pigs. This along with the table scraps and some grain fed the pigs. Dan had a smoke house to smoke hams and bacon for winter use. Dan usually had the wagon full of guests and kids who loved to ride with "Uncle Dan". They all loved him. He was a gentleman always. Never swore a word.

Various well-known persons spent summers at Phillips; one was Robert McNamara, who was quite young. I still remember his mother calling "Rooobert" before lunch and dinner. He was Secretary of Defense under

President Nixon. I'm sure he had forts in the big rocks that were on the side of the mountain.

Sidelight:

Alice Bryson Lyon, from the

Tahoe Daily Tribune, February 28, 1975

"It was a lot of hard work, but it was fun, too. In the early days, there was always a big bonfire in the evenings after supper, and there would be music and dancing for the guests. Sometimes, grandmother would take milk and cookies to the kids who were camping in tents with their folks."

"Those first years were pretty rough. We didn't have any electricity and our only refrigeration was by means of ice houses down on the river which we hoped would hold through the summer."

Fruits and vegetables were brought from peddlers out of Gold Hill, meat came out of Placerville, except for some frying chickens, and no one liked to ride to the Grove, now Camp Richardson, to pick up orders of fresh eggs and butter sent around the lake by rail and steamer from Minden.

"I hated those trips," Mrs. Lyon said. "The steamer would drop the eggs, butter, lard, ham and bacon off on the pier and you couldn't let it sit there very long. Se we'd go down with a horse and wagon and it would take all day because the grade was nothing but sand and we had to open and close about 1,000 gates to get through someone's property."

The resort didn't have a milkman, so a herd of about 20 head of cattle was maintained for that purpose. The only post office between Tahoe and Placerville was a little log cabin approximately where Little Norway is today. There was daily stage service later on between Placerville and the lake, but the highway "left much to be desired because the maintenance crew consisted of five men with pick and shovels," she said.

"We had to sacrifice looks for strength. There's nothing fancy or frilly here because everything was built to stay," she said – "even me, I think sometimes."

Phillips Station Burns

In 1876 the Station at Phillips burned again. At that time, JWD Phillips had a ranch at Garden Valley, which he bought in 1869. After the Station burned, my grandmother, Sierra Nevada, "Vade" Phillips, moved to Glenbrook where she had a hotel/boarding house. There she met and married A. W. Clark, a captain on one of the steamers on Lake Tahoe. In 1879 my mother, Mehitable Jane Clark, was born at Glenbrook, Nevada.

Sidelight:

From the Tahoe Daily Tribune, Feb 28, 1975

According to the Saga of Lake Tahoe, in the early 1870's John Sweeney took over as proprietor of Phillips and as part of the lease he was to keep the hostelry open and furnish meals and a stopping place for the few teamsters and other travelers who still used the road. However, Sweeney concentrated on producing dairy products and with the standard menu being hard tack biscuits and beans, he was well on his way towards establishing a reputation for the worst food on record on the entire Pacific Coast when the station burned down for the first time in 1873.

In 1886 Vade Clark bought Rubicon Springs. At that time mineral water was a very popular remedy for most any affliction and used as a palliative measure. My grandfather and Vade Clark build a 2 ½ story hotel and soon had a thriving business with many of the "Nabobs" from the prospering Comstock mines of Virginia City as guests.

Vade Clark operated the resort at Rubicon Springs for nearly 15 years when she sold it to Daniel Abbot. All this time Phillips Station was rented.

In 1904 Vade leased Rubicon Springs from Abbott and ran it for four more years until 1908 when she returned to Phillips Station.

Sidelight:

Alice Bryson Lyon from the
Tahoe Daily Tribune, Feb 28, 1975:

In 1908 my family returned to Phillips and immediately set about to rebuild the half-century-old station that had fallen in a state of disrepair through the unconcern of the various cattlemen who had leased the site.

In that year, all that remained of the once famous way station was a long building and one of the barns. It took just one year to develop Phillips into a full-fledged resort boasting a station, cabins, a general store, a "cocktail lounge" and a campground area with tents that could accommodate entire families.

"I'm not a good cook, but mother and grandmother were great ones," Mrs. Lyon said. "I remember once when mother said she was 12, she was over at the store where grandfather had sort of a bar for the teamsters. "She said she heard one of the teamsters say that they weren't going to get a good meal that night because Mrs. Phillips was gone. Well, that made mother so mad she went into the kitchen and really got to work. That teamster was embarrassed and stuffed himself to the point that he could hardly walk.

In 1911 a second hotel was built and it was also destroyed by fire in 1912. In 1912 a dining room, kitchen and office was built on the opposite side of the road from the previous hotels. Cabins were also built and named for guests.

Sidelight:

From the

El Dorado Republican and Weekly, March 22, 1912

The hotel at Phillips Station was destroyed by fire this week. Mrs. Bryson and family being fortunate to escape with their clothing. In addition to the loss of the building and contents, the destruction included a substantial amount in currency, which the occupants were unable to save. James Bryson has announced that he will rebuild the resort at Phillips' Station as soon as it is possible to haul lumber there. The building was burned down last year. It was one of the most popular places along the State Highway to the Lake. Considerable lumber now is on the ground and the rest will be hauled there as soon as the snow is sufficiently melted. The new building will be principally to accommodate autoists who will stop for meals. It will have a seating capacity of fifty. Phillips' Station is two miles from the Summit and sixteen miles from Lake Tahoe. The post office is Vade.

From the

Mountain Democrat, May 25, 1912,

Mr. and Mrs. James Bryson and Dan Phillips left for the Summit Saturday to prepare for the tourist season at Phillips' Station. Their hotel burned down last season, but several cottages and nearly all the bedding was saved, so they will have comfortable quarters while rebuilding. The lumber is being hauled in now for an addition, which will accommodate fifty people at meal time, and a large fireplace will make it a cozy place to assemble evenings, when the weather is too cool outside. Phillips' is one of the most popular resorts on the way to Lake Tahoe, and is a favorite stopping place with autoists, who appreciate a good meal, such as Mrs. Bryson has a reputation for preparing at all times.

Phillips Tract

After the crash of 1929 the hotel business fell to nothing. The cabins were turned into housekeeping cabins and a subdivision was opened with fifty-some lots. It was called Phillips Tract. Lots started at $75. The first year, a woman sat on the road, under an umbrella with a sign saying, "Lots for sale from $75 and up." Well, she only sold one or two. We supplied her with a one-room housekeeping cabin.

An advertisement for lots for Phillips Station

A SUMMER HOME IN THE HIGH SIERRAS

Own your own home where nature has lavished its beauties. Beautiful scenery, fine fishing, hunting and outdoor sports.

LARGE LOTS FROM $125 UP. THESE BEAUTIFUL LOTS AMONG THE PINES AND ALONG THE RIVER BANK OFFER WONDERFUL OPPORTUNITIES FOR THE HOME BUILDER DESIRING TO GET BACK TO NATURE. WATER & ELECTRICITY GIVE YOU ALL MODERN CONVENIENCES.

Spend your summer vacations away from the noisy city. Remember we are only thirty minutes from Lake Tahoe. Also that within a few miles of us are over fifty Mountain Lakes, all teeming with trout and awaiting the sportsman.

THE IDEAL RESORT * FAMOUS SINCE 1858 * LOTS OF HOMES FAMILY ALREADY BUILT OLD PHILLIPS STATION LYON & SICKELS, Proprietors

P.O. Vade, California
Phillips is located 98 miles east of Sacramento on the Pony Express Route, Highway 50 and is conceded to be the most beautiful spot between Sacramento and Lake Tahoe. Stop and see the place on your next trip. For further information and literature, address as above.

Mother had heard of this very honest realtor who did developing up at the north end of Tahoe, so she and Alice made a trip up to visit him about 50 miles away over a very crooked mountain road with the three mile Echo grade to climb. It was no easy trip from Phillips.

Mother was a dynamic woman 20 years older than Alice, so she naturally took the lead. This was in 1933. With times so bad, the lots were not completely sold for years. It was a complete failure for the developer, Mr. Ketman.

(Oddly enough, many years later, when I entered this retirement residence, one of the first persons I met was Mrs. Ketman. She wasn't just thrilled to meet me here. Later, we had a good laugh about it and are good friends.)

Through all sorts of good and bad times, Phillips is still held by the Phillips family heirs. Some of the land was sold for a store, post office, and some rooms. Our housekeeping cabins were rented until after my mother's death in 1963, age 84.The cabins were getting old and weren't worth repairs, so Alice Bryson Lyon, my aunt, and I were ready to retire from Phillips Resort. Alice Bryson Lyon died in 1983, age 84.

The 107 acres we still own include about 20 acres of the meadow. In memory of the five women who worked their whole lives to save Phillips Station, I have established a trust fund in their memory to pay the taxes and any upkeep. The Phillips heirs will be able to maintain the Phillips property into perpetuity.

Notes
Phillips Chronology
1860 - 1869

1862   JWD and family purchased 160 acres at Phillips Station from A. E. Clark for $2,000 and opened the resort.

1863   Lydia Maria Pollock and family moved to Illinois and settled at Foosland. She and her husband had eight children – seven sons and one daughter.

   Children: **1851:** David Wells Pollock, **1853:** Joseph Phillips Pollock, **1855:** Samuel Pollock, **1858:** Robert Martin Pollock, **1860:** Charles Pollock, **1863:** Milton DeWitt Pollock, **1866:** Grant Pollock, **1869:** Emma Pollock

1864   Relief Phillips married Cyrus Fields and lived in Little Beaver Township, Lawrence County, PA, not far from Enon Valley.

   Children: **1866:** Ira Phillips Fields, **1868:** Mary Lydia Fields, **1872:** Joseph Cyrus Fields

1867   Charles Carroll Phillips and his family moved to Illinois.

1868 Phillips family farm in East Moravia was sold. Pending their move to Illinois, Lydia and Mary lived with Relief and Cyrus Fields. Lydia Davis Phillips, her son Daniel, and daughter, Mary moved to Ashkum, Illinois. Daniel was living in Illinois where his Uncle Amos Davis lived.

Alden Church Phillips joined JWD's family in California.

1869 Alden Church Phillips died in California from internal injuries inflicted when a dog spooked the horse he was riding.

Spirits of Survival
1870 to 1879

Lydia's death left Mary at loose ends and without a home of her own. She inquired about teaching jobs in Illinois and traveled to Vermont, staying with relatives for over a year. Letters in this year, 1871, indicate some incident, we'll never know what, involving Cyrus Fields, Relief's husband, and Joseph McConahy, who would marry Mary a year later. JWD had referred to "the Joe McConahy affair," and Joseph says "he has received an apology from Cyrus expressing regret for anything he or Relief had said or done to offend him."

In the spring of 1872 Mary returned to the Fields' house in Moravia and married Joseph Hennon McConahy. It was a double wedding ceremony as Joseph's sister (Isabelle) McConahy married Martin Ritchie. The newlyweds took up residence in Enon Valley on the east side of the Beaver River. Mary's brother Dan, who often catches the vernacular of the time, writes, "I heard you was

> *It is pretty hard times cannot sell anything and get the money… potatoes a failure corn not half a crop.*
>
> —Lydia Maria Pollock
> 1878

goan to be married in a day or two. If it is so, I think you mite send me ten cents so I could take a glass of wine."

Although she received many letters, Mary wrote few over the next six years, perhaps owing to the birth of four children: Lydia in 1873, Rebecca in 1874, William in 1876, and Relief in 1879. Not much time for letter writing.

Great Uncle Dan Phillips, who claims to be a poor writer but is actually a good reporter of daily life and a committed correspondent, sold the farm at Ashkum two weeks after his mother's death to A. T. Addison. Dan writes of how he wants to "go west in a wagon," and he travels with his brother Charles to Kansas, buys property and returns to Illinois. Dan had lived all over—on his brother Charles' farm, with his sister Lydia and with Uncle Amos. "...For my part," he writes, "I'm am tired of playing gipsy." After much soul searching and wandering, Dan finally makes it to the Sierras and JWD in 1872. He is impressed with Lake Tahoe: "the watter in the Lake is so clear that one can see the botem where the water is 75 or 80 feet deep." He works as a rancher, farmer, miner, teamster, and forest ranger, and writes Mary, "I long to be my own boss but then I have not enough money to suit me..."

Health and "doctoring" are continuing themes in this decade. Mary writes of having been "bled and cupped," for $20, a bargain, she thinks. Lydia Maria seems to struggle with many health problems, saying she takes cotton root bark tea every month "since the change of life come on." Medicine is primitive, and tuberculosis (scrofula), sore throat (quinsey), typhoid, cholera and other diseases and injuries take an ugly toll. The crops are at the mercy of weather, and the letters often mention how drought or too much rain or late frost or heat cut the commercial crop in half or worse.

The Phillips spirit of survival and connection often comes through, as the following letters detail, and this excerpt demonstrates. In 1875, Dan writes from California to Mary in Pennsylvania:

> You spoke as if you would like to have me thare this winter. I
> should like to be back thare for a short time and I am in hopes

I may sometime but I cant say when. The coldest night we have had this winter is 30 above zero. Last fall when I came out of the mountians I weighed 154 lbs now 170. So you can see I feal some better than comon but I still have some akes in my old bones.

The Letters

Mary Phillips in Ashkum, Illinois to her sister Relief Fields in Enon Valley, Pennsylvania.

Ashkum, February 13, 1870

Dear Sister Relief,

I wrote to you on the 22 of January and was looking for an answer when yesterday lo! and behold! a letter came stating that you had not heard from us for "this many a day".

I don't see how it happened that my last letter did not reach you. But to proceed to business. As I see by your letter you are exceedingly anxious to know how we all are.

In the first place I was up at ____when I received your letter so did not answer until I came home. I went up there on the 6th of December and was there until the 20th of January doctoring with Dr. Marshall of Clifton who did not want me to come home as it would be so far for him to come. He said I never had the ague. My blood was out of order and did not circulate and what little did rushed to my head. My head didn't ache but sometimes felt as though it would burst, and the top of it burn as though fire was on it and chill at the same time. The first time he bled me my blood was so black and thick it would not run. He said he had never seen such blood but once before. He has bled me three times in the arm and cupped me twice on the small of the back, once since I came home. He was here last Tuesday, he said I had been a great deal worse than I really thought I was. He said he was afraid at one time I would have a fit of apoplexy. It was all caused by stopping of the courses. I paid him twenty dollars the other day. He said he would have charged anyone else $24 "but as it was me only twenty." And would not charge for any more he would give me providing nothing happened. He sent me a bottle full yesterday and a note telling me to take a tablespoonful of salts every other evening. I am very well at present, have done the work since I came home, the first of any account since the 9th of September.

For Mother had a chill on the 19th of January and has not been able to do anything since. She got better of that one and took another on the 26th worse than the first. She was very poorly and weak for about a week. Then she began to feel pretty well again. And on the 19th of February she had another but was light to what the rest had been. She is beginning to feel some better again but is very weak. Dan went for Dr. Bagley when she had the first two chills. He sent her medicine to stop them and is taking medicine now to keep them off. Dan has not been well since last Thursday, is better now. I guess he caught cold going to Ashkum to church. There has been preaching there for the last two or three weeks. I was at church last Sunday and evening, the first time for a year.

Charles & family are well as usual. He has not been well all last fall & winter, is doctoring with Dr. Marshall the same Mary Lutton is doctoring with. He says he can cure her. The last I heard from her she is not doing well. I guess she is as careless as ever. Beck Trimble is teaching school where I taught last summer. Johnny has gone to Mississippi to hunt work. They did go to housekeeping in Clifton after they were burnt out. I guess their things are there yet. The folks in Clifton were very good giving her things to go into housekeeping with. Johnny never came to Lutton's before he went away. Charles calls their boy Charles Alden. I received a letter from Geo Freeman stating that Ad was married the Thursday before New Year's in the Methodist Church to Robert W. Failor. George wants me to come out there as he wants a <u>Tader biler</u> very bad. "<u>Ahem</u>."

Mary

Cresse Kellor, a childhood friend from Moravia, to Mary Phillips in Illinois. Molly is Mary's nickname.

Black Hawk, Colorado
April 18, 1870

Dear Friend Molly,

I received your letter some time ago but did not intend to follow your example but I have been waiting for ___ but we don't get much here I had a letter from A__ the other day and she told me to tell you that Mr. Taylors eyes were the color of yours and if you would write to her she would send you one of his photos but I can tell you he isn't half as good looking as my fellow is I must tell you about him He is in Denver I look for him up soon and then I expect it will decide destiny for I shall decide for or against him but I will let you know the next time I write he is a good man and if I marry him I expect to go down in the valley to live probably in Denver and then I want you to come out and see me, Molly, for I know you will like Mr. Vanston that is the gentleman's name how do you like it

Mollie I wish you had never gone to Illinois and had come out to Kansas and then you could have found that man and probably you would have not been sick so much I think the best thing your Mother can do is to go back to Penn and stay this summer and improve her health and tell Daniel to sell out and come out here to the valley. George is going down as soon as he can to the mountain valley. There was a colony settled there this Spring and there was a great many going from here I would like very much to go there but I will not stay up here in the mountains any longer than I can help I never was so tired of a place there is very few here pay any regard to the Sabbath day Oh I cannot like this place we had quite a snow a few days ago and expect to have snow until June.

Mollie I am keeping house for a very nice old man his wife has gone back to the States he has a daughter here now but she intends to start to the States this week Ed went to Gulich mining about three miles from town   I could not have the children go to school there and they have a good chance here and this old man wanted me so I accepted I get four dollars a week and my children kept that is better than I have been doing since I came here

I was surprised to hear of those deaths You wanted to know how Davids folks were I have not heard from them for four months they were still at Edinburgh then I heard from Phobe a short time ago her and Sharp are getting along splendidly Did Johnny Tremble leave Becky for good I think she makes a mistake in getting married has Charles folks gone to Kansas yet give my love to them and to your mother and Daniel and write soon and let me know if you are wading through the mud this summer. More snow

My love to you
From your friend
Cresse Kellor

Mary Phillips in Illinois to her sister Relief Fields in Enon Valley. Mary refers to a land warrant issued to her mother Lydia for her husband's (Joseph) service in the War of 1812.

Direct your letter to Blackhawk, Colorado

Ashkum, July 3rd, 1870

Dear Sister Relief,

Your letter was received on the 11th and I should have been more prompt in answering but the fact is I have very little time to write a letter, but am very glad to receive them. Pen in hand to tell you how Mother is.

The first of last week we thought she was getting better her feet was not much swollen For several days they have appeared more natural but she is getting weak so very fast. She says has let up very little today. She says there is a change in her either for the better or worse she can't tell which.

I am afraid it is for the worse for that bunch in her bowels which I can feel from the outside is no less – I am inclined to believe larger. She has mostly had a pretty good appetite until very lately but can't eat much for everything appears to stop in her stomach.

She says she would like to go and see you and will if she ever gets well. I would have more hope of her if it was not for that lump. I am afraid that it will prove something pretty serious. There is to be a Sunday School celebration down in the timber tomorrow. She did think once that she would be able to go. Dan hitched up the team today and we all went out to see our ____. She was pretty near tired out when she got back. She takes one kind of medicine and then another. She took Dr. Kennidies ____ but it appears to gnaw in her stomach. Some one recommended Heatellers stomach bitters and she has taken some & also Dr. Cagouts Yellow Doc & Sasparilla. We often want to send for a "Dr" but you know about how much faith she has in them. I had intended to go to the celebration but will stay at home with Mother for I presume it is the last fourth I will ever have the chance of spending with her. You wrote that I never told you how long I took a school for. I took up for three months. Twenty five dollars per month. That is the wages they give for common school here with summer and winter to board them also. Just two more weeks to teach. If Mother keeps getting worse, I will stop school tomorrow. There will be a month or six weeks vacation. Then they want me to teach three more months but I never intend to teach again so long as we pretend to keep house.

We received a letter from Charles yesterday were all well intend to stay at Uncles [Amos] until fall and then start Westward Ho!

I was up at Clifton last week and was in to see Beck Trimble. She still ___ for the town. John is at home. He says the next time he moves he will move to PA. ___ Kiebert and Mary families are well but caught cold and was sick in bed again. I have not seen any of them since before Charles went away have not seen Rach since the first of March.

It has been pretty dry here so much so that the grain will be but half crop. The prospect for corn is splendid. Potatoes few and crop very poor. There was quite a storm here last Thursday night. Once the thunder roared as though it struck the house. There was a house struck by lightening and burned up four miles north of here. It was one of Luttons neighbors. Maloy is their name. Mrs. Maloy and six children were in the house. He has gone to Australia ever since last Spring for money. A few bedclothes was all that was saved.

Write often and I will try and do the same. Mother often says it appears more like home there and neighborhood than where we used to live.

Lovingly yours,
Mary

Mother took her land warrant down to Arcola with her. It was sent on to Washington and has never been heard from it since. Addie Taylor sent me her husbands photo he is real handsome.

Charles Phillips' daughter, Relief Lutton, to Lydia Davis Phillips. Both are in Illinois.

Appanoose,
July 25th, 1870

Dear Aunt,

I suppose you thought I was not going to write but I have commenced a letter now whether I will finish it or not. We are all well at present and I hope that these few lines may find you the same. We had our wheat cut & thrashed there was altogether 635 bu & Mr. Davis got some 1/3 of it Dan got a letter from you last Sunday. Pa & Aud is haying for Davis. Joe cut his heal on a sickle about a week ago he was moving hay he went to lift up the sickle bar & and his team started & tumbled him off his heal caught in the sickle just missed the bone then went a sloping for 12 inch and then cut that piece in two the pieces is gon all together but is getting well now. Ma says if you come out here you will have all the chicken gravy you want. She has about 3 chickens We milk 11 cows this summer so we have something to do Charley has got up here & spilt the ink on his self he cannot talk yet

Bill Davis was over home last summer for the first time for two years

Our school was out a week ago last Saturday I went through the arithmetic twice last winter I went to school 7 months last winter 3 to Froggy & 4 to the Mound

I want you to come out whether Dan does or not.

I have had my hair cut fore times since I seen you it is as short as it ever was Every time I get it cut I say it is the short time & it was longer the last time than it ever was.

We had a good bit of fun last winter at school. Franklin Porter let us do just as we pleased. We have had ripe tomatoes since the 4th of July & cabbage and corn. Where was you on the 4th. I was home all day. Well I must close for Ma & Joe is agoing to Navaoo and I want to send this.
Write soon.

Good by
Yours truly,
Liefie

& then cut that piece in two. one of the pieces is gon all to gather but is is getting well now. Ma says if you come out here you can have all of the chicken gravy you want she has about 300 chickens. we milk 11 cows this summer so we have something to do. Charley has got up here & spilt the ink on his self he cannot talk yet.

Bell Davis was over home last sunday for the first time for two years.

our School was out a week ago last Saturday I went through the Arithmetic twice last winter; I went to School 8? months last winter. 3 to Froggy & 4 to the Mound.

I want you to come out whether Dan does or not.

Appanoose, July 25th, 1870

Ashkum
Aug 31th 1870

Dear Sister

Yours of the 27th is at hand I went down to Pollocks on Saturday arrived there at ten o'clock at night Kansas is plaid out they having bought in Champaign Co he has 160 acres paid 22 Dollars per acre 80 acres built a small house on it they will move about the 10 of Sept. their address will be Saybrook McLean Co the children all have the hooping cough are all gitting beter. Emmy has it the worst.

The camp meeting was a failure in that place having moved it near Chicago. I went to church with David on Sunday Started for home on Monday at 7 in the morning arrived at Gilman at 9 in the night and walked home so I intend to work in the hay today. I will close

DD Phillips

P.S. I received a letter from Charles Rinehard he is with his uncle in Allegheny he sends his kind regards to Mother and you.

Lydia Maria Phillips Pollock in Illinois to Relief Phillips Fields and Mary Phillips, in Enon Valley, Pennsylvania.

September the 10th, 1870

Dear Sisters,

I received a letter from Daniel giving me the melancholy news of Mothers death I thought when we left we would see her no more in this world I hope she has gone to a place of rest we must all try the realities of another world.

We have bought in Champaign Co. Ill our post office address is Saybrook McLain Co. Ill. We will move Tuesday the 13th I have caught some cold and have been in the background am better now the Doct says my spleen is diseased am in a hurry to send the letter to the office I bid you all good by hoping to hear from you soon.

Lydia

We all have whooping cough
I have got it with the children
Emma has it pretty bad
And is too poorly to have her likeness taken

D.D. Phillips in Illinois to his sister Mary Phillips in Enon Valley at the Fields'.

Ashkum Sept 14th 1870

Dear Sister

I have sold the place to AT Addison of Joliett for 25 dollars per acre give possession the fourth of October 1035 dollars in cash and the nicest mare that you ever seen Where I will go I cant say What is there here that you want sent to you What will I do with the bereau.

I expect that I had better send your money to you. did Mother say what she wanted don with her money wright as soon as you receive this your brother

DD Phillips

P.S. Maria's address is Saybrook McLean Co

Mary Phillips in Enon Valley, Pennsylvania to her sister Lydia Maria Pollock in Illinois.

Enon Valley, Laurence Co Penn.
Sept 18, 1870

Dear Sister Maria,

I received your [next line unreadable] Should have answered sooner but I have had a great many letters to write. And such sad news that it is quite a task. Although you almost knew that our Dear Mother could never get well when you saw her last.

Yet I suppose the sad and melancholy news came unexpected at last when you heard that she had gone to her long home.

Little did I think the Saturday we came here that by the next Saturday we would convey her to the silent tomb. I had hoped differently but we almost knew she could not be with us long. The thought of getting back here was all that kept her up while we were coming. She was so very anxious to get here. She had not been able to sit up for a few weeks before we started. She knew she would never get any better for Monday noon before we started she told me she wanted to get ready to start by the next Thursday for if she didn't come then she would never come. Mrs. Davis and Mrs. McLerson were very good to help me get ready. And we started Thursday afternoon. Arrived at Gilman about dusk. Mr. & Mrs. Davis came along. Dan got Mr. Kirkman's spring wagon and put a bed it. It carried Mother in it. He got us through tickets to Pittsburgh by the panhandle route. We did not know our mistake until we got to Columbus O. Then it was too late and we had to go around by Pittsburgh. Arrived there Friday evening at dusk. She was sick at her stomach when they got her off the train. I told her she had better stop and rest that night. So I possessed a room and two big Negro waiters carried her up three flights of stairs in a chair then brought her a cup of tea & crackers – felt well as usual. The next morning she was very low, had intended to take the morning train but waited for the eleven o'clock express. I just got her up in time for that and that was all. Rung the bell and they came and carried her down. I just had time to get my tickets and baggage checked. Arrived at Enon in a short time. She had her large chair all the way to Pittsburgh. It would not go into the car door there so from there it came as baggage. And at Enon the conductor carried her into the hotel in his arms. As soon as he got her in she fainted. We thought she was dieing for some time but she revived and was able for Cyrus to fetch her out that afternoon.

She appeared better than usual that evening and next morning, after that she kept getting worse as fast as she could. Tuesday morning Cyrus went for Dr. Smith. He came Wednesday morning one of the toes on her left foot commenced to pain her. She had me call the Dr. back to look at it. He said he could not see anything. It kept getting worse and most finally all over her foot and in her ankle. Next morning it commenced in her other foot too. She told me to make a spikenard poultice and put on them (which I did). She said that was good for mortification. They pained her so she could not lie still or anything. They were cold as clay all the time. She said they felt so dead & cold. The Dr. looked at them that day. He told her it was not mortification but her nerves. We could not get them warm. She felt it in her back and in one of her fingers some.

Thursday night the pain eased some but then she was short of breath. About three o'clock AM we thought she was dieing. She revived some and was so very hungry. At a quarter past nine she was short of breath and had us raise her up in bed. She said it looked dark outdoors. Then we knew she was dieing. She knew us all until the last but did not say much. The last thing she said was "Don't fret for me Mary and make yourself sick." Before that she had said "That nothing in the future troubled her all her hope was in Christ." She passed away just as though she was going asleep. We could scarcely tell when she stopped breathing closed her own eyes & mouth. Her request was to be laid beside the rest in the old place. Rev. Miller preached the funeral sermon.

Sept 18th 1870

JWD Phillips in California to his sister Mary Phillips in Enon Valley, Pennsylvania.

Sept 18th 1870

My Dear Sister

Yours containing the Sad news of Mothers Death is at hand One year ago we mourned dear Aldens death now our dear mothers it admonishes us that time is passing us also at the undiscovered country may we be deemed worthy of meeting our Mother & Brother again Although the news was expected it makes us feel Sad very Sad the thought that we shall never see her again can hardly be realized

I am glad she was able to reach Pa to be laid beside Father I want an Iron Fence & Head Stone erected I will pay one half the costs if the other children will the other half. If Jo McConahy will do on the Acct get him to if you have to pay him well for doing so. I have written Jo when I get a reply will write Fields Is he with property so anything can be collected

We had the misfortune to Lose another good cow got drowned at G Lake

Did Mother leave any word about Aldens Estate what should be done with it

I have just heard from below the dry feed and most of the fences are burned had hard work to Save the buildings. This is my year for hard luck

Write soon Love to all

Yours Affectionately
J.W.D. Phillips

D.D. Phillips in Illinois to his sister Mary Phillips in Enon Valley, Pennsylvania.

Ashkum
Oct 9th 1870

Dear Sister

I sent you a box yesterday marked CP Fields I was down to Marias about a week ago her health is not so good as it was when she was up here. I want her to go out and spend the winter with you but she thinks that she cant leave home

I sent the land contracts to Chicago when you left they have not come back yet the Station agent is goan up tomorrow and see if he cant have them sent down I want them on Tuesday 4th for I expect Addison down to settle up and then I will send you some money

I have not sold the cow and calf yet Polly only offers 25 for the cow & 15 for the calf I think I can do better

As to Aunt Mary Prescotts address I can find nothing here I think that you will find some letters in Mothers trunk from her I think it is South Fairlee I will wright in a day or so yours as ever

DD Phillips
I will send you the shiping bill in this

Lydia Maria Phillips Pollock in Illinois to her sister Mary Phillips in Enon Valley, Pennsylvania.

November 4, 1870

Dear Sister,

Your welcome letter came to hand in due time and was glad to hear you ware all well Daniel was here he came here on the 22nd of October staid until second of Nov when he left I was sorry to see him leave all alone but we are all scattered it is hard to tell whether we will meet again as regards my health I was pretty bad after we moved the trip was a little too hard about 27 miles a days drive I got a good deal better and went out of doors I have no doubt as yet but that it is the spleen I am worked so strange as long as I am quiet I feel pretty well as soon as I stir around I have some strange feelings I think if I could be quiet for six months I would get well but there is so much to do and it is like that braking out that I had so long as there is any of the disease left it got to work with new vigores.

We are living in a little house 14 by 16 but are building one 16 by 24 besede the old one story and half height intend to plaster 2 rooms this fall have it weather boarded it is raining today the road will be bad for Dan we have to get pretty well of the whooping cough

Now Mary we have made one payment and have to pay some more in the spring if you have your money on hand and don't want to use it Harvey wants to use it and give lawful interest with security we cannot make anything on the farm until fall you will get more interest here than what you can get there unless things have changed since we left I think we will like this place I think we will not have so much ague [malaria] here.

Our post office is 7 miles so a letter may lay 2 or 3 weeks

Our address is Saybrook McLean Co., Ill

Lydia M. Pollock

Lydia Maria Pollock in Illinois to her sister Relief Phillips Fields in Enon Valley, Pennsylvania. Dan is preparing to move to Kansas.

December 6th 1870

Dear Sister Relief,

We received yours of Nov 20 was glad to hear from you. I am improving and I will tell you last winter I lifted some sacks of turnips and strained myself I had an inward weakness and inward burning and it extended down to my legs and feet It was caused by my womb being strained it effected my spleen. I think I might have been well long ago if I had known that I should have to be so careful of myself I take cold with the least dampness and I would go to work a little and I aught not to lift anything I did not know anything about that disease I think the Doct is doing very well.

Mary, Dan sold the bedstead and chairs to Mrs. Davis stove to Wallace for 15 dollars boiler to Davis for what it cost table left with Davis to sell he left his two plows harrow and bureau to be shipt when called for he left coffy mill wash board sifter rake hoe lamp don't know wheather to keep or not he gave me tea pot brown bowl the round white dish that had a piece out of it scissors 4 milk pans strainer jars soap pickles/tub/but went to tares and he gave it to someone.

I do not know about what he had in his wagon for I was not able to go out to the wagon the sugar bowl I did not see it would not be prudent to expose myself to go it would do me more harm that good this winter. Poor prospect for spring would like to go and see you if I could. Mary I expect you would have some old black veil or something and make me a bonnet if you please to send one that you think would suit me Dan gave me Dr. Fitch and the history of California that old comfort made of your light calico dress he put it on his mare and she tore it in two he gave it to me. As regards money we have one hundred to pay the first of April and five hundred by the middle of August and no chance to make money before to pay on that Harvey expects to teach school this winter that will be a little $40 per month but we must live on something. As regards Mary's clothes anything that you do not need will be exceptable that box shipt to Mahomet Champaign Co Ill it is 12 miles from us

write to Saybrook when you ship it

Lydia M. Pollock

I made 2 check shirts for Dan
Ship in Harveys name

D.D. Phillips in Illinois to his sister Mary Phillips in Enon Valley, Pennsylvania.

Appanoose

December 11th 1870

Dear Sister

I received yours of Nov 8th was glad to hear from you and that you had received the money all right. I am well and so all the rest.

The stove I sold to Peter Wallace for fifteen dollars to be paid on the first of June I left part of the dishes and the sugar bowl at Marias also the history of California & Dr Fitch As to her health I'm afraid there is not much hopes of her giting beter I oferd to give her money to go there but she thought that the trip would be to mutch for her

I have been gathern corn ever sence I cam here have about seven thousand bushels gathered and about as mutch more to gather Uncle thinks that he will have twenty thousand bushels

It is raining & snowing today will start the hay in the morning he has about two hundred & fifty tons

Eathen has been goan to school at Ft Madison all summer has been at home for a week he intends to go this winter

I paid Charles for the chickens ten dollars I sold five again at two dollars & a half making 12.50.

I paid Dr Bagley twenty dollars

Lizzie [Charles Phillips' wife] wants to know if Mrs Robertson is in Moravia if not where she is they received your letter but never answered it

I am as ever

DD Phillips

Manhattan [Kansas]

Jan. 8, 1871

Miss Mary Phillips

Dear Friend,

I have not heard from you for a long time and I thought I would write to you once more I heard that you was in PA I am well I am staying with Phoebe [his sister] this winter in Manhattan her and her man and baby is well I heard from Chris and Ad the other day they was all well but Ad has been sick this winter but she is better now they live in Denver I wrote to them and never got answers from them   tell me whare to write to them and give me all the news about them and if you are ever coming west again give my respects to Mr. and Mrs. Fields and tell them to write to me and I will answer them

Write soon

No more now from your friend

G. H. Freeman

Address

Manhattan Kansas

D.D. Phillips in Illinois to sister Mary Phillips in Enon Valley, Pennsylvania.

Appanoose Ill
Feb 13 1871

Dear Sister

Once more to wright to you Im goan to try in the first place I must tell you how I am for my face and neck is all sore with the scarfula am some beter at present

Uncle[Amos] has been sick the Doctor was afraid for some time that he would not git well at present he is able to tend to his business he left this morning to go to Springfield to tend to his hay Suit the same one he had when you was here the hay and cost amounts to about two thousand dollars we see at present ressing hay and hauling to the station about six miles east of here

Charles and family are well the children have all had the hooping cough this winter I fetched Joes box to him

Uncle & I git along beter than we did before we have not had a word out of the way

Chloe wants you to come here

I received from PE Wallace of Ashkum he said that he had not heard from you and that he expected to git your school monny soon and he wants to know how and where you want it sent so you had better write your self I will send you Wallaces letter I expect to leave about the first of April

DD Phillips

Lydia Maria Pollock in Illinois to her sisters Relief Fields & Mary Phillips in Enon Valley, Pennsylvania.

Feb 28, 1871

Dear Sisters

It has been some time since I have written but it is not every day we have a chance to send to the [post] office. David went and got the box about the 13th of this month all right not anything damaged. Most of the clothes you sent Emma are large for her you drest her up in style. Grants suit a little large but can where it it is better a little large than small. Mary Emma has grown so fast this winter and is so fat. In Sept she was so poor She was not half as heavy as when you saw her. That wrapper you sent just fits it is the nicest make and fits the best. Mary I did not expect you to send your veil. I thought you would have some black to make a bonnet I did not want you to take the clothes off from your back. As regards going on a visit it looks very slim. If I get better it will be hard for me to leave and if I do not I will have to take the means to Doctor with. I expect to have to take medicine for some time. My nerves are a great deal stronger than they were. When I was at your house and before I thought it was the same that Mother had when I got worse and I would take them weak spells I did not know that it was my nerves until this Doc that we emploid said so Ellen is not very stout for the lest two months. She got cold think she will be better in a week or so. The boyes have to do most of the work all the heavy work. Think by warm weather I will be able to get about better than I can now I must close or I will have all the bad spelling there is in the Country in this one letter. I am writing to Relief you ought not to send 2 of your dresses.

Write as soon as you receive this Lydia M. Pollock

Relief Fields
Mary Phillips

Lydia Maria Pollock in Illinois to her sisters Relief Fields and Mary Phillips in Enon Valley, Pennsylvania.

May first 1871

Dear Sisters

It has been some time since I wrote to you but I have been waiting for to send to the [post] office but they are so busy plowing with the teams that we have no chance to and have not gone for six weeks. Suppose there is a letter for us there/ David is going to Mahomet tomorrow and I want to send it/ My health is better than it was last fall but not as well as two months ago/ the Doct gave me a bottle and I recuited right up on it he left me another and it was weaker than the other and I went down on it. I have got some more and am better than I was. Mother done wrong to travel around with prostration of nerves. Daniel wrote once to David and has written 2 letters and received no answer/ let me know about him how Charles and he feels about Kansas. I will try and write to Wells if you give me his address. Ellen has got pretty well/ They are planting corn today/ we set a quilt together with the pieces of calico you sent me

Mrs. Barker (where we eat the prairie chicken) had the measles and got better and went out to feed the stock and took cold and died. The scarlet fever was at Champaigne City in the fall and winter was very bad this spring it got around here but was very mild the Doct said if it was in the winter it would be very bad all of our children had it but David and Robert David's lungs apere better this spring after having the whooping cough than he has been for 3 springs before

I have not been able to get our pictures taken but will try when the weather gets mild I have to go so far and the wind blows so hard it blows a great deal harder here than in the timber.

I remain as ever
Your Sister
Lydia M. Pollock
Relief Fields
Mary Phillips

From an old neighbor from Illinois, to Mary Phillips in Enon Valley, Pennsylvania.

May 5th 1871

Dear Mary
Received your very welcome letters several weeks since but have neglected to reply for the want of time. I shall say nothing about your waiting so long before writing to me as I think I waited long enough to balance all accounts. The family are all as well as usual except Mother and my self. Mother has had a felon (?) on her thumb on the right hand it has been nearly three

weeks since she has been able to work. I have been at home two weeks but have not been able to do much this week on account of a very severe cold/ the three girls go to school they have a new teacher by the name of Emma ___. They like her very much she boards at Mr. ___ and is some friend of his Abby likes it first rate now. She went through compound fractions last winter. Phillie Clarke is at home now she spent the winter with her Uncle at Campaigh she has not been to school any since you taught. The other girls are going now and learning finely. Mary, Hattie, and Abbie study grammar together. Now Willie and Richard go to school this summer and now the teacher has as much trouble with Willie about laughing in the class as you did. Mrs. Fanning has gone to Peoria again and poor Rose has to stay at home and keep house for her Father. Mrs. Hays was here last night and inquired after you. Olly has got to be a large stout boy and is just beginning to walk. Harry ___ is larger than Olly and can creep. Mr. and Mrs. Wallace are well. Mrs. Horrons folks are well but they have got a selling fever on and will sell as soon as they can get a chance. We have not got any candytuft seed but will send you some migoinette [forget-me-nots]. My brother Ed is at home helping Father. They have got some 60 acres of corn planted. We have not got much garden started yet but what is planted is doing well potatoes corn and peas are all up. We have had a very early spring very little rain until this week weather has been stormy and rather cold have not had any frost since the middle of April and the prospect is a good for a beautiful crop.

The folks that bought your place have moved into it a part of them consisting of Miss Alison four boys and a girl about sixteen years of age. Mrs. A died last fall I have been there once and think they are a very nice family. It made me think of you everything seems about the same that it did when you were there and I noticed your rhubarb was growing finely. I believe

I wrote to you in that other letter that I was going to school in Ashkum.. Well I went just 2 weeks 2 days when the teacher was taken sick and was obliged to give up and go home and the school broke up   never the less I went to Mr. Pacard and examine. I passed the examination alright but the trouble is to get a school. I do not expect getting a school this summer. They are agitating church building very strong in Ashkum just now. I think there will be one up by fall. They had ___ last winter. There has been about 20 united with all the Baptist ones. And ---- and I was among the members   I was baptized a week ago last Sunday but I am coming to the end of the paper and I must close excuse mistakes because I was obliged to hold my head up with one hand while I wrote with the other. Please write soon.

And believe me you friend
___ Davis

From Addie Taylor, an old neighbor from Moravia, now in Colorado, to Mary Phillips, in Enon Valley, Pennsylvania.

Denver City,
May 14, 1871

Dear Friend Mollie,
    Months have elapsed since I last wrote to you & I thought today I would make amends for my long neglect
    There have been changes with both of us since we last heard from each other directly I have heard with regret that your dear Mother is no more. I can sympathese with you in your bereavement She was a good mother and a sincere friend

and memory of her recalls the time when my own dear Mother lay on the bed of death She so longed to see her friend your Mother but as that could not be she said that they would soon meet where parting is no more and I have no doubt they have it is sad at any time of life to be deprived of a Mother but we should be thankful that ours were not taken from us in childhood but let us look forward to a glad reunion with them beyond the hereafter.

I was living on the other side of the range when I received your last letter but have neglected to answer it We left there the last of Sept and have been living in Denver ever since I like to live here very well it is a very pretty city but I expect we will go to the mountains again this summer Mr. Taylor thinks he can do better there than here but we will not go across the range its pleasant in the mountains in the summer and not as pleasant in winter as it is there. We did think of going to ranching but not this summer There is money to be made in stock raising here There are a great many coming here this spring so many that it is very difficult to get houses enough to live in.

I do wish you would come out here and I know you would do well You could get ten to twelve dollars a week sewing at dressmaking girls have a better chance here than there do come and try and persuade Relief and Mr. Fields too.

Well Mollie we have got the sweetest little baby he is most three months old he looks just like his pa and you'd say he is good looking do you know what baby looks like we call him Willard Freeman.

Crise and her children are well and doing well and our folks in Kansas are well George wants to come back here again I heard that Charles and Daniel are going to Kansas again I think they had better come here Write me all the news about the folks over on the Beaver remember me to Relief and family Tell her I would like to hear from her I will try and not be so remiss in writing My kind regards to your self and hoping to hear from you soon.

I am your friend,
Addie Taylor

D.D. Phillips in Illinois to his sister Mary Phillips in Enon Valley, Pennsylvania.

Appanoose
July 30 1871

Dear Sister

Your welcome letter come to hand one week ago but I have been so busy haying that I had no time to answer it until the present so will do the best I can I have not been very well this summer but have work all the time have lost but one day since I come here and that was the coldest day last winter. We finished haying last night will go to the timber in the morning to finish sawing will be there about three weeks Mary Shafer is at work for her uncle in Nauvoo Fany Isenburg is maried to Amos Swageit they live about two miles from here on a rented farm I'm sory to here that Maria is so poorly if she is able to travel I think it best for her to go east and stay this winter but I expect she wont do it for fear she would be in the way If she will go I will pay her way there and back if she will only go

As for you coming out West I have nothing to say If I was located my self in a good place I would say come but as I am on the go you will have to do as you think best if you want to go along west in a wagon if you are out here about the first of Sept we will go Charles and family intend to go along as for my self nothing would please me more than to have you along I am well I should like to hear from you before I leave here

DD Phillips

To Mary Phillips in Enon Valley from an unknown friend.

Wampum PA
Aug 1st 1871

Friend Mary

I arrived at this place yesterday all ok after a good walk after I left you took the wrong road and went about three miles out of the way I got to Manes N at 3 pm took supper and went to Logans and staid all night left at 8 am & from their to Edinburgh & mist the train there / I struck out on foot arrived at Mahoningtown on time I would not do it again for any money When I got to this place I was about gon up & this morning I don't feel very well at all.

When I went to Jackson I found a letter awaiting me staiten if I was coming home I had better do so at once & read one here staiting the same.

I telegraphed that I would start in a few days Cy has not made any arrangements yet As soon as he makes the arrangements I will know what to do if I go home I will be out in six months/ have you decided yet wheather you will go or not I say pack up and go.

While at ___ I herd compliments passed on you that you was a beauty and one of the finest young ladies around this part of the country. I thought so to Well I have given you news that I have

If I go home I will start Thursday next if you will be in town I will stop if not I will go on

Give my regards to all & let me hear from you soon you can answer this at this place if it reaches you in due time if not answer at Arcola. My regards to the Miss Youngs

Yours & c

T. L. __ Jr.

From an affectionate friend in Ashkum, Illinois to Mary Phillips in Enon Valley, Pennsylvania. The name is illegible.

August 2, 1871

Miss Mary Phillips

My dear friend it is with pleasure I take my pen in hand to answer your very kind and welcome letter. All of the folks you were acquainted with are well they inquire after you very often. The girls were very much pleased with your picture. Ella is going to send you one of hers immediately and I presume Hannah and Louisa will send theirs when they have them taken. You must send me one of yours and if I ever have any taken you shall have the very best of them.

I am all alone this afternoon the rest have all gone to hear Mr. __ preach. It has been very warm here for a month past and there is a good deal of sickness. __ Gifford is quite sick. We have no school now. I expect it will commence the first of October. The Congregationalist have commenced to build a church in Ashkum and there has been a few large buildings put up this summer. Mrs. Robert Lutton had a boy about three weeks old. If I do not get a chance to teach hear I think of going to Iowa and staying with my sister.

Fannie Packard is married his brides name was Gridley. His Father requests me to say that your school money is safe and he will see that you get it as soon as this years taxes are collected the reason you did not get it last spring was because the roads were so bad that Wallace did not go down to present your order until the money was all paid out.

Have you taught since you have been gone I should like to see you again but do not expect I shall in this world What has become of Dan has he gone where the grasshoppers live yet

Well Mary I must close this letter it is getting dark to write

Hoping to hear from you soon I remain your affectionate friend

___ [name illegible]

Abbie Benton, a cousin in Vermont, to Mary Phillips in Enon Valley, Pennsylvania.

So Strafford, Vermont
August 31, 1871

Dearest cousin,

We are all very anxious to hear from you if you receive this please write that we may hear from you

Abbie Benton

From Amoret's son, Henry Junior, in Illinois, to Mary Phillips in Enon Valley, Pennsylvania.

Arcola, Ill
Sept. 1st, 1871

Dear Mary,

Your very welcome letter I received today and very glad to hear from you as I have been looking for a letter from you for a week Today is the first time I have been without doing something there is nothing to do now for everything is dull and no water yet don't know what we will do for the want of water if it don't rain soon have been getting it in the country for a long time for the stock at the stable They all want you to come out and would be glad to see you All delighted to here that you have some notions of coming

But cannot get a school this fall but will be a chance to this winter I will send you a paper and mark where you will see names of teachers and when commence You will please in your next letter state the time when you will start for the West You must not give it up Mamie is going to school when it commences

Father sais you are welcome to come and stay here and go to school and you must come Mind that now   how are you Joseph McConahy he will come some of these fine days and will not take you back so soon Yes I was sorry I did not get to see you again before I came home did not know I was going home so soon Well the best way for you to come is to take the P.F.W & Chicago road and go to the crossover near Chicago and from their take the ICR Road to Arcola or when you buy a ticket buy it for Akaw for that is the name of the station and known on the Ill Central by that name don't come the way I did anyway. There is a good school here as good as in the States and no road but you will get the first chance in teaching if you will come soon. I have wished for you a many a time to be here I tell you we would have gay old times together I have had a good many young ladies to call in the last few days and all have invited me to call on them but have not yet

James is going for the girls lively every night with one of the best livery rigs and having a gay time tell Mrs. Young the next time I am East I will call on her but don't think I will be out for a while and give her my compliments

Whear do you expect to go as you say you will not be at home by the 19th Mother wants to know where your sister is in Champaign County Ill Please stait

Well I must close Give my regards to all and yourself

Good night
Yours V C
Love, Henry Jr.

P.S. Please send your letter to lock box 11, Henry

D.D. Phillips in Illinois to his sister Mary Phillips in Enon Valley, Pennsylvania.

Appanoose Sept 3, 1871

Dear Sister

I received your welcome letter and was glad to hear from you and that you was well I am some better that I was when I rote you last

I intend to leave here in the morning I am all ready to leave if Uncle [Amos]gits my money he has gone to town? _____

now for it CC [his brother Charles] is goan with me if he finds a place to suit him he will move his family in the spring or in fall.

the paper that you sent sometime ago came to hand all right it is about dark and I have my team to tend to I would close

I almost forgot to tell you about Eathen [Uncle Amos's son] he was haling logs to the saw mill yesterday and the log he was setting on rold off and he went under it his knee is sweld up his back is hurt some and his face is all bruised up but the Doctor says he is not dangerous

You will have to excuse bad riting for it is dark and I cant see Yours as ever

DD Phillips

Sept 10th 1871

Charles & I are at _____ about 200 miles from A. Davis's will cross the river at Kansas City if all is right on Wednesday morning

DD Phillips

P.S. Mary your money on the Iroquois place Mr Addison was to pay it by the forth of oct to Mr. Lutton you had beter send out after it for I think it will be paid & Lutton may be slow about sending it to you

DDP

From a friend in Illinois to Mary Phillips in Enon Valley, Pennsylvania.

Arcola, Ill
Sept. 12, 1871

Dear Mary

I have not yet recd any answer to my last letter as it has been some time ago since I wrote you and about time I should here from you and would like to know when you are coming out. Would like for you to come   as soon as you come or know when you will come

It is very dry here and about out of water Water is selling at a great price just now.

Please answer on receipt of this and give my regards to all and yourself

Yours truly, Tl Cluny

From Lydia Maria Pollock in Illinois to her sisters Relief Phillips Fields and Mary Phillips in Enon Valley, Pennsylvania.

Oct 3 1871

Dear Sisters

It has been a long time since I wrote to you it was neglect of me I kept putting it off the supporter works as I thought it would as long as I have it on I can do the work very well it makes me nervous to ride in the big wagon if you ever try the supporter Dr. Fitch thought that was all that I would need to bath my bowels with salt and water that all gone feeling at the pit of the stomach I had it ever since we moved here until I got the supporter I could not lift anything nor walk but it would come on Dr. Fitch would be my Doct for lingering disease as for going on a visit before I got the supporter I was not able now I am able I cannot leave the work   As regards your coming I would like to see you but unless you want to stay a while I do not want you to spend your money unless you stay out west do no think hard and think I do not want to see you for that is not the case I do not want you to spend your money for nothing Charles & Daniel have started for Kansas there is some ague in the country Harvey feels like it this week we have not had any of it since we came here. I remain as ever

Lydia M. Pollock

D.D. Phillips in Illinois to Mary Phillips in Enon Valley, Pennsylvania.

Appanoose Ill
Oct 8th 1871

I have been to Kansas and back again we landed here on Thursday evening When I left here I intended to stay out west but my health is so poor I thought the best thing I could do was to come back and see if I could git better I don't know yet whether I will Doctor here or go to Chicago I'm no worse then I have been for the last two or three months but I have come to the conclusion that if I dont git better I will be worse before long

I only bought 16 acres of land at 6 six dollars per acre
Charles bought 72 acres he paid the same it laise along side the
Indian reserve and I expect it will be in market by next spring if
it is I will see if I can git som more We bought about four miles
from John Lauflin and about six miles from American Lion Co
You need not answer this until you hear from me again

DD Phillips

D.D. Phillips in Illinois to his sister Mary Phillips in Enon Valley, Pennsylvania. Dan is at the Pollock's.

Mahomet

Nov 14th 1871

Sister Mary
I arrived here on last Sunday noon & found the folks as
well as I expected. Maria is some better than she was when I
was here before for myself I am some better that I was when I
rote to you but I have not made up my mind not to work mutch
this winter I will stay here about a week and then I intend
to go to Arcola and see what I can do there I sold the mules
to Charles he intends to go to Kansas in the spring or fall I
intend to have him brake up the place I bought & then it will
pay for itself for the rent of it for my own part I never expect to
go on to it myself
Wells wants me to come there I don't know but what I will
in the spring I am gitting tired of living the way I have for the
last year & if I go there I will make it my home with Wells I
will rite again in a week you need not answer this

DD Phillips

November the 14th, 1871

Miss Mary L. Phillips

I received your letter yesterday concerning the money. That money is not on our hands nor will be before some time. That man has had bad luck since he came here his wife died and left him 2 children and he sowed a great lot of oats to make the money for you and the chince bug eat all the oats and wheat in the country. The oats was a total failure. The man is honest but you will have to wait a while on the mony. He has to pay off the railrode with his ___ or lose it for got badly burned in Chicago. Had I known sooner I could have maid a turn D Robinson but I paid him his payment. I can make a turn on the next payment which comes due on next November 12 2 hundred and 50 dollars. I can make a turn on that so I make it safe for you the man is I believe pretty honest he will pay you soon as he can I know the money is safe all you want is the interest

We can't sue for money only in open court and that don't come til next March so if you allow me to make that turn let me know soon.

Mary wrote you all the news so that is all. Write soon.

Lutton

Mary Cloke, a former student, to Mary Phillips in Enon Valley, Pennsylvania.

Ashkum, Ill
November 22nd 1871

My Dear Friend Mary

I am almost a shame to write for it is so long since we received you likeness but it is not to late yet. We all think your likeness looks very natural. Sister Ellen has sent you one of her pictures.

Well I must tell you a little about our school   we all wish very much that we could have you back here to teach our school for we have got a lady from Dupage Co and there is not one of the scholars that like her and she is teaching this fall but the most scholars she has is six and most of the time she only has one or two scholars but we had a splendid teacher last winter and all the children learned very fast

Ellen is in the fourth reader and William and Richard and Roda are all in the third reader Sarah Hattie and me read in the fifth reader   Hattie and I have been more than half way through our arithmetic (I suppose have heard that Emma and Abbie Davis is away from home) Emma is in Iowa and Abbie is in Littleton. The young lady that is living on your place lost her Mother a few weeks before they moved down here and so it makes it very lonesome for her as she has no sisters. She is keeping house for her Father and Brothers and she is only sixteen years old they all send their best respects to you Mary you must excuse this poorly written letter as I am in a hurry to finish it so as to get it mailed it is very cold here now but we have had very fine weather here this fall to do our fall work in the crops are very good here this season.

Mrs. Padley has had three parties this fall and Father and Mother was to two of them. I hope this will find you enjoying the best of health as I am very thankful to say it leaves us all quite well at present.

I must tell you of the weddings. Mr. pling Packard is married to Miss Sophie gridley and Mr. William Mellon is married to Miss kaylet up north and also his sister Amy was married the same night only three days ago.

Mr. Davis has been very sick but he is on the mend and also Mrs. Witchstrav has been very sick indeed this summer and she has got another little boy and Mrs. Merkle and Mrs. Eden have both got another little boy.

Please write to us for we would so very much like to hear from you and write us all the news you can. I have not much more to say this time but I must wish you a very merry Christmas and a Happy New Year and many a good sleigh ride.

Mary please pardon my blots and blunders this time I must close with love from all to you.

Phoebe is not at home this winter she is living in Ashkum with Mr. and Mrs. Notttingham. It is good sleighing here now. We have not got our house finished yet. Mr. Merkle has put up a large new house and had it painted over a fresh.

Well Mary time and space demand a close please write soon

I send my best and kindest love to you I still remain as ever your kind and loving scholar and friend Miss Mary Cloke
I believe you know our address it is Ashkum Iroquois Co Illinois

Arcola

Nov 28th 1871

Sister Mary

    Once more I find myself pen in hand to scratch a few lines to let you know where I am I arrived here a week ago found them all well times are dull out here this winter I heard from Charles he says that he wants me to come there and I have some notion of goan What do you think about it for my part I am tired of playing gipsy

    I am some beter than I have been for some time I have been Doctern with SS Fitch of New York it cost me ten dollars per month John wants me to stay here this winter he thinks that by Spring I can find something to do if I cant find any thing to do until then I will find some other place I think for I cant stay in one place so long and do nothing I want you to write and tell me what you think Amoret is about the same old thing I want you to write a soon as you can for I want to hear from you Have you received your school & the money on the place yet [Addison's payment on the farm] Well Mary if you are a gone to do nothing only run around like myself let us go to Kansas in the Spring by puting our money together we can git a long well by buying young stock & if you want to teach school there is a good chance about a mile from where I bought

    I dont want you to go unless you want to & think it is best for your self I remain as ever

Your Brother DD Phillips

Arcola
Dec 13th 1871

Dear Sister

Your favior of Dec 9th came to hand today and I hasten to answer it as best I can in the first place John intends to start east on Monday next 18th of the month and if your are goan along with him he wants you to be ready to go

I received a letter from Wells last night he wants me to be sure and come there this winter or in the Spring John thinks it is the best thing I could do but I can hardly make up my mind to go for I long to be my own boss but then I have not enough money to suit me to start on Wells address is Forest Home Amador Co I intend to stay here until John comes back and it may be I will find some thing to do and go to Colorado or California on account of my health

As regards you Mary on the place I think it is as safe in the hands of Mr Addison as it would be in Luttons but then he is a strainger to me but then I think it is safe

Mary I have some notion of goan to my place in the Spring and improve it that is plow it and set out a orchard and keep batch if I do that I may be there in the Spring but if I go to Cal I will not come I want to hear from you as soon as you git to your journeys end

Anney [Amoret's daughter] received a letter from Cyrus wife She said that you was goan to be married in a day or two if it is so I think you mite send me ten cents so I could take a glass of wine

Yours as ever
DD Phillips

Relief Phillips Fields in Enon Valley, Pennsylvania to her sister Mary Phillips in Vermont.

Enon Valley Jan 28th 1872

Dear Sister

Thinking a few lines from here might be of some interest to you I will try and write a little. We are all in reasonable health. It was three weeks after you left here before we received any mail from you. I began to feel quite uneasy was glad to hear you was alright. I have not anything to write that will be of interest to you.

Mr. Berge came week before last with three men Amzi and Milton. Chopped with them four days that week and the teacher was here two nights. Mr. Berge came back the first of last week with his men and finished hauling the timber. Will not be back until spring to frame the timber.

Cyrus received a few lines from Wells to know what he was doing with the Joe McConahy affair so he will render the necessity of going to see him. Wells wants to know what has become of you that you can't find a little time to write to him. I wrote to Dan since you left and asked him if it would not be a good plan for him to marry and settle on his land, he answered he thought it would be if he only had good health but as he was now he would not, his back and hip pains him so much, says if he cannot get into something to do that suits him there, thinks he will go back to Uncles [Amos] and stay until spring and then go to Kansas. I wanted him to come and see us and have Maria come along if he thought she was able and he would like to but that was out of the question at present. Have not heard from her yet perhaps she can come out with you when you come. Don't want you to come until you think you would be contented if you was here.

Emmet Russle died the morning after you left.

The little Daniels girl that her mother was a McCandles died three weeks ago of cholera infantism.

Mrs. Polly Robertson was buried two weeks ago today. She was brought to Mr. Brothers and the funeral went from there to McClelands Church as she had requested. Mr. Reed thought the shroud was got in Youngstown as her remains were fixed and brought in a coffin from there. He said it was something very gay looking and all fixed off with lace, she had the chapter selected to be read at her funeral.

Mr. Samuel Davidson buried a little girl yesterday had (I think) inflammation of the brain. They thought she was better, gave her some medicine and she died in about four months.

Almost all the children in school have had the measles.

Ira and Mary talk about Aunt Mary coming home every day. Ira goes to Aunt Marys bed to sleep every night. Hoping to hear from you often I will close. You must not expect me to write as often as you do. For you have a double chance what I do and you can imagine we are plodding along about the same old way, if anything unusual takes place we will try and let you know. Give my love to uncles and aunts and cousins and reserve a share for yourself

Relief Fields
(Written across the top of page 3)
Westfield Church was burned the 9th of the month.
(Written across the top of page 1)
Dan said there has been four cases of Scarlet Fever in Arcola two died, one got well, one has it yet.

Peter Wallace, a friend in Ashkum, Illinois to Mary Phillips in Vermont.

Ashkum, Illinois
February 12, 1872

Miss Mary Phillips
Dear friend,

I recd you letter about a month ago were very glad to here from you that you are having a nice time we are all well here at present Mr. Davis had quite a hard spell of sickness in the fore part of winter but is well now his daughter from Iowa is here on a visit that smart little woman he used to talk about

I had a letter from your brother Daniel from Mahommet Ill he is well Ashkum has grown considerable since you left here. Warful built a new store and Packard built one and Payson built one but he never fills his

About the school I don't think they will have any school before August they voted last fall to have only six months school in the year and they are having it all this winter so they will have no summer school unless they hire a teacher out of there private funds some of them talk of doing so if they do they say they like to have you teach for them I will find out more about it and let you know I will get your money on the 15th at least I expect to if you would have no real use for it I would like to borrow it till about the 15th of June or the 1st of July I will pay you 10 percent for it and be obliged to you besides I have corn to sell but I want to hold it till then if I can please let me know as quick as you can

Our boy is getting to be quite smart he runs all about and talks some Mary is afraid he will soon be boss

We will be very happy to have you come to see us when you come to the states and I suppose you will be happily surprised to see a new Methodist church in Ashkum   they are going to build one right away they are to buy the lumber today

Please excuse haste and a bad pen

Yours & ____
Peter Wallace

Relief Phillips Fields to her sister Mary Phillips in Vermont.

Enon Valley Feb 22 1872

Dear Sister

I will try and write a little this evening to you. Your letter was written on the third but did not come to Enon Valley until the seventh for Cyrus was hauling lumber last week from the station and was in the [post] office every day to get a bottle of Kenedips medicine for me for they had none but was looking for it every day. I had a turn of nettle ras two weeks ago last Saturday and Sabbath and also a very severe cold and the children were almost sick with a cold. I think it was because the weather has been so changeable but we are all well now.

I think it has been so long since you wrote that I had better send this to Strafford.

As I told you before you went away and also wrote to you and now tell you again we want you to stay there until you are perfectly satisfied and when you want to come back then come.

I had a few lines from Maria once since you left. Her health is not as good this winter as it was in warmer weather. She says she is strong enough but it is her nerves. Dan was there when she wrote. Thought if he could get into work he would stay around there until spring and then go to Kansas.

You know where Wm Brooks lives this side of Widow Young's, his brother in law and wife came there last week on a visit from Pittsburgh. Since he came there she was taken sick with small pox and is lying there with it. Now if that gets into the neighborhood it will be more alarming than the typhoid fever.

I want you to see if they know what ever became of Willard Martin's Mother (Mary Molton). You will be apt to see some of her brothers and sisters they live some place there. If you live to come back Aunt Polly will want to know about them.

Feb 23 Belinda Wilson and Kat were here today. Kat wants that piece like her white dress for fear she has not enough for a over skirt. Shall I let her have it and you take the money and get more of something else for Mollie a dress or not.

I do not think of anything more at present. Wishing you a pleasant time I will close.

Yours as ever,
Relief Fields
Mary L. Phillips

P.S. Remember and not come back until you are satisfied to do so. They used Rev. Miller so mean that he applied to presbytery to grant him a discharge and they done so, now the congregations can get supplies or go without preaching.

Moravia,
March 4th, 1872

Friend Mollie,

Yours of a still more recent date is at hand its contents masticated and the contents satisfactory

There has been some change in my intentions since I last wrote you I have concluded to sell out my interest in brick making will not farm any but keep two teams in the limestone trade until fall then, God knows the rest.

Have rented my farm to Alfred Aley for one year will either sell or buy some of theirs

Don't know which have some first thoughts of going South and teach for one year Am waiting for something to turn up if I should take a notion to get married this Spring you had better gather up your little change and be ready. If I do get robed in matrimonial majesty I will buy Belle or Wilkison out so as to have an interest in the old homestead

Saw Mr. Fields a few days ago he expressed himself as being very sorry if he had ever said or done anything to me, contrary to the most modern style of common decency result differences of opinion as to what constitutes the abuse described element of our present greatness.

He denying having never expressed or thought an evil intention toward me his wife likewise being a fast friend up to our latest _____ I prevaricated and retired midst great applause I don't know of anything surprising or particularly so except the recent introduction of a smart fox into the city of New Castle.

As to the weather it is cold and dry it has neither rained snowed or thawed since you left or anybody else

The Beaver is very low and supports a heavy coat of ice said to be 7 feet thick at Wampum Do you intend coming home in the Spring to await my arrival if the former I will meet you at some remote station escort you to home I don't like the style of name in your ever green garden Belle and Mart cooing in the other room like two mice in a cake of gingerbread Mons Ritter is also here on a visit looking gay as ever The Goodle family have also just arrived making letter writing difficult Capt Malty demands the table for dinner

Yours as Ever
J. H. McConahy

Relief Phillips Fields in Enon Valley, Pennsylvania to her sister Mary Phillips in South Strafford, Orange County, Vermont.

Enon Valley,
March 1872

Dear Sister,

We received your letter yesterday wanting that receipt, it found us all well. I will write a little this evening to & by Cyrus to the [post] office in the morning. It has been too cold to either rain or snow here of any account all winter it has snowed two or three inches today. That man that had the small pox has a very light turn of it and they went home to Pittsburgh last week. Ella Young went with them (they are cousins) Nan Young said her Mother and Tom was opposed to her going but there was no use to give her advice for she would do as she pleased. There has no person taken it around here.

You know John Hannah that went with Mary Ann Scott he and a younger brother were chopping a tree down two weeks ago last Saturday it was a leaning tree and before they thought of it, the tree split and flew back some way so that it hit Robert knocking him back ten or twelve feet, mashed his head all to pieces broke both arms killing him instantly. He had been to Kansas two or three years and had lived there had been home only three weeks.

They say Jim Davidson and Lizzie Leonard are married they and all Woodses went to Pittsburgh where they were married. Woodes came back and Davidson went on to Virginia to some of her friends.

It is late and I must close, hoping it will prove well for you in the end for going there. Give my love to all that inquire for me.

Yours as ever,
Relief Fields
Mary L. Phillips
I expect you will be at Strafford by the time this gets there.

[Ed. Note: Mary (Relief's daughter) made her mark on this envelope with a pencil.]

Bell Flower Ill
March 12th 1872

Dear Sister

 I received yours of Feb 12th sometime ago but I had nothing to write I have neglected to answer I am in the same fix yet but will do the best I can Maria is not enjoying very good health this winter Charley has the ague & all the rest have colds I am some better than I was last fall but I don't know what I will do next summer I don't want to work out & eat pork for I think that is the reason I am so unwell this winter for when I was at Uncles it was pork all the time James Henry & I was thinking of starting a drug store but John would not help him enny So it has plaid out. There is a Rail Road to be built this summer about a mile from here Harvey wants me to stay & start at something here in the fall and Wells still wants me to come there & I received a invitation to join a colony to start with teams [wagon train] about the first of May from Manhatten Kansas for Oregon or Washington Teritory GW Freeman & Robert Sharp and Lady (Pheby F) is goan As I am afraid that I cant never enjoy good health in this stait I have some notion of goan Will find out in two or three weeks James Freemans mother died on the 10 of Feb

 John Henry came home on Friday run around town on Saturday Sunday & Monday was home drunk & Thursday he went to Danville on Rail Road Business & I left & that is all I know about him

 Harvey dont want me to say enny about Charley having the ague for fear you will never come to the State So when you write say nothing about it

I think you had better stay where you are please write by
return mail

Yours as ever
DD Phillips
DD Phillips to sister Mary
Direct Bell Flower Station
McLean Co. Ill

JWD Phillips in California to his sister Mary Phillips in Vermont.

March 17th 1872
Forest Home Amador Co Cala

My Dear Sister Mary

Yours of Jan 31st was received about two weeks ago delayed
by the snow blockade and I have delayed to get our photographs
they are not as good as might be Jane & Ida have been down
to see Esther I met them on their return in Sac City Nevada
was not with us and cannot send hers but will send as you direct
prior to June Esther has another daughter making 3 girls and a
boy to date all well.

You will perceive that my beard shows age it shows more in
the picture than in person I am 45 it seems difficult to realize
that I am on the shady side of life

You speak of snow we have none here but can look on the
snow capped peaks of the Majestic Sierres from 50 to 75 miles
distant from us in depth from 5 to 30 feet deep not mentioning
huge drifts of perpetual snow In 1863 I packed hay on mules
over snow 20 feet deep in the month of August and within 12

feet from the edge of the snow could mow a swarth of grass it was as solid as ice Lay on the north side of a ridge.

Your description of where Uncle Steven lives is very definite but might be improved by stating what hill he lives on & what road ends there.

I was not aware that Uncle Steven wife saw me or I her when I was in Vt. where they married then Dec 1852 I think I should enjoy a visit to Vt. very much but that is among the improbabilities We would gladly receive all our relatives photographs & herewith send our good wishes to all. I would gladly correspond with any that think my brief messages would compensate

Yours Lovingly
J.W.D. Phillips
A letter directed to Placerville will find me wherever I be in mt or vall [valley]

Child Chloe, daughter of Uncle Amos Davis. She was 8–9 years old when this letter was written to Mary Phillips in Vermont.

March the 27, 1872
Appanoose, Ill

Dear Cousen,
it is in the Greatest of pleasure that I take my pen in hand to tell that I am well and hoping to find you the same my pa is dead he died the 22nd of march at Half past 3 in the Night dear cousen I must tell you that we milk 18 cows I rote you a letter Before this one and I had to Burn it up so you must please Answer my poor writing my little Sister Mary Jane is

the sweetest Girl you ever saw she is leazing in the Cradle asleep while I am riting my ma is _____. By now dear cousin I must tell you there been no fire in here today just got through washing and canning I am eating an Apple is that fine enough cousin Dear cousin I must tell you that the fire is burning know Dear cousin I wish you were here to tell me something to rite you so I will turn over

I wish I could see you again We would have a jolly old time

Oh dear cousin I Guess I will have to stop riting this time and Another time I will rite more news to you I guess that I am the prettiest cousin you halve got Dear cousin I love you to your Halo if you love me as I do you no knife can cut our love in two

To my cousin Mary from her cousin Chloe Davis
Direct your letters to Chloe, Appanoose Hancock County Ill

Dear Cousin
Send me a Kiss
My pen is poor
My ink is pale
My love for you
Can never fail

march the 27. 1872,
Appanose
Ill.

Dear Coosen

it is in the Greatess of pleasore
that I take my pen in Hand to
tell that I am well and hoping
to find you the same my pa is dead
he died the 22 of march at Half past 3
in the Night dear Coosen I muss tell you
that we milk 13 cows I rote you a letter
Before this One and I had to Been it up
so you most please Anewer my poor riting
my little Sisster mary fone is the Sweetest Girl
you Ever saw. She is Leaying in the Cradle
Aleep while I am riting my ma is coing her
Hand rite By me Dear Coosen I muss tell
you there aiues Been to hire in here today
I Joss got through washing and coming
I am eating an Apple is that fine Enough Coosen
Dear Coosen I muss tell you that the fire
is Burning know Dear Coosen I wish you were
here to tell me something to rite you
so I will turn Over O and Over

March the 27, 1872, Appanoose, Ill

Joseph H. McConahy in Moravia, Pennsylvania to Mary Phillips in Vermont. This letter was written two months before their wedding.

Moravia,
April 6 1872

Friend Mary,

After a protracted lapse of time I once again as in days of yore command the _____ to hold sweet communion with absent ones. Every age of the world has had its wonder the earlier age had its flood another its Tower of Babel another crossing the Red Seas on dry land and later its Christ and his crucifixion. Yet later one had its Dark and gloomy ages. Still later one had its Luther and grand Reformation. Yet all these sink into one huge grand mass of utter significance when compared with the unrivaled wonder which I am presently about to relate but at present will exultingly pass on to the next which is as follows to _____.

This leaves us all in ordinary good health – nothing unusual or frightfully absurd having taken place since I last advised you. George Morrow and brother Jim have bought the old Homestead. Bell and I individually I myself own the Zeigler Farm. Would like to have had an interest at home but was not able to buy myself and could not find out by you how much you was willing to invest. I concluded to do the next best thing and let it go. We hold possession until after harvest and then will make a deal and sell out so we will have no place to go as my place is rented for one year.

You say you are willing to sacrifice all you have for those you love now that is one grand mistake of your life. Since I do not wish or ask you to sacrifice anything for me if you had put anything in the common crib you would have received bond with interest until you were paid. I am not quite as destitute of principle as you may suppose as to take the last cent of my wife's money and squander it. I had hoped you thought better of me than that.

You seem to be somewhat patriotic. You say as Ruth of a former date whenever thou goest I will go thy people shall be my people and they God my God. That is perfectly correct but what need has a man of a traveling companion when he has neither country people nor God to visit but going in whatsoever direction the wind blowith.

The poet says very truly I suppose there is a divinity that shapes our ends. That Divinity seems to be opposed to new arrangements and may utterly cast them asunder unless we come to a better understanding. I cannot say as to what I will do this fall and winter as I know not the future.

You say you expect you made me mad. That is a mistake. You did annoy me from the fact that you seemed to evade and made no definite answer.

If your answer had been positive I could have shaped my ends to suit. The answer to the first wonder is a negative one. How can anyone do as they please in this world when each is dependent on the other. It is well you revealed your intentions before the contract was closed. You seem to be infatuated with <u>Yankee Liberty</u>.

Yours truly,
J.H. McConahy

D.D. Phillips in Illinois to his sister Mary Phillips in Vermont.

Bellflower McLean Co
Illinois April 14th 1872

Dear Sister

Yours of March 11th is at hand & to answer it I loose no time. I expect before this reaches you that you have heard of the sad news of the <u>Death of our Uncle Amos Davis</u> he died on 22th of March twenty minutes to three in the morning with lung feavor was taking sick on the 19th & was buried the 24th he is buried on the mound beside his wife

I am glad you still enjoy your self in old Vt I should like to see our friends but think that I would not like to live there it is too cold. I never intend to spend another winter in Illinois it is too cold & windy

Harvey Pollock is going to South West Mo after he plants his corn & if he likes will sell out & move he wants me to go along I have some notion of goan for if I farm I want fruit of all kinds & I can sell out in Kansas enny time & I will do all I can so we can live handy to each other for my own part I should like if it would suit you to have you come out West & you can buy land or stock or if that don't suit you I will buy land & give you a morgage on all I have & I will give you ten per cent on your money

I will let you have the land & stock in your name So at enny time you want your money you can git it We will start about the first of June & I would like to know by that time what you intend to do. I think it would be better for you and myself to if you come

Monday 15th I received a few lines from Charles he has rented the big Medow at 3 dollars per acre he wants me to come out & help him farm it but I have come to the conclusion to leave that State my health for the last two weeks is very poor I am still Doctern with SS Fitch

Uncle [Amos] made his will the day before his death using them all alike including Mrs Davis As I want to write to SS Fitch & CC [his brother Charles] & want to go to the Station by noon I will close let me hear from you often

DD Phillips

From J. H. McConahy in Pennsylvania to Mary Phillips in Vermont. The wedding is for J. H. McConahy's sister Isabelle to Martin Richie.

Moravia, April 29th 1872

Friend Mollie,

Yours of the 28th is at hand in reply I would say state the time at which you will meet me at Buffalo and make it soon as possible if you wish to see Belle & Mart married as it will come off on or about the 20th of May

I believe Belle wishes you here to help her get fixed that is to get things ready for hostilities

Yours as ever
J. H. McConahy

[Ed. note: Hostilities—joke for festivities?]

Chloe Davis [Amos Davis' daughter] to her cousin Mary Phillips in Pennsylvania

Appanoose, Ill
May 18, 1872

Dear Cousin

I received your kind letter and was glad to hear from you We are all well and hope you're the same   Yes we have his picture No I hant such a big girl I am only 9 years old read in the fifth reader Dick says he will rite to you and send you his picture if I had mine taken I would send it to you I must tell you that I am a going to school in September and going to learn music and talk Dutch Dear Mary I just got done eating dinner Say cousin tell me who your middle name is You got the 1st letter L   What does it stand for tell me please or do you know Ethan is downstairs by the table Well today is Sunday don't look at the bad writing do come over I would like to see you awful well if I send you my picture I can tell you something that it will do for to set out in the yard to keep things out of it So many miles between to Friends that love each other At the end I hope we will meet together some time in another world or else in this one

O my best cousin do come and see me. I love you Every where I go I send 2000 kisses and 90 more   I send my love to you and all who inquire after me

From Chloe
To her good cousin

Belleflower June 16 1872

Dear Sister Mary

Once more after a long time to pen a few lines to you I am going to try but who you are I know not i.e. what name to call you by So if I should call you rong I ask your pardon but I will venture the name of Mary & if Joe is my brother I wish you & yours health wealth & happiness and may peace be with you

I will stay here til the first of August & then I will go for some warmer place than Illinois for I never intend to winter over in this state enny more there is no news to write My box is down at Charles and what there is in it that you want let me know and I will have him send it to you for I never intend to have enny use for them As Maria intends to write I will say no more

Yours as ever
DD Phillips

Lydia Maria Phillips Pollock to her sister Mary Phillips McConahy

Dear Sister as Daniel has wrote I thought I wold write it is a shame I have not wrote before but I still heard from you was glad you enjoyed your self so well but was disappointed that you did not come this way when your way was paid Amoret was to see us 2 weeks ago came on the last day of May and left the third of June She said you had not wrote to them she thought you might She did not fetch any of Logans clothes did not expect it

My health is improving am pretty smart now the cold winds do set pretty hard on me was not out of the house more than 12 times from the first of Nov to the first of June was able to be up most of the time and able to work a good deal if kept warm it was nervous prostration but it was on account of my monthly turns stoping they would come and stop to soon

Write soon hope if you have changed your name you may do well would like to see you give my love to all inquiring friends

Lydia Pollock

D.D. Phillips at Lydia Maria's in Illinois to his sister Mary Phillips McConahy in Pennsylvania. Dan wants Lydia Maria to return to Western Pennsylvania for a visit. He thinks the visit will improve her health.

Bellflower McLean Co
Sept 9th 1872

Dear Sister

I am goan to try to pen a few lines after a long silence in the first place I have had the ague & Billious Feaver combined I have not been able to do enny thing since the 13th of August you cant go into a house without finding some one sick. I intend to leave this part of the world by the first of Oct where I will stop I cant say at present will go from here to Hancock Co but will not stay there longer than a week or two I am through writing for myself from this point on it is for Maria they all have had the ague for the first time since they came out here but not hard She is talking some of goan out there this winter. I think that she ought to leave this State and see if it would not do her good Harvey has all he can see through at present to pay for the farm but when he has it paid for will have a good thing the new Rail Road station is a mile and quarter & they intend to have the cars running this fall and then he can sell out for 40 to 50 dollars per acre I will pay her way out there & I expect that you & Relief will have to keep her until you can send her home

Yours as ever DD Phillips

D.D. Phillips in California to his sister Mary Phillips McConahy in Pennsylvania. Dan took the train from his brother Charles' in Illinois to California.

Sacramento,
Nov 11, 1872

Dear Sister,

I landed here about an hour ago. I left Charles on the sixth. They was well I sent you a package & I expect you have received it before this As I wana write a few lines to Maria & I am now riting by gas lite I have been on the cars [train] so long that I am almost plaid out Will write when I git rested & give you a small idea what I saw on the road I will go to Wells in the morning

DD Phillips

Forest Home
January 27/73

Dear Sister

Yours of the 16 is at hand & I hasten to answer you wanted to know what I thought in regards Maria I am afraid she will never be enny better & I think that the breaking up of winter will go hard with her. I gave her money last fall to go & see you all back there, thinking the change would do her good & I think Harvey mite have seen her start I wish I had staid & went with her & came here in the Spring. there is one thing this is the nicest winter I ever seen only about a week the nites froze ice & thin at that nothing more than a good frost

As regards that money at Ashkum I hardly know what to think I thought at the time it was all right I think I will write to Addison he is the one that bought the place & see what he says this is a hard world it is hard to tell who to trust. Who will lie and who wont

Wells and family are at Placerville this winter the girls are goan to school G.H. Freeman & another man & I have been batching this winter Freeman left yesterday he is goan to work for Wells next summer. I intend to by some stock and go to the mountains in the Spring. has the boats quit runing on the canal?

I sent my bed to Maria to ceep until I cald for it & as you want me to have the quilt I want you to take good care of it for me & then if I cant remember you, I will try and think where my quilt is My health is better than it was and I think that I will be all right soon As I have a chance to send this to the office

I will close but I will try some of these times and write a sheet full Kind regards to all and I remain as ever your Brother

Dan

J.W.D. Phillips in California to his sister Mary Phillips McConahy in Pennsylvania.

Placerville Feb 21st 1873

My Dear Sister

I am just up from Forest Home prior to leaving your letter was received glad to hear you were well We are all in usual state of health Dan is quite well & satisfied to make this his abiding place.

The coldest indicated at the Ranch is 30 degrees above zero or two below freezing -- hanging on the North & outside of the house What do you think of that compared with your 60 degrees colder (makes me shiver to think of it without the experience.)

I have answered all letters received from you.

Dan and I have bot a small band of goats ranging in grade from the common to 7/8 cashmere have 16 live kids from 14 Ewes They will have another litter in July & August. My 12 ewes last year raised me 33 kids worth to me $4 per head. have about 60 Ewes more to come in

My family lives here in town so the girls can go to school I am with Dan most of the time at the ranch heard from Charles a short time ago all well

I expect to sell my valley range and buy higer in the mts suitable for goats.

Write all the particulars about our old neighbors.

I think I could enjoy myself at your Literary meetings particularly to hear Uncle Billey A. Spout

The last word we heard from Maria she was better.

I have no word from our Vt friends would like to hear from them.

Dan has been out and killed a deer The first & only shot he had

Write soon and oblige
JWD Phillips

Lydia Maria Pollock in Illinois to her sister Mary Phillips McConahy in Pennsylvania.

Belleflower McClain Co, Ill
April 17, 1873

Dear Sister,

I received 2 letters and was glad to hear your health is good as it is and getting along with your babe as well as you are now don't do as I did do as much as you can and don't go in damp places you see I overdone myself in lifting and it affected my nerves and that is the cause of my turns stopping I have not been since I wrote before it is retention of the menses in place of suppressions (?) on the kidneys ... Dan thought his disease was seryola he was doctoring for his blood the most of the time but one doctor told him it was his liver and he thought he would doctor for that more. He thinks we all have got the sercfula if anything ails us in regards that rocking chair it would not pay to send it what it would cost to fetch it would buy another of a cheaper kind such as that would cost more than a bed would you need not send it it has been pretty wet this spring can not get to work for the ground is so wet they plowed the potato ground yesterday intending to plant today but it rained so will have to wait we received the paper you sent I would like to see the Awlsworth folks but it is hard to tell when that will be it looks as if it would be nice if some of the large boys was girls but the boys are very good to work … I have to wear my supporters all of the time before I got them if I would left the tea kettle I could not get over it for several days I can work now if everything is warm but cannot touch anything that is cold in the least so I cannot do much house work in cold weather I am going to write Relief and tell her the particulars a little more than I wrote to you for you are too young to know everything. I expect you think you know considerable by this time more than you want to know again Mrs. O'Neil died of congestive chill that woman that was at our house that time you and Mother came in the wagon for lunch from uncle Amos I do not think of anything in particular and will close

Lydia M. Pollock

Lydia Maria Pollock in Illinois to her sister Mary Phillips McConahy in Pennsylvania. The pictures that Lydia refers to are Mary and Joseph's wedding picture.

July 20, 1873

Dear Sister

   We received your letter yesterday stating the death of John Smith we had not heard of it we have not heard from them for over a year and when they did write they did not say anything about the children. One time John wrote that Rebecca was going to keep house he did not say who it was with nor whether she was married or not. Wore they parted and what for and how long do you know what they are doing the boys and girls how are they behaving Now give us all the information you can we know nothing only what you write Harvey wants to hear all you know was it heart disease he died with.

We have not heard from Dan for a long time we are as well as usual have had considerable rain since I wrote

Fall wheat half a crop young wheat good corn looks well a great deal of it planted late. Your letter and pictures came all right Joseph does not look much as he did when I last saw him do not know when I saw him last have not heard from Relief lately I will bid you good-by

Lydia Pollock
Answer as soon as you can

D.D. Phillips at J.W.D.'s ranch in California to his sister Mary Phillips McConahy's in Pennsylvania.

Garden Valley Oct 1873

Dear Sister
Your faviour came to hand some time ago to answer it I will try I have been very unwell all Summer having the chills every once in awhile it is liver chills not ague but I have felt better for the last two weeks -- I have been down here fixing a place to

fetch the stock to this winter -- will start for the mountain on the 20 will be gone some three weeks with the stock

You wanted to know when I intended to come back there that is more than I can say I would like to see you all -- & you know I would like to go a fishing in (the) Beaver next month Old Jane & I don't git along very well & if we don't get along better I will sell my stock & hunt some place else & live a happy (life) back in a cabin by the sea -- they are going to live in Placerville this winter so I will not be bothered with her for some time and I won't bother her you bet

yours in hast
DD Phillips
Direct to Garden Valley

Lydia Maria Pollock in Illinois to her sister Mary Phillips McConahy in Pennsylvania.

August 2nd,1874

Dear sister

It has been a long time since I wrote to you my health is about as usual it is very dry corn will not be more half a crop the chints bug took part of the wheat if there is no rain there will be no late potatoes there is no early ones of any account Polly [a Pollock relative] wrote to Harvey that there was hard times there could get no work and she said she did not know what she would do she thinks some of the people will starve if things do not change what is the trouble is all the work stopt is there no work for good hands can you go and see her and see what is the trouble I should think the girls could get work our boys have to work do not miss a day in working time and we are not able to do for more than our selves and not do that right.

As regards my going on a visit I expect that has fell through cannot help it I cannot get off like some people crops failing and land to pay for there is a railroad 1 ½ miles and a station there there is a express office it is called foos station our post office address is foosland Champaign Co. Ill write immediately and let us hear how things are there   do not forget I got the handkerchief

Lydia M. Pollock

Lydia Maria Pollock in Illinois to her sister Mary Phillips McConahy in Pennsylvania.

Dec 8th, 1874
Foosland, Champaing Co., Ill

Dear Sister,
It is a shame that I have been so long writing but I keep putting it off we are well as usual my health is some better than it has bee for some time You heard from Dan he was at Wellses but was going to take leave soon   I suppose he will get it to write there I think you had better write to him   he is a little odd you know and might think hard if you do not he was not very well

Corn is not more than third of a crop dry weather and chints bug the cause. Some late potatoes after the fall rain the children are going to school all but David and Emma We received yours some time ago

Mary if you have any more babies you take care of yourself for 3 months there is not anything gained in being so you can say I done my work in two weeks and loose your health and may be your life excuse me I bid you all good bye

Love to all
L. M. Pollock

D.D. Phillips in California to his sister Mary Phillips McConahy in Pennsylvania.

Garden Valley
Dec 20th 1874

Dear Sister

It has been a long time sence I have heard from you I have no reason for not writing before & I should like to hear from you often but if you think that I hant worth writing to why of course you are right in keeping quiet. I have been in the mountain all Summer it commenced to snow in Oct and we had about three feet and we had to stay some two weeks waiting for the snow to settle so we could git out we left the mountain on the second of November and there has been no storm sence and we are having a fine winter the grass growing until about a week ago when the night became to frosty So at the present time we are having cold nights with warm days

Wells family is living in Placerville this winter Ester & family was in the mountian for two months She & all of children was sick but when they left they felt almost well Ester is like the old woman (i e her mother)they are as alike as two yellow peeps. the last that I heard from Charles he was in West

Wichita Sedgwick Co. Kansas if you can read this you can do better than I can let me hear from you

I remain as ever
DD Phillips

Relief Phillips Fields to her sister Mary Phillips McConahy. Both are in the same area in Pennsylvania.

Enon Valley,
February 17, 1875

Dear Sister,

I received a few lines from you about two weeks after we was to see you/have not heard if you got along well after that or not. I suppose it will be some time before the weather gets so you can get over to see us and I feel anxious to hear how you are so I thought there would be no harm done if I should write a few lines thinking you would take the trouble to read them.

As you are in about the same latitude of us there is no use in giving a description of the weather but will just say I am really tired of so much freezing. I don't know how you get along without a spring, for almost everything we have is froze except our spring/ around the watering trough the ice is higher than the trough, and in it, the ice is almost solid to the bottom and every morning Cyrus has to chip it out.

I had a few lines from Maria since I saw you. She said her health was better last summer than it had been. Have not had any word from Charles since they went to Kansas. I will write a few lines and send to the office to them when I take this over.

There will be Sacrament at our church next Sabbath. I wish you could be over and hear our preacher – he is a splendid preacher. It would do you good to hear him. We have a very nice organ in the church and expect to keep it there. Anna Alcorn plays on it. Christmas Eve they had a Christmas tree in the church for the Sabbath School. We all went over. It was very nice. The class that Mary was in all got a little china doll/ there was seventeen of them.

Do you know how Charles is getting along this winter? It is such hard times there. There is an account of a woman named McAnamay being froze to death at Wichita going home from a neighbor. The last word I had from Daniel (must be since I saw you) he had gone to Garden Valley. The snow was three feet deep in the mountains in October before he left and had to hunt about a week in the snow before he could find all the stock.

I suppose you know Leander Faddis has another wife (Emma McCard – cousin of Jennie) they have divided the house and left a partition through the kitchen. Now Young has a little daughter about three weeks old.

It may be I have wrote more than you care about reading. What I commenced to write for was to have you let me know how you are getting along.

Your tired sister,
Relief
Be sure and come over as soon as ever you can. Try and come so as to go to church at Enon.

Garden Valley
Feb 28 1875

Dear Sister

I received your favior some time sence but failed to answer. So now I will try and see what I can do in the line of wrighting We are having a warm & dry winter the early rains of last fall started the grass & it being warm all winter that young cattle are doing well without enny feed in fact the feed has been better all winter than it was last Spring in April but we nead rain very mutch for every thing is on the stan still for the want of it

I will be left alone for about two weeks. Wells has gon to see his old friend J.B. Wilson of Vellejo he used to be his mining partner he is worth some thing over a million & he thinks he is about to die and he sent for Wells to come and see him

I have not been over to Placerville this winter there fore I can give you no news from the family only Vade is in Amador Co She has lernt the dress making traid & has started out to try her luck

We bought three goats (in) Spring payed fifty dollars a piece one was poisoned and died on the way up to the mountian. I will send a lock of the wool or rather hair you can wash it & it will look some better.

You spoke as if you would like to have me thare this winter I should like to be back thare for a short time and I am in hopes I may sometime but I cant say when. the coldest night we have had this winter is 30 above zero. last fall when I came out of the mountians I weighed 154 lbs now 170 So you can see I feal some better than comon but I still have some akes in my old bones I always expect GH Freeman is still at Damacus Oregon Shaefer (?) and Family out thare. they landed thare on Nov

I remain as ever yours
DD Phillips

[Ed.note: Angora goat hair is still in envelope]

Relief Phillips Fields to her sister Mary Phillips McConahy – both are in Pennsylvania.

April 28, 1875

Dear Sister,
As we talk of going tomorrow to the station I thought I had better write a few lines to you. When I was over to see you I forgot to say anything about ashes or soap. If you will bring your grease over with you we can make it here without much trouble to anyone.
The turkey that I spoke of was fighting with the rooster and got killed but that makes no difference we can find enough of something else that will stop hunger while you are here.
Mary I want you to be careful about taking cold or lifting much until you get stronger than you are now.
Walace Fields wife was confined the day after I was to see you the child was dead and she died Friday night after and was buried Sabbath. George Douglas' boy was buried the same day.

Remember I expect you all over here as soon as you are able (but not until you think you can come without hurting you)

Yours as ever
Relief

D.D. Phillips in California to his sister Mary Phillips McConahy in Pennsylvania.

Slippery Ford
Aug 10 1875

Dear Sister

it has been along time sence I have heard from enny of you and I would like to hear from my old Home once and a while -- I am well Jane is sick but is giting better and I think she will be all right in a few days I am working for Wells this Summer -- but think after this I will stay below Wells hit his eye with a stick and has been blind in one eye for a week but he can see some now he was out deer hunting last week and killed a nice one -- there is 1500 men working on the Placerville Ditch you can tell Joe that they are taking the water out of the American River a little above Sugar lofe and they are runing a tunel to top of Echo Lake it will cross the road hand the old North America House -- they have surveyed all of the land a round here this Summer and the land sharks are taking all of the good pine timber in Lake Valley and have been looking at the timber up here but as it is mostly fur and it wont last under ground they dont want it At present the lumber goes to the Nevada mines. there is not travel on the road but Fruit teams

I would like to hear from you all and tell me what is goan on in that part of the world give my love to all my friends if you know them

DD Phillips

D.D. Phillips in California to his sister Mary Phillips McConahy in Pennsylvania.

Garden Valley
Oct 19 1875

Dear Sister

Yours of Sept 21 is at hand I received the papers you sent me but I expect I neglected to mention them when I wrote to you I am always glad to receive papers from that part of the world for there is a grate menny things that interest me in them that you would not notice

I dont expect to write as long a letter as you have to me I am not mutch of a letter writer but there is no use of me telling you that for you new that years ago and I dont improve line of business

I still think that I may come back to Laurence County some day but it is hard to tell when I still think of the dear ones I left there but I expect that it would not apear like Home to me enny more

did Retchel Lutton and Dr Marshall git married you wrote me some time ago that they was engaged give my kind regards to Jane Bruce when you see her in fact to all my old friends if you know them (you need not count the Book girls in)

I'm baching all alone at present intend to start back to the mountain the first of the month after the goats & when I come back I will have someone with me. Wells and Family are goan to Glen Brook to ceap a Boarding House that is on Lake Biglar (or Taho)

I was over the day before I left the mountain to visit the grave of our dear brother Alden it is on a little nole with about a dozen other graves about two hundred yards from Lake Bigler [Tahoe] it is one off the nicest places I ever saw there is a hotel cep by Tom Roland nown as the Lake House two stores and five or six other houses the water in the Lake is so clear that one can see where the botem where the water is 75 or 80 feet deep there is three steamers runing on it the Lake is nearly round and I think it is about 12 miles acrost it is a grate place for the big bugs to visit in the Summer time

Oct 25

I am like yourself I have taken a fresh start but dont expect to have mutch to say for I want to write a few lines to Maria tonight I intend to start up for the goats on the 27th will be gon from here about eigt days -- it is about seventy miles by the way I will have to go -- I will go to the Georgetown Road will come out on the Placerville Road at the Junction house -- about ten miles from Wells place (Joe will know about where it is) I expect by the way the wind blows I will git a good weting before I git back -- Kind regards & love to all

I remain as ever your Brother
Dan

Pampanoose, Vermont,
November 5, 1875

Dear Cousin,

Little did I think when you were here & spent these few months with me so pleasantly (so pleasantly for us) that it would be four years before I should even write you or have the pleasure of hearing from you but it has been so and now I think I can spend a few leisure moments quite pleasantly in conversing with you of the past, present, and future through the medium of my pen.

This leaves us all well with the exception of Mother she has been quite poorly for the last few months but is better now I think we all remain about as we were when you were here Uncle Prescott's family as somewhat changed My son is married has one child he lives with his wife's father Ky (?) expects to be married this fall & will take his wife home Aunts health is very poor Hettie & her hubby & little one spent the summer months with them it is wonderful to state that she is as happy as ever

Uncle Stephen has moved to Massachusetts with his little group which is larger by three than when you were here. Uncle Ephriam & family are well.

Abbie lives in Manchester N.H. she was married last August to Mr. Hutchison his business very often calls him west and he often says he will go and see you but has not made the attempt yet he expects to go west this winter if so will use your ticket if possible some say it is not good others say it is I hope it is if so we will send you the money as soon as he returns Alice is with Abbie going to school but Julie and Jake at home to poor old folks, an old bachelor and old maid. Well they are honorable are they not?

I nearly forgot to tell you of Relief she has been at work at Manchester since you were here until this fall She has come up for a rest is at Uncle Prescotts.

My dear cousin Mary, you will value this worth answering for we all want very much to hear from you. Yes we are over anxious. Please write as soon as possible and accept this with love from us all to you and yours

From you affectionate cousin
Lizzie C. Waterman

Relief Phillips Fields to her sister Mary Phillips McConahy in Pennsylvania. The McConahy's seem to be having financial difficulties. I don't know why Mary lost her property or if she got it back.

Enon Valley,
Feb. 28, 1876

Dear Sister,

I don't know as I have any thing of very much interest to write. Only seeing the sale of your property I feel so anxious to know if it is in reality sold, or if it was bid in with an understanding that Jos. could redeem it and keep it on, or if you do really have to let it go. I feel very sorry for you but that does not help the matter any.

When will you have to leave it if you have to go and where will you go to?

The way the weather is and the roads are so bad I do not know when we will get over to see you.

Our horses have had the distemper for a long time. Have not drove to the church for four weeks. Jack's throat broke on the inside and out. Dick's only on the inside. Will be fit to drive in a few days.

Mrs. Matthew Young (Amanda Festher) died about three weeks ago very suddenly sitting on a chair supposed it was heart disease. Mrs. Robb died two weeks ago had been unwell for a long time. They said it was her liver and stomach. Maggie Grubb died this forenoon of pneumonia of the lungs.

It just now occurs to my mind that his will was that at her death their place was to be sold and the money equally divided amongst the children only the lame one was to have two shares. There is only twenty acres.

If you have to leave where you are if Joseph could get that _____would not that suit him very well   This is only my own notion and I'll say nothing about it to anyone only just mention it to you.

I'll send you a seed catalogue. There was two sent to me I like. Mary's gem papers all come but in December I'll send another year for it and send one to Maria and send the Cherry Girls to you for Lydia.

If you have to leave there I want to know when and where you are going to be.

Yours as ever,
Relief Fields

P.S. We are all in usual health.
Mary McConahy's address was Moravia, Lawrence Co.

Lydia Maria Pollock in Illinois to her sister Mary Phillips McConahy in Pennsylvania.

Foosland Champaign Co, Ill

[Ed. note: no date]

Dear Sister

It has been a long time since I write to you but think of writing every day there has been quite a bit of ague about here several of the children have had it I have had better health this summer than I have had for 5 years but have to take special care of myself I got some cheap pictures taken and they are getting all white but I will send one and send one of Joseph to you and Relief for he gave me nearly all away to the girl.

You have heard of the rain and mud in harvest they had 20 acres of oats 90 acres of flax they had a terrible time to get part of it half of the oats fell off and a great deal of the flax/ the cabbage was rotting considerably

Does Mrs. McConahy keep house & will you gather some spearmint seed if they have any and send it to me and gather a few chestnuts for to plant Just a few send by mail send as soon as gathered they ought not to be dry before planting

I suppose you have heard of the talk of the hoppers [grasshoppers] flying over they were fling around and I do not know what kind they were (time will tell) I would like to see you and your family and see how you look we have lots of potatoes – 2 hills make up a wooden pail full

The boys are all at home only Joseph is in Bloomington going to school/ he wants to go for a while

I will close by bidding all good by

L. M. Pollock

J. P. Pollock in Illinois to his aunt, Mary Phillips McConahy, followed by a letter from his sister Lydia Maria Pollock. Mary is in Pennsylvania. Uncle Charles is in Kansas.

Monday, June 18, 1876

Dear Aunt,

You must think something strange has happened because I impose the present opportunity of writing to you You must not think it strange that I would discharge my duty even at this late date. Although I do not write often to you, I believe I think as much of you as is my privilege and duty. We are all well at the present time that is as well as usual. We are all here father mother "sisters brothers" David has come home from Kansas. He has been at home for some time probably two months. He has secured a quarter section of land in Kansas by preemption which required him to stay there six months being on the place at least once within a month and improving some and paying government price for it. His land is 30 mile south west from Uncle Charles.

We are having rather poor weather for farming this spring wet and cold. Our prospect for large crops is at present not very flattering but may do well with good weather from this theory David Samuel and myself think of going to Kansas this fall. All depends however on having good crop this year. We feel like taking Mr. Horace Greeley's advice "Go West young man, go West" I believe have nothing more to write Mother will finish this letter.

Your affectionate nephew
J. P. Pollock

Lydia Maria Pollock writes:

Dear Sister,

It is a shame I have put off writing so long I put off at first to hear from David to see if he had sent his picture to you when he came home I did not write.

My health is pretty good for me   I weigh one hundred and fifteen last Sept Now I weigh 105 but have to take cotton root bark tea every month since the change of life came on but the Doctor gave me another kind of medicine to take if you take cold and other medicine fails try cotton "root bark" the cotton that grows in the South

Did you get your place back how is your health how is Thomas Hennon and Hannah getting along Ethan Davis [Amos' son] went to Charles' him and his wife went out for his health in a wagon he has the consumption so they say he was between 2 mules and they pushed against him and mashed him so he spits blood he married his step mother's sister. The talk is he is running through his property Liefy is married a mile or so from home has a farm but not fixed up much he not been there a great while. I must write to Relief love to all good by Samuel and Robert are working for a neighbor

Lydia M. Pollock

Mrs. Lutton has the consumption Mary has good health

Unknown author to the McConahy's in Pennsylvania. The note is money for the Phillips' farm in Ashkum, Illinois.

Ashkum, Ill Jan 1st, 1877

Mr. and Mrs. McConahy, dear friends

We wish you and your family a happy new year and are all well now but we have had quite a bit of sickness through the fall and up till now. We hope this will find you and your family all well and that you …

[Ed. note: part of the letter is missing] …as far as I know about your mony Mr. Addison gave Dan a note for $200 and when he went away he left the note with Jacob Lutton and when it came due Mr. Addison found it at Smith & Gages and paid it to them and he has the note Gages is dead and Smith has gone away and I don't know anyone who could tell me anything about it except Lutton and I would not like to say any things to … (letter torn)… you again I should have thought Dan would have told you about it if he knew for my part I thought you had your mony before now but I know Lutton sold the note and it was paid write soon and let me know if you would like me to go and see Mr. Lutton I will do you any favor as far as I can see you are on the same farm yet all the old neighbors are the same except Davis who sold his place to Ralph Mitstoke who was married last week to a young lady from Michigan Davis folks are living on the McHerton farm their youngest son died last October and left a wife and two children McHerton's sons sold out and went to Bloomington, Ill there has been quite a number of deaths around Ashkum lately one of whom you may remember was Paipons youngest daughter she was buried 8 days ago

I almost forget to tell you about our little family we have two boys and three girls our baby is 8 weeks old tomorrow the boys are...

[Ed. Remainder of the letter is missing. We don't know who it is from.]

Relief Phillips Fields to her sister Mary Phillips McConahy. Both were living near Enon Valley, Pennsylvania.

Enon Valley,
Feb. 13th, 1878

Sister Mary

I will write you a few lines this morning not time to write much. Cyrus is going to visit the schools with ___ today at Enon. Chisbart and Cy Henrys wife was here Monday   She said you was very sick I want you to write and le me know how you are if you are any better or not We just have the old mare and some young colts to drive and Cyrus makes so much fuss about crossing the creek   Write and let me know how you are as soon as you can We are all well only colds Liefie was married New Years Day to Anthony Chambers

Relief
Belinda Wilson is not expected to live from one day to another.

Lydia Maria Pollock in Illinois to her sister Mary Phillips McConahy in Pennsylvania.

Nov 22, 1878

Dear Sister

I received your kind letters and was glad to hear from you. Last year we moved the stove into a plank kitchen it joined the house but there was too much morning air and I took cold and them pills did me no good I sent to the Doct sent me some medicine and it drove it down and hurt my breast and appeared to go back to my breast and head. See if Caroline Smith was worked that way   if I had not taken cold and it had not taken another turn I think I might have gotten along but as it is it is hard to tell the rest are well only colds.

It is pretty hard times   cannot sell anything and get the money I could not go this fall I could not go out of the doors but I do not say much about going East potatoes a failure corn not half a crop

As they are going to the office and must close

Good-by to all
L M Pollock

Garden Valley
April 20th 1879

Dear Sister

When your letter came to the office I was not at home was up to Onion Valley it is about 30 miles from here in the mountain Went up there to mine but there is no water where our mine is -- we could do nothing to amount to enny thing so we only staid two weeks -- if we could git water I think we could make about 9 dollars per day but all the water is taken up by the Ditch Company so we will have to wait thare own time -- last fall was dry & cold for this part of the world but it's making it up this Spring for it rains almost every day & the clover is as large as it is most years by the first of June

I have not done mutch work this winter for last fall I was thrown from a load of hay & put one of my waists [hip] out of place I could not use it mutch all winter but it is all most well at the present time I have tried my luck some this Spring at mining here at home but have not cleaned up as yet and I am not sure I will get enny gold after I do -- but if I should I will send you a little to look at

As for me coming back there it is out of the question I can find all the work I can do out here & I am not able to buy the old place if I was thare & my health is better than it was when I came out here & my health is more to me than money I will try & come & see you sometime if we all live long enouf Wells is here at the present time so when you right to him direct to Garden Valley I expect that he will go to Glenbrook in the Spring when we drive the stock to the mountain his family lives at G.B. [Glenbrook] Ida was to see me this winter from here she went to Petaluma to see Ester & to show the folks her Toney Meloche he is clerking in the saw mills at Glenbrook: he gits $150 one hundred & fifty dollars per month -- Vades husband run a engine last summer for 80 dollars per month Vade has a daughter named after her mother [Hettie] I will close for the present

Regards to all
DD Phillips

Robert M. Pollock in Illinois to his aunt Mary Phillips McConahy in Pennsylvania.

Foosland, Ill
May 23rd, 1879

Dear Aunt,

As Mother has written today I will pen a few lines. I am staying in Foosland this summer clerking for C. Dyer. Don't know how long I will stay. Have hired for just as long as we can agree. I receive twenty seven dollars per month

Enclosed I send my picture and love to all. As Mother has written all the news I suppose and I have no more time at present I will close hoping that we may all meet again. I remain as ever your nephew

Robert M Pollock

[Ed. note: C. Dyer was a dealer in dry goods, groceries, hardware, hats caps, boots, shoes, drugs, lumber, coal, etc.]

June 27th, 1879

Mary,

The children are in bed and I have seated myself to write a few lines. Cyrus was saying today that there was going to be a picnic on the fourth near Darlington and unless something prevented more than he knew of now we would go to it if I wanted to.

Now I want Joseph and you to come over here the evening before if you can (if you have no previous engagement) and go down too and you will have a chance to see Mr. Wilkinson folks there or go to their house. You can surely get somebody to milk your cows until Sabbath evening. I did not get half a visit with you over there. Now be sure and come if you posably can. It will do you good to see all your old neighbors and you never was at Darlington I believe you will see some of the world you never saw before.

I have no notion of wanting to interfere with any of your affairs nor do I want you to look at it in that light but write to you just as I was talking to you. I have thought so much about you since I came home. You looked so bad that day we was there. I think you should not put it off any longer without trying to take something to restore your health.

I would like to write a great deal more but hope you will come over and we can talk better than write.

If you cannot come at that time do try and come soon

Good night
Relief Fields

A Collection of
Family Photographs

Phillips family homestead near
East Moravia, Pennsylvania
Rebecca McConahy & Lydia
McConahy Brown Dowds

Phillips' family homestead near East Moravia, PA

Lydia Davis Phillips

Joseph Wells Davis Phillips

Charles Carroll Phillips

Lydia Maria Phillips

Relief Phillips

Alden Church Phillips

Daniel Davis Phillips

Daniel Davis Phillips

Mary Phillips
(as a young girl)

Mary Louisa and Daniel Davis Phillips

Joseph, Mehitable
Jane and Ida Phillips

Mehitable Jane Phillips and Child

Ida and Vade Phillips

Left to right: Hettie Sickles with Wells (son),
Vade Bryson with Alice (daughter), Mehitable Jane Phillips

Left to right: Hettie Sickles,
Sierra Nevada Bryson,
Mehitable Jane Phillips,
Unknown, Jim Bryson In
front: Alice Bryson

Left to right: Vade with Alice Bryson (daughter), John
Meloshe (Ida's son), Mehitable Jane Phillips and Hettie Clark

Relief and Cyrus Fields with Ira

Mary Phillips and
Captain Freeman

Captain Freeman

Illustration of
Great Uncle Dan

Great Uncle Dan
and Nieces

Great Uncle Dan, Jane
and Betty Lyon

Uncle Dan at 83 in 1922 with Jane and Betty Lyon

Great Uncle Dan's Birthday Hettie, Wells, Louise, Babe
Sickles, Great Uncle Dan and Niece

Mary Phillips McConahy
(Possible Wedding Picture)

Joseph Hennon McConahy
(Possible Wedding Picture)

Joseph and Mary McConahy's Children Back row: Relief, William,
Lydia; Front row: Rebecca, Myrtle, Wells - about 1895

Lydia Maria Pollack

Harvey Pollack

Pollack Family
Note: Another son is only partially visable, on the left, as a
result of damage to this photo.

1921 at Phillips Station
Left to right:
Dan Phillips, Mary
Phillips McConahy, Wells
& Hettie Sickles, Alice
& Henry Lyon with Jane
In front: Louise Sickles,
Rebecca McConahy

Alice and Henry Lyon
with Jane - 1921

Sickles and Lyon Families - Babe, Wells, Hettie and Louise Sickles -
Betty, Alice, Henry, Sally and Jane Lyon

Mary Phillips McConahy,
Great Uncle Dan Phillips,
Vade and Jim Bryson,
Alice Bryson

Myrtle McConahy and
Alice Bryson

Myrtle McConahy at Meeks Bay, CA 1908

Phillips Station

Phillips Station Featuring Phillips Crag

Phillips Station Meadow

Phillips Station Dining Hall

Louise Sickles at Phillips Riding a Goat

Alice Bryson

Lydia and Rebecca McConahy

Great Uncle Dan Phillips at Meeks Bay, CA 1908

Stage Coach that Great Uncle Dan Phillips Drove To Rubicon Springs

Notes
Phillips Chronology
1870-1879

1870   Mary Phillips returns to the home of Relief Fields in Western Pennsylvania near Enon Valley from Illinois with her mother Lydia, who was ill. Lydia died here. Daniel remained in Illinois.

Phillips Station was leased to John Sweeney.

1871   After visiting relatives in Vermont, Mary Phillips returned to Western Pennsylvania.

1872   Mary Phillips married Joseph Hennon McConahy on June 11.

Children: **1873:** Lydia Mabel, **1874:** Rebecca, **1876:** William Charles, **1879:** Relief, **1883:** Wells, **1886:** Mary Myrtle

After living in Illinois and Kansas near or with various relatives, Daniel joined JWD in California.

1873   Phillips Station burned for the first time.

1874   Charles Carroll Phillips went to Kansas and later to Victor, Colorado where he mined gold.

1876 Phillips Station burned for the second time.

1879 Mehitable Jane Clark was born at Glenbrook, NE. She was known as Hetty or Hettie.

Still on the Face
of the Earth
1880 - 1889

Great Uncle Dan, who lived until 1933, continues to write during the 1880s and 90s, but many of the other correspondents from the prolific 1870s are quiet. Relief Phillips died in 1881 at the age of 48. Lydia Pollock's daughter, Emma and daughter-in-law, Barbara, are heard from as writers for the first time, as well as an important figure in the early 20th century, Vade Phillips Bryson, JWD's lively daughter, also known as Sierra Nevada. Postmistress, innkeeper, resort manager, Vade was well known in the community for "meeting everyone with a joke and sending them away with a smile" (*Mountain Democrat* May, 1921).

In 1883, JWD lost a daughter, Ida May Meloche, 25 years old, from "inflammation of the bowels." However, Louise Sickles Day writes in a letter dated December 28, 1993 that Ida "aborted herself." Vade took over the raising of Ida's year-old son,

> *I am still on the face of the earth*
> *& I find lots of work to do but little money for it*
> *but then there is lots in the same boat.*
> *Be sure and come out to this State in the Spring*
> *I think it will do you good*
> *& what is this life only what we see & enjoy*
>
> —D. D. Phillips,
> November 28, 1888

John, and a few months later lost her own son, Joseph Wells Clark, three years old.

About this time, Charles Phillips moved to Kansas and later went to work for a mining company in Colorado. Although he mined in Colorado, his home base remained in Kansas. He died in 1889 in Victor, Colorado six years later, at age 70.

Always the wanderer, Great Uncle Dan traveled to Washington Territory in 1884, but after finding it more settled than he expected as well as too cold, he returned to Garden Valley, California and started ranching "on his own luck." In 1888, Dan helped Vade build a house on property she had bought at Rubicon Springs.

In January 1889, Great Uncle Dan writes Mary the sad news of JWD's death at home. His obituary in the **Mountain Democrat** describes him as, "…gifted with more than common ability, although in all his ventures luck seemed to be against him. He was one of our most industrious and energetic citizens…."

Relief and JWD—two pioneering Phillips gone in the same decade.

The Letters

Lydia Maria Pollock in Illinois to her sister Mary Phillips McConahy in Pennsylvania. Lydia is referring to her sister Relief's death. Relief died in January 1881.

Champaign Co., Ill
Feb 15th 1881

Dear Sister
     It was a very sudden and hard stroke to receive the sad news of dear sisters death it does not seem as though it could be that

I shall see her no more in this world but may we strive to meet on that other place to part no more

[Ed. note: the rest of the page is missing, second page – beginning is torn]

I am not as well as I was last summer   Emma had a bad spell of diphtheria this winter How old was she [Relief] when she died and what was Alden's age   David is still in Colorado does not talk of coming home   The children are all home but Robert as I don't feel like writing much   I will close

Give my love to all
Lydia M. Pollock
Want to know all your childrens names

J.W.D. Phillips in California to his sister Mary Phillips McConahy in Pennsylvania. He's writing about his sister Relief's death--possibly of pneumonia.

Garden Valley
March 9th 1881

My Dear Sister
Your very welcome letter came duly to hand containing the sad news of our dear sisters death It surprised us very much as we supposed her general health to be good I think if she had taken mullein tea freely when she was first attacked it would have saved her life   I think it is the best herb for all common complaints and particularly coughs catarrh [an inflamed condition of the mucus membrane, usually of the nose and throat] & all throat infections   I know a case of apparent consumption where cough night sweats emaciation pains in the

chest all existed in a marked degree that was perfectly cured he used it freely drank it with his meals and all times when thirsty He saved the seeds when past bloom and cut up the whole stock.

Our winter was very wet and dry Trees leafing Peaches in bloom Snow fell last night enough to whiten the ground. Only once has snow fallen before this season. We were plowing yesterday and burning brush today sitting by the fire We are all in apparent usual health

Charles intends going to Colorado next summer I think from the tone of the letter he contemplates moving the entire family I may be mistaken in that

A letter from Esther reports all well there

Ida and family spent about two months with us have just went home to Glenbrook Nevada

Nevada [Vade] is still here. She has two children Boy & Girl

Where are the Roberstons and what are they doing

What Allen Cameron was it that was injured by the fright on the PR Truck Has Hard Scrabble dam all gone   Has Wm Allsworth sold out

I have rented the Summit Range and house for three years & intend teaming across the mts next summer I prefer it to any other occupation I feel better

I hope this will find you all well. I should much like to see your little babies

Accept love and good wishes

Write soon & oblige

Yours Affectionately

JWD Phillips

Home June 15 1881

My Dear Sister Mary

Yours of recent date duly at hand May not answer as freely as I should not having your letter before me We are all in usual state of health I have been about the two past weeks hauling lumber for a stamp Mill go again today for another week. Dan has been haying today plowing corn will cut wheat in a day or two the best in the county C.C. Phillips home address is Good River Sedgewick County Kansas. Present Schofield Gunnison County Colorado After July 1st and until in September Sherman Heinsdale Co Colorado He is at work for a mining company pay him five dollars per day and expenses but it takes his wages to pay his assessments has hopes of making a raise. If he should I think he will visit this coast

The past month very cool and dry had a good rain last week too late to benefit this section but 7 miles East will help the wheat most of it in bloom there – here the most of it cut great difference in climate in that short distance Singularly Charles and I are together Politically (greenbackers) [The Green Back party wanted to make green backs the only paper currency] I think the old parties have no principles to carry out but what the Banks and Corporations propose Strange that the People cannot see it

Family all here but Ida She is at Glenbrook I propose to go there shortly and will likely spend the most of the summer there.

All join me in good wishes to you all   Please write on receipt and greatly oblige

Your Brother
JWD Phillips

D.D. Phillips and J.W.D. Phillips in California to their sister Mary Phillips McConahy in Pennsylvania. Louise Sickles Day writes in her letters that Ida aborted herself and died in the process.

November 24, 1883

Dear Sister

Your favor is at hand & it is my sad duty to inform you of the death of Ida May (Phillips) Meloche. She died at Truckee with the inflammation of the bowels & was buried Oct 1 1883 And on Oct 31 on the ranch near Garden Valley Joseph Wells Clark son of Nevada died aged 3 years and 8 months he was sick but 5 days with some thing like the bloody flushes – I thought more of him than enny boy that I ever saw for he was always with me & when enny one would ask him whose boy he was it was always Dans boy & when he was in death struggles & the last thing he said was O Danie. We had the best doctor from Placerville for him – the rest of us is well – I think it would be the best thing you could do would be to come to this coast & spend a year with us Spend the summer in the mountains & the winter on the coast – I think if I had staid in Illinois that I would have been dead long before this – I think that I could have made more money some other place but I have to be careful with my health for it is none of the best

I think you had better come out here in the spring
– DD Phillips

My Dear Sister

I have the pleasure of addressing in good health   that is for me   I am not very vigor some time   And I thank you for the honor you do me in giving your boy my name & I hope to have the pleasure of entertaining you here for I do not think you could invest money that would pay as much percent towards improving your health in any other manner come spend a year If Joe cannot stay so long you can return alone Dan has written of our great loss in the death of Ida and Vade's son Joey.

Love and good wishes to all

Yours affectionately
JWD Phillips

Lydia Maria Pollock in Illinois to her sister Mary Phillips McConahy in Pennsylvania.

Dec 3, 1884   Foosland Champaign Co

Dear Sister
Harvey came back home the Saturday morning before the election it rained the day he intend to go over to your house we was very sorry Emma was too she wanted all you folks to write in her book
My health is better than it was not well yet I went to meeting last winter and sat with my feet damp and cold I took a burning in my arms and feet and inward burning
David is home and I will send it to the office love to all

Lydia M. Pollock

Foosland Ill
Dec 9th 1884

Dear Cousin

I was glad to hear from you and you wanted to know if Pa was well he was feeling very well but was tired he had to stay at Chicago twelve hours and I was sorry you did not get to write that pretty verse in my album. I don't think I will get to go to school this winter but I am studying at home.

I have commenced to take music lessons for the winter. We have not had any snow to amount to anything but it has been raining a good bit. Well it is about night and I am going to a party tonight and I will have to close for this time.

Your cousin
Emma Pollock

J.W.D. and D.D. Phillips in California to sister Mary Phillips McConahy in Pennsylvania.

Garden Valley
-- Apr 12th 1885

My Dear Sister Mary

Your two letters to Daniel received the one last Spring by me while Dan was away in Washington Territory and do not hold myself blameless for it being answered no sooner. Well we are all well mine has been excellent since last August I attribute it mainly to abstaining from tea & coffee and the use of hot water instead.

We had a remarkably warm winter & but a light sprinkle of rain in Feb & March & but two little showers thus far for April Grain in this vicinity looks fair but lower in the valley very bad. Black Oak in full leaf for three weeks Fruit looks promising Frosts may dissipate that

I had a letter from Charles not a great while ago all well was looking for Joseph [his son]to return from Colorado where he had been absent four years. We are all pleased to hear from you You must not conclude we are indifferent because we are negligent in answering

All join in love and good wishes to all

JWD Phillips

[Ed. note: letter from D.D. Phillips on same paper]

Dear Sister

it has been a long time sence I have written to you I sold out here last Spring & on the 17 of April one year ago I started for Washington Territory & the letter that Lydia rote to me came to Garden Valley & was not sent to me so I could not answer it I found that part of the world settled up more than I expected and it is to cold for me so I came back & on the way home I stoped at Portland Oregon & staid for one week with G.H. Freeman he is on a ranch eight miles from Portland Phebe Short (Freeman) is there has seven children her husband has the consumption & I do not think he will live long I have started a ranch on my own hook and I am in the hope that I will make home for myself so I can do better than I have sence I came out here give my Love to C.P. Fields & Family & the same to you all Tell Lydia to write again & I will answer

DD Phillips

Foosland, Ill
October 17th 1885

Dear Cousin

I received your welcome letter and was glad to hear from you We are all well except Ma She is not very well she would of wrote to you long ago but her nerves are so weak it hurts her to write thinks she is improving She can not do any sewing or any thing like that does some of the housework & I have to do the rest of the work think she may be able to go to see you by next fall

What is the reason Lydia doesn't write to me anymore tell her I would like to hear from her is she still going to Wampum to school yet I will not get to go to school this fall nor do I think I will go this winter. Ma cannot get along without me. I am studying what I can at home our school commenced about a month ago We have the same teacher that taught our summer school. Well I will stop talking about school at present.

About at week ago it rained for a week and you may know it wasn't very pleasant staying in the house a week but it has cleared off and hasn't rained any since. The boys are away threshing and I will have to go to town so I will close for this time remaining

Your cousin
Emma Pollock

June 12, 1886

Dear Sister,

I am almost ashamed for not writing sooner. We wanted to get them before David went to Colorado and there was a traveling man came along to hang out doors ... hurt our eyes in the sun and wind Emma had the diphtheria about 18 months ago and went to school as soon as able She came very near going blind her eyes are weak yet She lost 3 terms of school she started to go to school this summer but took the measles the 3 youngest had them what appears to be the matter with you if it is your monthly send to Dr. Webber Bloomington he can if any person can if you feel wore out make hop tea and drink as you can drink 2 or 3 cups a day it is good

Wells wrote to me that a man cured himself of consumption with Mullen tea I have read in a paper of a person curing himself with it after lungs commenced to bleed

Joseph had the sore throat and all out of order he doctored with Dr. Pierce he wanted 15 a month but finly he came to 6 a month he doctored for over a year he looks well now

Lydia Pollock

[Ed. The letter continues written by Lydia's husband J. H. Pollock.]

Dear Mary

At the request of my wife your sister I add to her epistle as follows I wrote to P. Wallace about one month ago requesting him to inform me by return mail in regards to your interest pay there that you had imployed him to look after & that I was intending to go up there if necessary after hearing from him to see after the matter & get it in a satisfactory shape for you. After waiting one month I received a postal with the simple statement as follows came up sometime before the last of the week and I will give you all the information in my power in regards to Mrs. McConahy's interest in Clifton now what I wanted to know was whether it consisted on obligation or claim on Mr. Lutton or was it invested in real estate in Clifton in your name or had Lutton simply used your money in the purchase of a lot deeded to himself for some reason he has evaded giving me any information as to the shape in which your claim stands but after a long delay says simply come up and I will tell you all in my power about it the circumstances creates suspicion in my mind – if you desire & request I will go up and look up the mater & see how it does stand

Your in law and otherwise
J. H. Pollock

PS I would be very glad if you could find out & give my sister Pollys address I have written to Newcastle and the letter goes to the dead letter office by return to mefeel very anxious to know where she is or what has become of her.

Charles Carroll Phillips in Kansas to his sister Mary Phillips McConahy in Pennsylvania.

Clearwater, Kan
March 28, 1888

Mrs. Mary McConahy,
Dear Sister,
      Your card and letter were both received   you must pardon me for not ancerin promptly for I haven't wrote a letter for

about a year not eve to Jo [his son] we are all well weather cold & backward will commence planting corn next week

In regards to your coming to Kansas I am unable to advise men do live here or will as in every country Wichita is quite a city I presume he could git work still it is dull at present if you want to buy land now is a good time for land is cheap you ought to come out and judge for yourself For my part would not like to advise

For my part I should sell soon as I can & go to Colorado Garfield Co, thear where Jo is I was thear when the Indians were thear   I think it will be a very rich country & it is very healthy I will mail you a paper from thear Jo is overseeing the coal miners for the Midland Railroad His address is Carbondale, Garfield Co Colorado you had better drop him a line He will give you the particulars

Your brother and well wisher
C C Phillips

Addresses included

Mr. Joseph Phillips
Carbondale
Garfield Co.
Colorado

Mr. C C Phillips
Clearwater
Sedquick Co.
Kansas

Miss Emma Pollock
Foosland P.O
Champaign Co. Ill

Mrs. Maria Pollock
Foosland
Champaign, Ill

Emma Pollock, Lydia Maria's daughter, in Illinois to her aunt Mary Phillips McConahy in Pennsylvania.

Foosland, Ill
May 1st 1888

Dear Aunt Mary,

I take the present opportunity to write you a few lines We are all well as usual Mother is not feeling very well Hope you are all enjoying good health. We have had very warm weather until last week it has been very cool. It has been raining now and then for several days.

Aunt Lizzie from Kansas has been visiting us this last week. She went to her Father's in Iriquois Co first and stayed six weeks found them all well, then come to here and stayed about a week, started home the 30th would have stayed longer but there was an excursion going to Springfield (the capital of the state) on decoration day, and some of the boys and their wives were going so she wanted to go so as to have company part of the way. Mother says she would not have known her for she is so fleshy and large to what she used to be and looks so much like her Mother used to look.

Milton & I will send you one of our pictures. We went to Bloomington about a month ago & had them taken. We would like to have some of your pictures if you have any to spare. Mother sent one of Joseph's and his wife's pictures to you over a year ago. You never said anything about it in any of your letters.

Nothing further I will close for the present time

Please write and let me know whether you received them or not.

Excuse bad pen

Your niece,
Emma Pollock
PS Aunt Lizzie had her youngest girl Every (Evra) with her.

Emma Pollock, Lydia Maria's daughter, in Illinois to her cousin, Rebecca McConahy, in Pennsylvania.

Foosland, Ill

July 30th 1888

Cousin Rebecca,

I received your letter of the 13th and also the papers. Thanks to you for your kindness. I wrote to Aunt Mary in March never received any word whether you received it or not and told about bro David getting married.

We will send Uncle and Aunt a picture of David and his wife and also one of Grant's. David is living with Bro Samuel yet for Samuel's wife has very poor health and they are staying to help her. There has been quite a rage about pictures here. There has been a good artist in Gibson which we never had before. Father had his picture taken and will send one with David.

How is Aunt Mary's health? Robert said you wrote she was sick. My health is not very good, yet it is better than it was in the winter. I have been thinking some of going to Pennsylvania or to some other state for my health have not decided what I will do as yet. Grant has had a bad neck it kept him home the fourth the doctor called it an abscess. It was three weeks before it was ready to be lanced. It was the largest one I ever seen. He is able to run the reaper now. You can't guess how many binders the boys have sold this summer. They have sold fourteen. What do you think of that?

You ought to be here to see our gasoline stove. It is the nicest thing I have seen. It is called the Jewel makes but little heat only when we bake then it makes considerable heat

You asked if we ever hear from Uncle Dan or Charles. No we never hear from Uncle Dan. Grant is going to send his picture to him and try and hear from him. Mollie Phillips and I correspond together. Joseph is married and lives in Colorado. He is a manager of a mine or some other work up on the mountain. I forgot just what it was anyway he gets $150 a month and expenses paid. Do you know where Rebecca Smith is? Well I fear you are weary reading this uninteresting discourse so I will close and remain,

Your cousin
Emma Pollock

D.D. Phillips in California to his niece Lydia McConahy, daughter of Mary Phillips McConahy in Pennsylvania. Lydia was 15.

Garden Valley
Nov 11th 1888

Miss Lydia McConahy
Yours came to hand some time ago but I failed to answer I have been in the mountian all Summer Came down in time for the Election -- I am sorry to say that we Democrats lost but it may be all for the best but I can not think that way -- I have been to Soda Springs sence the first of July helping my neace Mrs Clark (Vade Phillips) build a house she bought what is known as the Poter Springs last winter & this summer she bought the Rubicon Springs. She is to pay $6.500 for the two places I once think she gits started she will do well

We have not had enny rain since the first of last April &
today it is 70 in the shade & clear in fact it looks as if it never
would rain but I think it will soon I intend to mine this winter
Wells left this (morning) for his old place on the Placerville
Road he intends to be back in about a week they are all well
-- Some of these days when I think I am good looking I will go
to Placerville and have my picture taken & send you one

They all send their regards to you and all the rest. I remain
as ever your Uncle

DD Phillips

D.D. Phillips in California to his sister Mary Phillips McConahy in Pennsylvania.

Garden Valley Jan 16th 1889

Dear Sister

It is with a sad heart that I wright to inform you that our
Brother Wells is dead he died on Sunday morning the 13th he
went to bed Saturday night as well as he has been for some time
– he intended to go to Placerville on Saturday but it looked so
much like rain he did not go & at six o'clock in the morning
(Sunday) Mrs. Phillips heard him give one long breath and he
was dead without a struggle

And on the 15th he was laid in his grave in Placerville

Yours in hast
DD Phillips

Fowler, Colo
June 27, 1889

Mrs. Mary McConahy Ellwood City
Dear Aunt,

You no doubt will be surprised to get a letter from me at this place. We are not even in Fowler but about 2 miles out in the country. We are camping here and on our way to Uncle Charles Phillips. Guess I wrote you about Joe's poor health and that we were to spend the summer in Colorado. We came to Colo the first of April and expect to stay until the middle of Sept.

Joe is some better than when we first came but is far from being a well man yet. He is so thin but is tanned until he is brown. We thought it would be impossible for him to stand it at home this summer attending to business so we have a clerk in his place and he is trying to take things easy. I was afraid for him to start out on such a journey but there are so many camping out for their health here that we could not coax him out of trying a camping trip too. We have a large spring rig with a good top on it and a tent and are taking it as easy as we can. We do not drive very far a day but just stop when we are tired.

Joe has a good shotgun and rifle. Leeland has a 22 rifle and we have fishing poles so we hunt and fish and take things easy as possible. We do not know when we will get to Uncle Charles but want to get there by the 4th of July. We think often of when we spent the fourth with you. I know I never had a nicer visit anywhere or enjoyed myself better than I did at your house.

And we would like so much to come out there again but don't know whether we will ever have a chance or not.

I am wondering if I will like Uncle Charles as well as I did you. He has moved back to Victor so we won't have quite so far to go at first. We go through Pueblo, Colo Springs, Manitou, Cripple Creek and to Victor. We are expecting to stay through July and maybe August as it is always so hot and then they are Joe's poorly months and it will surely be so much cooler there. We will go out to Glenwood Springs and want to go up Pikes Peak from the West Side. We were to Manitou about a month ago and went up as far as the half way house from the east side. If Joe is able for this trip we want to go on to Yellowstone Park but am afraid it will be too much for him.

We were talking about you yesterday and we thought how we would like to have you with us on this trip through the West. And to visit Uncle we were sure you would enjoy it so much. Have you hear from Mother Pollock lately? She is not very well this summer.

This is Sunday and it seems so merry to sit around all day and not go to church. We so seldom miss church. Joe is lying on a comfort with a pillow under his head trying to get a sleep. The boys are playing around. I wish you could see our boys Aunt for I think they are very nice and I know you would think so too. Joe has awakened and says to tell you how he wished you would come from the east and Uncle Dan from the west and meet us at Uncle Charley's. And I can see a tear in his eye as he said it so you may be sure he meant it. Can't you come out this summer? We will have our buggy and team and can come and go as we please. We are all dying for company and we expect to take Uncle Charley and Aunt if they can go and go on lots of excursions and be gone 3 or 4 days at a time and if you could be there we would surely have a time.

I sent these cheap rates from the east back here if there is none come and then go home with us when we go and stay this winter with us. We would enjoy it so much. Write us what you think about it and say you can come. Write to Victor as we will make that our home through July if we can stand the high altitude. Write soon.

Love to all
Your loving niece,
Ida

D.D. Phillips in California to his sister, Mary Phillips McConahy in Pennsylvania.

Garden Valley
Nov 28, 1889

Dear Sister

I am still on the face of the earth & I find lots of work to do but little money for it but then there is lots in the same boat. Be sure and come out to this State in the Spring I think it will do you good & what is this life only what we see & enjoy I am sure you would like at least one Summer in the mountains – we all went behind in last Summer at the Springs but it may be better next Spring there was to many went to the Worlds Fair & the Silver Mines in the State of Nevada all stoped work but as long as we all ceep well we will come out all right be sure and come out in the Spring give my love to all inquiring friends if I have enny left in that part of the county.

DD Phillips

Notes

Phillips Chronology
1880 - 1889

1881   Relief Fields died near Enon Valley, PA.

1886   Vade Clark bought Rubicon Springs resort.

Lotus post office established.

1889   JWD Phillips died at his home near Johnstown, CA.

Not Getting Rich
Very Fast
1890 - 1899

Vade Phillips Clark bought The Rubicon Mineral Springs Resort and Hotel in 1886, a fairly polished operation located on the Lake Tahoe Indian Trail next to the Rubicon River. She successfully operated the resort and the mineral water business started by the previous owners, and was a general whirlwind, doing much of the resort cooking and entertaining herself. An essay included in this chapter details her life at Rubicon Springs.

Her charm and hard work kept the enterprise alive until 1895, when, as Dan writes, it closed "on account of silver being so cheep the silver question has broke lots of people up on this coast."

Just before she had to give up Rubicon Springs, Vade invited her aunt Mary McConahy to California to be cured of her ills by the mineral water. Aunt Mary never made it, and Vade soon settled for running a

> *Well, what do you do with a dead horse in your barn?*
> *You simply leave the horse there and hope he freezes solid and stays that way until spring.*
>
> —Louise Sickles Day, 1994

boarding house and the post office in nearby Kelsy. In 1898, Dan writes that Vade married her second husband, James Bryson, and had a baby girl, Alice, twenty years younger than Hettie her oldest daughter. Great Uncle Dan has taken up mining, and writes to Mary, "I did think I would come to see you before this but it seems not -- if luck comes my way I will, if not I will ceep on diggin and live in hope."

Also included with the letters of this period is a wonderful story from Louise Sickles Day about a trip Vade and family members made to the infamous Donner Pass and Donner Lake in the winter of 1899.

While herbal remedies are popular -- Lydia Maria Pollock writes of a man "who cured himself of consumption with mullen tea" -- medicine is starting to inch toward science. In a reply to Mary McConahy about sending her daughter Rebecca to Colorado for her health, Robert Pollock asks if any "microscopical work" has been done to tell what the illness is. It's not clear if Rebecca was tubercular. Lydia Maria Pollock's two sons, Milton and Robert graduate from medical school in Chicago, while their brother Samuel earns a degree in dentistry.

`My mother and Mary Jo's grandmother, Mary Myrtle McConahy, was born in 1886. In 1895 her parents, Mary and Joseph McConahy, moved from Moravia where Joseph owned a general store and was postmaster, to Ellwood City, Pennsylvania. During the last few years of his life, Joseph was a tipstaff at the Lawrence County courthouse in New Castle. It was rumored that he had gone bankrupt, and that he had a reputation for not being able to hang on to a nickel. At the age of 61, Joseph was hit by a runaway horse and buggy while crossing the street in New Castle. He was nursed in a nearby hotel for a few days and then taken home to Ellwood City where he died.

`Family legend says that each time my grandfather put his pants on the bedpost, my grandmother became pregnant. My grandmother Mary was left a widow with six children, aged 22 to 9 years old.

J. H. McConahy in Moravia to his friend and classmate the Honorable W. B. Dunlap in Moravia, Pennsylvania. Joseph McConahy studied at Westminster College in New Wilmington, PA and graduated with a law degree from Washington and Jefferson College in Washington, PA. He never practiced law. Joseph was seeking a position as postmaster of Moravia, PA and apparently solicited recommendations from former college classmates.

Moravia, Pa. July 14, 1893

Hon. W. B. Dunlap Dear Friend & Classmate,

Yours of June 29th with letter of recommendation secured. except many thanks. I would have waited in Washington [PA] in order that I might have had the pleasure of shaking hands with you all but I wanted to see the Hon Sipe and understood that he was at that time in the City of Pittsburgh and thought if I delayed too long he might escape me.

Did see him but will have to wait the result. In finding Hon Sipe I made another discovery that was the finding of Noah W. Shafer you remember him he was in the class of 59 (?)

He seemed to have made a success of life as he has built up quite a practice in his profession of Law and accumulated some good property.

Through him I heard from Alf Kerr and Fritz McClaren He tells me that Alf has become a total wreck don't even have an office and spends his leisure moments loitering around saloons.

Sorry to hear it as Alf was a good fellow and should have done well.

Such is life. Just what you make it.

I looked out of the train as I passed through Canonsburg both ways but failed to see any of you.

If I had seen you or known particularly that you were there I would have stopped off Did not see one man in Washington that I knew or ever had known.

Hence it was not very hard to back away at an early moment.

Your friend
J. H. McConahy

Sierra Nevada Phillips Clark (Vade), J.W.D.'s daughter, to her aunt, Mary Phillips McConahy in Pennsylvania.

Garden Valley, Cal
Nov 27th, 1893

My Dear Aunt Mary

Your dear letter Dan recd in due time and he will write soon, so here goes. We were so pleased to hear from you and Dan said he answered your last. I intended to write you so many times but I have so much to see to that it keeps me busy

I hardly write to any at all.

You speak of coming out next Spring   hope you will and come to my Soda Spring [Rubicon Springs] and it will cure you. I am going to San Francisco to see about getting a lodging house for this winter during the Mid Winter Fair.

My sister [Ester] lives in Petaluma and her health is very poor. She has three daughters married and one daughter and son single. Her boy is of the best.

We are having a terrible storm, and Dan has just got the grain in, and if it doesn't let up I'm afraid it will wash out.

Mother's [Mehitable Jane] health is pretty good now. She had quite a sick spell since I came down from Rubicon but generally speaking her health is just splendid. She has no internal complaints nor rheumatism, as old people are subject. She will be 78 years in March. Uncle Joe died at 78 [Mehitible Jane's brother] two year's last spring [1891].

As soon as we have any photos taken I shall send you one. I have a big girl who is six inches taller than I. I am 5 ft 1 in. And she is an awful good girl [Hetty]. We rec'd your girl's photos, they look like nice girls. I hope we will be able to meet in this world. Love from us all. Write soon. Again

Your loving niece,
Vade

Milton Pollock, Lydia's Maria's son, in Chicago to his aunt, Mary Phillips McConahy in Pennsylvania.

Chicago,
May 22, 1895

Mrs. Mary McConahy
Dear Aunt,

I sent you an invitation to our commencement exercise which takes place today. I presume that you noticed that both Robert and I graduate this year. We have studied medicine four years which seemed a long time ahead when we began but the time has soon slipped by.

Brother Samuel graduated in dentistry this spring also. Don't know but what he sent you a card at the time.

I send you by mail today a photo of myself with graduating gown, would like if I could have sent each of my cousins one but it would take so many that I feared to begin on them. Maybe can send them one later.

We do not know just where will locate yet. May go to Colorado where we were prior to going to school. Unless we change our minds Samuel & I will stop in Pueblo Colo a city of over 30,000.

Last Thursday was one of the eventful days of my life taking upon myself new responsibilities being that of married life. It would scarcely be proper for me to attempt to describe the girl of my choice for you know I would think her an ideal and could only describe her as such so will leave this for someone else.

Hoping to hear from you I remain your affectionate nephew

M D Pollock (Milton DeWitt)

PS Better address me at Foosland as do not know what my permanent address will be

[Ed. note: Printed on stationery, Rush Medical College Cor Harrison and Wood Sts Chicago]

Part of a letter from J. P. Pollock in Foosland, IL to Mary Phillips McConahy in Ellwood City, Pennsylvania. The "old country" Pollock refers to is Moravia, PA. He is going to a convention in Boston and wants to visit Mary on his way back to Illinois.

1895

My Dear Mary,

The International Christian Endeavor Convention will be held in Boston in July from the 10th to 15th. My wife and I have our minds made up to go to this convention and on our way back will stop at the old home place if we can succeed in getting the R.R.C. to allow a stop off. We are going to Chicago Monday and will make a big effort to get the priveledge of stopping.

… I want so bad to be able to do this. It does seem since I have been thinking about it a good deal in connection with this trip that I ought to see you and the old country once in my life & I am going to if possible and also I wish you could give me by return mail the names and addresses of any of the folks back in Vermont. If I had their addresses I might make arrangements to meet any who might go to Boston during the convention. If any of you people are going I would like to know it before that time. This is all about the convention.

I was out home last evening and found Father and Mother in their usual health. The rest of the family are well. Samuel graduated in dentistry last month and Robert and Milt graduate next month from Rush Medical College where they will be thoroughly prepared to practice medicine. They will locate probably in Illinois. This is all for the present. D.W. and I are still in the store. Health only middling good.

Sincerely yours,
J. P. Pollock

Part of a letter from Ida Pollock, wife of J.P. Pollock, in Foosland, IL to Mary Phillips McConahy in Ellwood City, Pennsylvania. Ida and J.P. had wanted to visit Mary on their way home from a convention in Boston. The train was making up time and did not stop. Ida and J.P. waved to Mary and her children as the train passed by.

1895

…what made us feel worse than we did was when we heard Lydia was coming back with us. If we had known that we would have gotten off the first stop after leaving you standing on the platform so unceremoniously. But they did not stop for so long. They were making up for lost time and only stopped a few times that night. We did not enjoy our homeward trip as we should have because of our disappointment at not seeing you folks. We saw you on the platform and thought you were all there. Did you see us? We were waving our handkerchiefs as hard as we could. It was a shame and that is all there is of it. Tell Lydia not to wait on us coming again but for her to come anyway. Don't send my basket until she gets the frames done unless she can't finish them for quite a while for I should like to have something she had made ever so much. I have a shell for you that we got in Boston and a piece of chocolate stone from the floor of the Capitol in Washington. They were taking up the floor in one of the corridors and I picked up several little stones as keepsakes. Send our basket by Pacific Ex Joe says. I asked Joe what to tell you and Joe said there was not much chance for him to say anything after I had written a letter he supposed I had said it all only he would send his love to you. Well Aunt will have to close as it is dinner time hope this will find you all well as it leaves us.

Love to all,
Ida

This is a little of Boby's hair I cut it off this spring This is the shortest one of all I had give all the rest away. Some of the braids were twice as long this is a short one from the lower side Here is some gum for Myrtle and Wells.

J. P. Pollock, Lydia Maria's son, to his aunt, Mary Phillips McConahy in Pennsylvania upon the death of Joseph McConahy, her husband.

Foosland Ill
Dec 3, 1895

Mrs. Mary McConahy Ellwood City PA
Dear Aunt,

We are all very sorry to learn of Uncles death. I had fears of it from what you wrote as regarding his injuries. It seems terrible sad news to me and of course very very much more so to you and the family. I just felt that I must rite you a word of sympathy. It may be some consolation to you to know that we heartily sympathize with you. I know you have learned to trust in the Lord and look to Him for comfort. This is the best I can do to recommend the Blessed Master & his grace. Let the truth come to you that He suffered even to the death and by this knows how to sympathize and help. Trust in Him and cast about to make the most out of life. I hope your health will hold out and that you will be able in some way to get along well. Give my love and sympathy to the family.

Sincerely yours,
J. P. Pollock

Garden Valley
Dec 8 95

My Dear Sister

I was glad to hear from you but sorry you had such bad news for me but we have to look on the bright side of life & say thy will be done O Lord not mine we are all giting old & we do not (know) how soon our work on earth will be done nor in what way we will be called hence I think it is best we do not try Mrs Clark (Vade Phillips) has been very sick She is giting along all right now She had to give up the Springs on account of the mines of the State of Nevada closen down they closed on account of silver being so cheep the silver question has broke lots of people up on this coast I am sorry for her for she is a hard worker & tride to make something but fate seems to be against her She is keeping a boarding house & has the Post Office at Kelsey (about 5 miles from here)

About me coming back there it is all most out of the question at present for I can not sell what little I have at present. times is to hard out here but I am in hopes it will change soon & I am afraid I have lived here to long to stand the cold winters but if luck comes my way I will come to see you once more & I mite take a notion to stay but my health is so mutch better here than in the states. I am all most afraid to try As for making money I think it is beter there than here I would not think of coming this time of the year & it may be by Spring I change my mind let me hear from you often I remain as ever your Brother

DD Phillips

Garden Valley Oct 22th 1896
Dear Sister

Your favor is at
hand I received a letter from
you & one from Lydia last
Spring but when yours came I
was Sick ahead for one month
Wade Said She would write
to you but She neglected to
do So & Lydies came when I
was in the Harvest field
& when I got through, I moved
the Old Lady & Wade to their
old place in the Mountains &
as I was not feeling well
I went to the Rubicon Springs
to rest but when I arived there
they wanted me to drive Stage
from the Springs to Lake Tahoe
So I don So for two months
then I moved Wade & her
mother out of the Mountains

Garden Valley, Oct. 22, 1896

D.D. Phillips in Garden Valley, California to his sister Mary Phillips McConahy in Pennsylvania.

Garden Valley
Oct 22nd, 1896

Dear Sister,

    Your favor is at hand I received a letter from you & one from Lydia last Spring but when yours came I was sick ahead for one month Vade said she would write to you but she neglected to do so & Lydie's came when I was in the harvest field & when I got through I moved the old lady (Mehitable Jane) & Vade to their old place in the mountains & as I was not fealing well I went to the Rubicon Springs to rest but when I arrived there they wanted me to drive stage from the Spring to Lake Taho so I don so for two months then I moved Vade & her mother out of the mountains Vade is 14 miles from here running a boarding house at a mine

    I want you to do all you can for Bryan I would like to come back to see you all but times is to close at present to think about it as your letter with C.C. Phillips address has been lost I can not think of his P.O. I would like for you to send it once more I have not had enny letter from him for years I never hear from enny of the Freemans if you find out where George or Sharpes is let me know Do you know what Brother Charles boys is doing if I had plenty of money I would come and see you all but that is the trouble with lots of us I expect or at least I am a feerd so

I remain as ever, your brother
D.D. Phillips

D.D. Phillips in Colorado to his sister, Mary Phillips McConahy in Pennsylvania.

Direct to Kelsey, El Dorado Co

Kelsey
Jan 7 -- 98

Dear Sister

Yours came to hand I thought I had your last answered but perhaps not. I have ben mining for the last year but I spend more than I make so I am not giting rich very fast but it may come yet I still have hopes. I am well the Old Lady [Mehitable Jane Phillips, J.W.D.'s wife] has gone to Petaluma to Ester Vade is married again to a man by the name of Bryson

I did think I would come to see you before this but it seems not   if luck comes my way I will if not I will ceep on diggin & live in hope

Durant is to be hung today I will send you the paper he is the one that killed the two girls in the church in San Francisco

Kind regards to all as ever your Brother
Dan

Placerville,
October 5, 1898

Dear Niece

I expect that you have come to the conclusion that I never intended to write to you but you're mistaken. Last Spring I went from here to Auburn from there to Grass Valley and staid all night at Nevada City & from there to Downerville Sierra Co there we staid for 1 month mining & from there we went to Gold Point for two weeks & then to Sierra City then to Gold Lake & went fishing it is the best place to fish you bet from there we went to Garden Valley & stoped at Camels Hot Springs & then to Truckee & then to Lake Tahoe for a week then to Rubicon Springs and Placerville again landed here on the 12th of Oct we maid nothing all Summer

Vade was married last Spring to James Bryson & lives in Placerville

I wrote to CC Phillips last Spring but when I came back I found my own letter waiting for me – I wish you would write to him if you have his address & tell him I want him to write to me direct to Garden Valley El Dorado Co.

The Old Lady is not well [Mehitable Jane] She was 89 years old the 22 of last March She sends her love to you all & when you write be sure and send some words to her it makes her feel so good to think you all think of her You will have to excuse this letter for I do not know if you can read it.

DD P

D.D. Phillips in California to his sister, Mary Phillips McConahy in Pennsylvania.

Placerville
Oct 18th 99

Dear Sister

it has been a long time sence I have riten to you I have been in the mountians all Summer I was at Glen Alpine Soda Springs -- I have jest come out. We had the deepest snow that was ever known in the mountian for this time of year five feet on the Sumit -- I came to the conclusion that I have all the snow I want for some time. I see by your letter to Vade that Brother Charles & JH Pollock is dead When I look in the glass I see my one gray harre it look as if I to would soon go the same road -- I am well in fact I feel beter than I have for years & I intend to spend the rest of my Summers in the mountians of California I think you had better come out here in the Spring and spend a summer camping where you can have all the fish you want & the nicest climet in the world.

I intend to go mining this winter I do not as yet know where but you direct all letters to Placerville in care of Mrs James Bryson

I remain your Brother
DD Phillips

Vade Phillips Clark Bryson, J.W.D.'s daughter, to Mary Phillips McConahy in Pennsylvania.

Written on Uncle Dan's letter of Oct. 18 1899

Dear Aunt Mary and All

Your letter was rec'd and I forwarded same to Dan who was at that time at Lake Tahoe, and as he did not answer while there thought we would both write. Was very sorry to hear of Uncle Charley's death also Harvey Pollock. Aunt Mary will send you some photos one of these days of Mother & my baby [Alice] (5 mos old).

Sister [Esther] lives in Petaluma Sonoma Co. She has been in miserable health for years, but at present feels pretty well. She has five children, four girls and one boy. All married but the youngest girl.

Mother feels quite smart. She will be 84 yrs in March. Dan seems to feel better than for a long time, looks fat, so don't worry about him. My daughter Hetty is still with me but talks of going into business for herself.

We all send best love to you all.

Hoping to hear from you soon again. I am as ever Your loving niece

Vade
PS Excuse pencil

The Special Lure of Rubicon Springs

From *Along the Georgetown Divide: A Collection of Stories and Reminiscences About the Famed Georgetown Divide* By Georgia Gardner, Published Privately by Georgia Gardner, 1993 and *Jeepers Jamboree The First Years*, Compiled & Arranged by Bud & Peg Presba, 1983 Rubicon River Enterprises, Inc. First Edition.

Rubicon Springs, located in the desolate, primitive Rubicon River area along the old Georgetown – Lake Bigler (Tahoe) Indian Trail was probably known to early day trappers and explorers, but official credit for their discovery goes to John and George Hunsucker, miners from Kelsey, who located there during the summer of 1867. Here the brothers felled pine trees and built a rough log cabin in the meadow south of the springs.

By 1877, they added outlying shacks and a pine sapling corral for their stock. Three years later, the Hunsucker's began bottling Rubicon Springs water, packing out by mule train to Georgetown and McKinney's resort at Lake Tahoe.

After almost twenty years, the brothers sold out to an energetic, enterprising woman by the name of Sierra Nevada Phillips Clark, or "Vade" as she was affectionately called. She added Clark Potter's Springs one mile east, up the canyon, as part of the resort's outdoor attractions. Her hospitable instincts came naturally, having inherited her business ability from her father, Joseph Wells Davis Phillips.

The Rubicon Mineral Springs Resort and Hotel, a two-and-a-half story hostelry was envisioned. Carpenters were hired at $2.50 per 12-hour day (or less than 21 cents per hour). Lumber was unloaded from wooden barges on Lake Tahoe at McKinney's and brought down the rocky road to the chosen building site, adjacent to the Rubicon River.

The 16-room hotel was a palace in the pines with curtained glass windows, a parlor, complete with organ and a fine dining table set with white linen and silver cutlery. The hotel was always filled to capacity and if more showed up, bedsteads were built on the spot from fresh-felled pine, and everyone shifted to make room for more.

No one complained about sleeping on the floor or out underneath the trees and the stars. Often the meadow was full with as many as 100 guests.

Vade, too, marketed the mineral water. She was apparently great in getting publicity for her springs, because hundreds came to experience the flavor of the water of which she also boasted, with the slogan, "tastes better than whiskey!"

Vade foresaw great things for her resort and enlisted the aid of the county to establish better roads and she put into service a six-passenger coach, drawn by four horses. "The Rubicon Flyer" made daily trips between her establishment and McKinney's at Tahoe over a road that would make the 'rocky road to Dublin' look like a 'flowery be [sic] of ease.' Still others made the trip on horseback or private carriage, taking only 2 ½ hours to cover the nine-mile distance between Lake Tahoe and the Springs.

The road improvement, her charm, and the lure of the Rubicon soon had her booked beyond capacity throughout the entire summer season. Young and old came looking for answers to their health problems and to find diversions from the city at this wilderness retreat. It is amazing that some of them survived the trip over the rugged terrain between Georgetown and the Rubicon – or even the nine miles of backwoods wilderness between the Springs and Tahoe.

Comin' 'Round The Mountain

from *The Saga of Lake Tahoe* by E. B. Scott

… you are coated with dust, your eyes are smarting, your tongue is clogged, your hair is caked, your limbs are sore, your flesh is inflamed, you want to go home… but the brute of a driver, unmindful, tears madly on — jolting over rocks, goading his horses into an insane gallop sending the battered inmates of the stage to the roof, where their heads are banged and beaten. (Wasn't a lady killed and the Concord broken all to smash not very long ago?) Now you are skidding around a jutting and dangerous precipice where one inch too near the edge will pitch the stage, crashing through pines, to destruction."

… Up we go to the roof again and then down to be crushed on the hard-as-iron seats…sea sick and sore and in a truly pitiable plight but no one to blame but ourselves and other traveled monkeys who have endured this style of tail cutting."

Such were the trials and tribulations suffered by the early day stagecoach passengers when crossing the Sierra Nevada.

The water was not the only attraction to Vade's Rubicon Springs. Her natural hospitality and her pleasant manner were her greatest assets. The meals on which she prided herself gave her the reputation as "the best cook in the Sierras." Her food, her personality, and her integrity assured her a loyal clientele at $25 per week for room and board.

Running a resort 100 years ago was not easy. There was no electricity and the refrigerator was an icehouse on the river, which would hopefully last through the summer. Fruits, vegetables and meat had to be brought in. Fresh eggs came from Tahoe by stage. A herd of 20 cows was maintained in the meadow to provide fresh milk and butter for the three daily meals. Laundry was done at the resort by hand and Vade's meticulous eye for cleanliness had every piece of furniture spit-shine and polished regularly. Her instinct as hostess and entertainer gave her the flair to amuse her guests in the evening by providing them with organ music to dance and sing to … All adding up to the special lure of Rubicon.

Sidelight:

From The Saga of Lake Tahoe by E. B. Scott

… the fishing was good and there was even a rowboat although an occasional rattlesnake or two was bad… "unsettling" was the word perhaps.

Wine bottles, playing cards, croquet mallets, knarled walking sticks, double-barreled shotguns, repeating rifles, fishing rods, tackle and sewing baskets constituted the more obvious personal effects of the guests.

In just four years Vade had won herself fame and a publicity bonus within the pages of *Mineral Springs and Health Resorts of California* published in 1890:

> These excellent mineral soda springs are romantically situated in the beautiful Garden Valley on the Rubicon River, some eleven miles west of Lake Tahoe. Everything surrounding them partakes of the picturesque – the tall mountains covered with groves of pine and spruce and capped by century-old cedars. Here and there are traces of the slow yet persistent march of huge glaciers of bygone days; here and there are seen the volcanic sentinels in the form of huge granite pillars silently watching the Rubicon as its bright, silvered stream silently glides along

the moss covered banks. The hillsides are covered with sweet-scented shrubbery, and the valley with flowers, imparting their fragrant aromas to the mountain atmosphere – a most valuable combination for consumptives, asthmatics, persons suffering with chronic bronchitis, catarrh, etc., etc.

The mountains afford ample opportunity for exercise with the gun, as the river does with the rod.

The atmosphere is bright, clear, pure and invigorating, imparting new life to the overworked brain and under worked body of the busy city life.

The Mineral Springs themselves belong to the alkalocarbonated class of water, so valuable in the treatment of many diseases, such as dyspepsia and gastric catarrh, torpidity of the liver and constipation of the bowels, Brights Disease of the kidneys, inflammation of the bowels and bladder, etc., etc. For a tonic the waters are excellent. This action is also diuretic, aperients, and antacid.

They are located at an elevation of 6,200 feet above sea level and are pure, clear and sparkling, containing besides the mineral ingredients, large quantities of carbonic gas, so useful in the treatment of stomach disorders.

New and excellent roads have been built, and the trip to Rubicon Soda Springs is full of picturesqueness and romance as the waters are full of health-giving and restorative qualities.

With the improvements to the road being maintained by five men "with picks and shovels", Vade was allowed to open a Post Office at the Springs in 1901. Her daily Rubicon Flyer transported the mail, and it transported tourists and vacationers in and out of the meadows. Due to the rough route and the inconveniently located buttons and tucks on the well-upholstered seats, they were nicknamed bun-bun-busters.

In 1901, Vade sold out to Daniel Abbott. In 1904, Vade who had remarried and was now Mrs. Bryson, leased the hotel from Mr. Abbott which she continued to operate for four more years before finally leaving the area permanently.

Ralph Cowell of Moana Villa purchased the Rubicon Springs Hotel in May 1908, but by this time the health spa craze had begun to wane and the once booming business steadily declined. Finally, in 1930, Cowell sold the land and its improvements to the Sierra Power Company. The deserted hotel stood silent until 1953 when heavy snows that winter leveled the sixty five year old structure and by the spring of 1954 nothing remained but splintered timbers and a pile of rubble.

Rubicon Springs Memories by Louise Sickles Day (1988)

In all the ventures "Vade," my grandmother made, one summer after Rubicon Springs was sold and before returning to Phillips, the Murphy's had an emergency occur, so "Vade" ran the hotel for them one season only.

My mother, "Hettie," a young woman in her twenties, was a waitress in the dining room. Mother had a snapshot of two-year-old little Louise, standing in the dining room holding a syrup pitcher overhead pouring the syrup that was cascading down over her face onto a waiting tongue, and, of course, enjoying it immensely.

I don't imagine little Louise had dining room privileges again very soon, at least after breakfast.

My grandmother, "Vade" was 5 feet 2 inches tall and weighed not over 105 pounds. Imagine the energy she had.

In E.B. Scott's "Sage of Lake Tahoe," I shall quote him in writing about Rubicon Springs. "Vade Clark was indefatigable. She quickly established the reputation as the finest cook in the Sierras. White linen tablecloths with polished silverware and generous quantities of substantial food enticed her patrons three times a day, and it was commonplace for Vade to whip up a meal for one hundred of her ravenous guests."

In all the various establishments she ever ran, her delicious food was a great feature. Of course, as "Vade" grew older, the heavy cooking was taken over by a chef. However, as I wrote before "Vade" made all the pastries through the summer of 1920 before her death in 1921.

"Vade" had a second marriage to James Bryson. I do not know the date of that marriage, but "Vade" was in her forties. James Bryson was 22 years younger than she . My half aunt Alice was born in 1899, the daughter of James and "Vade" Bryson. That marriage lasted about fifteen years.

Winter at Donner Lake
by Louise Sickles Day (1988)

This story took place in 1899 at Donner Lake. Donner Lake was where a party, led by George Donner and his brother, was caught in an early snowstorm of three feet of snow overnight on October 10, 1846. It was a disaster. Some later made it out over the snow, but others were completely stranded and too weak to leave. They ate their oxen and horses and some people starved to death. Those who lived resorted to cannibalism.

In 1899 Sierra Nevada ("Vade" Phillips Clark Bryson, her daughter Mehitable Jane Clark, 20 years old, and second daughter Alice Elaine Bryson, six months old, Vade's mother, Mehitable Jane Phillips, in her 80's, and Vade's nephew Johnny Meloche spent the winter at Donner Lake. Johnny had active tuberculosis. It was such a common disease those days. They wanted to stay at Donner Lake thinking it would help Johnny's condition. His mother, Vade's sister, had recently died. Vade and Jim Bryson hadn't been married too long. Dan Phillips, JWD's brother was there and Dan said, "Well, that is the dogondest idea I had ever heard of," and Jim thought the same way. However, they said they would get in enough wood and help get in their supplies, but wouldn't stay.

Many winters are light and they decided they would keep a horse and buggy so Hettie could drive into Truckee for mail, newspapers, and supplies. Finally all was ready and the men left saying, "Good by and we'll see you next spring." The women expected to have a wonderful winter.

Hettie, being young, would sometimes drive into Truckee for parties with her young friends and spend one or two nights. An invitation came up and Hettie decided to take Johnny along for a change. It was a beautiful day when they left. Hettie drove in the buggy. It was three miles into Truckee. When she first arrived she did shopping and picked up the mail to be all set to return.

The following day when the party was over it suddenly began to cloud up. Hettie and Johnny decided they should start for home and beat any real storm.

Well, it soon began to snow and turn into a real blizzard, with howling wind. It wasn't long before neither Hettie nor the horse could see anything. They found themselves up on the side of the mountain. Hettie got out and put Johnny in the bottom of the buggy, covering him with the lap robe. She tried to lead the horse down the mountain to find the road without turning the buggy over. It wasn't a very good predicament to find themselves in, especially with Johnny in the buggy yelling and crying, "I think I'm going to die!" over and over. I'm sure Hettie thought so too, and the horse would rather have been anyplace but the side of a mountain hitched up to a buggy.

Hettie, with long hair streaming down her back, soaked and frozen to the bone, managed to get back on the road. Finally they reached home. Johnny, of course, got in the house and lived to tell the tale along with Hettie.

The poor horse caught a cold and finally got pneumonia. Hettie had to take hot mash every day to feed and water the sick horse. After about a month, the horse finally died.

Well, what do you do with a dead horse in your barn? You simply leave the horse there and hope he freezes solid and stays that way until spring. To make matters worse they had bought a copy of the Donner Party to read out loud. You can imagine how that uplifted them. From then on Hettie would make trips to Truckee over the snow on snowshoes to pick up supplies and mail and get news of the outside world. That was a time of no radios. Hettie would pull things home on a sled. Without radios the family was anxious for news.

All perishables were hung down a well on the back porch so they wouldn't freeze, since any liquids in the house at night would be frozen by morning.

The next year Johnny died from a hemorrhage. I never heard of any dishes being sterilized. They must have all had a lifetime of immunity from tuberculosis as they all remained healthy and robust. With a fire in the stove all day, with boiling water, no doubt the dishes were boiled.

The transcontinental railroad crossed the mountain above Donner Lake. The snow sheds can be seen and were literally over their heads. There was heavy rail traffic to and from the east over that route. If it were a long train, it would take three to four engines to push and pull that train over the steep grade. Very often the family could hear the mournful sound of the whistles wailing.

What was going to be a mild winter turned out to be a heavy one and needless to say they never again tried any outlandish idea. They were brave and determined women to have carried out their plan.

In the spring the men returned, as they promised they would, but they never returned during the winter.

All survived and stayed well except Johnny and the horse that finally had a decent burial.

Notes
Phillips Chronology
1890 - 1899

1895   Robert and Milton Pollock graduated from medical school.

Samuel Pollock graduated from dental school.

Joseph Hennon McConahy died at home in Ellwood City, PA.

Amoret Phillips Henry died in Arcola, IL.

1898   Vade Phillips Clark married James Bryson.
1899   Charles Carroll Phillips died in Victor, Colorado.

Alice Bryson was born (Vade's daughter).

James Harvey Pollock died in Foosland, IL.

Below the Clouds, In the Clouds, Above the Clouds

1900 - 1919

After her husband, Joseph's death, Mary Phillips McConahy and her family continued to live in Ellwood City, PA. I know my grandmother took in boarders for a while because my mother had (and I still have) a small pitcher a boarder gave her as a Christmas gift. As for her children:

Lydia secured employment as a chief operator, indeed the only operator, at the local telephone office. My mother, Myrtle, worked nights in the telephone office while going to school. When a call came in, an alarm would sound, she would answer, and then go back to sleep when the call ended. In the morning she'd go home, eat breakfast, pack her lunch, get dressed and go off to school. She was 14.

I feel very proud of my relatives, so far.

—Mary Phillips McConahy,
August 19, 1907

Rebecca attended school in New Castle because Ellwood City did not have a high school. She also graduated from Grove City College and taught school. She seems to have been ill often. William was interested in drilling for oil and traveled around Pennsylvania, Ohio, and West Virginia.

In 1900 tragedy struck. Wells left home at 17, presumably in search of employment. He eventually worked his way west, ending in Oxnard, California, working at a sugar beet factory. It was the last time he was ever heard from and it is not known what happened to him.

There were happy moments too. Relief married C. A. Hartung of Beaver Falls, PA in 1902, and in 1904 Mary's first grandchild, Charles, was born. A daughter, Florence, arrived four years later.

In 1905 Mary's daughter Lydia married Ralph Brown, a mail carrier from Swissvale, PA and moved there. The family was growing. Myrtle contracted typhoid fever presumably from drinking water from a neighbor's well and was very sick.

By this time Mary Phillips McConahy had sold her house and moved into the third floor of the Hartung's new house with Rebecca and Myrtle.

Sad news came from other Phillips'. Lydia Maria Pollack died in Foosland, Illinois during 1903. And in California, Esther Doss (Vade's half-sister) died in Petaluma and John Meloche (Ida Phillips' son, raised by Vade) also died of tuberculosis. He was 19 or 20.

Vade was operating the Inn at Tahoe City and in December of 1901 Great Uncle Dan writes 'it is rumored that Hettie Clark (Vade's daughter) is married to Frank Sickles." The rumor was true and Vade's first grandchild, Wells Sickles, arrived in 1902. In 1904 Vade leased Rubicon Springs from Daniel Abbott to whom she had sold it in 1900. She ran the resort until 1908. Vade's mother Mehitable died in Sparks, Nevada in 1906 leaving Phillips Station to Vade. Hettie's second child Louise was born in 1906.

Meanwhile Mary Phillips McConahy was searching for a place to live and finally in the summer of 1906 she and her daughter Myrtle headed for California stopping on the way to visit with the Pollack's in Rocky Ford, Colorado (Lydia Maria's son).

In the late summer Mary Phillips McConahy and Myrtle were at Rubicon Springs with Dan, Vade and all. The family spent the winter of 1907-08 with Vade, Jim and Alice at Garden Valley. The summer of 1908 they were all at Meeks Bay because Vade was running the resort for her friends the Murphy's. That fall Myrtle decided to leave California and return to Ellwood City, PA. On the way back Myrtle stopped in Denver and stayed with Aunt Lizzie Phillips (Charles Phillips' widow). She worked as a clerk in the Denver Dry Goods store, probably to earn money for her trip home. Mary remained in California at the ranch in Garden Valley and seems to have bought property at Galt. Vade also began to rebuild Phillips Station after the fire.

Myrtle returned to Ellwood City in early 1909 and later that year Mary returned home because Lydia was ill. In October she went back to California with Lydia and her son Cecil. They stayed at Sea Bright, Santa Cruz, and Galt.

In 1911 Phillips Station burned again, and was restored again. In April 1911 Dan writes, "Mr. Sickles had gone crazy and tried to kill everyone in sight." In May, Mr. Sickles was in an insane asylum in Stockton. Later it developed that Frank Sickles suffered from Huntington's disease, an inherited disease, and spent his life in a sanitarium. The same year Hettie's third child, a daughter, Eleanor Nevada Sickles (Babe) was born. Of Hettie's three children only Louise escaped Huntington's disease and lived to be 88 years old. Her son Wells developed the disease and died from it in 1945. Babe also inherited the illness and died in 1963 at age 52.

In April 1916 Relief and Bert Hartung had their third and last child – Grace Myrtle. And in California Alice Bryson, Vade's second daughter married Henry Lyon and had a daughter Betty in 1919.

In 1918 Lydia married a widower, D.D. Dowds, of Beaver Falls, PA. He was a lot older than she and had children her age, but she was anxious to have a father for Cecil. The marriage was short-lived because he died September 11, 1921.

Frank Sickles, Hettie Clark's husband, introduced Huntington's disease to the Phillips family. Louise Sickles Day writes,

> *My father had a gene disorder. He died in an asylum. Both my brother and sister inherited the faulty gene. Each was normal until they entered the University of California. Both flunked out, which was at the beginning of complete mental retardation – a very tragic happening. I fortunately escaped the faulty gene. My mother Hettie had much tragedy in her life, but she was a very strong person. She worked so hard to save Phillips. She always seemed happy and beloved by everyone.*

Gene mutation has been identified as the cause of Huntington's, and genetic testing is now available to those who want to know if they have inherited the gene.

The 1997 Merck Manual of Medical Information contains the following entry about Huntington's:

> Huntington's disease is an inherited disease in which people in midlife begin having occasional jerks or spasms and gradual loss of brain cells, progressing to chorea (repetitive, brief, jerky, large scale dancing-like uncontrolled movements that start on one part of the body and move abruptly, unpredictably and often continuously to another) and athetosis (a continuous stream of slow, sinuous, writhing movements generally of the hands and feet) and mental deterioration. The gene for Huntington's disease is dominant. Therefore children of people who have the disease have a 50% chance of developing it. Because the disease

develops subtly, the exact age of onset is difficult to determine. Symptoms usually begin between 35-40. During early stages people can blend the spontaneous, abnormal movements into intentional ones so they are barely noticeable.

However, with time the movements become more obvious. Eventually the abnormal movements involve the entire body so that dressing, and even sitting still, becomes nearly impossible. Distinct changes in the brain can be seen on computed tomography (CT) scan.

Mental changes are subtle at first. People with the disease may gradually become irritable and excitable. They may lose interest in usual activities. Later in the course of the disease they may behave irresponsibly and often wander aimlessly. They may lose control over their impulses and become promiscuous. Over years they may lose memory and the ability to think rationally. They may become severely depressed and attempt suicide. In advanced stages almost all functions become impaired and full-time assistance is required. Death, often precipitated by pneumonia or a fatal falling injury, usually occurs 13-15 years after symptoms first appeared. Although drugs can help relieve the symptoms and control behaviors, no cure exists for this disease.

The Letters

Page three of a letter from William McConahy to his mother, Mary Phillips McConahy in Pennsylvania.

I cannot leave until I pay my bord, so you will find enclosed an order on the tin mill for the rest of my money there also an order for my money from the insurance co and if you send me $5.00 out of what you get that will help me out. Will send it all back in another month & more with it as I will go on tool dressing next week you can send it to my address as I will watch the post office the tin mill pays next Sat from 30 between 12 & 2 o'clock but if this does not reach you in time you can get it Monday I have two days coming at $1.72 ½ a day or a total of $3.45. In regard to getting Wells a job here I will say that there will be no chance yet for a while. There is no use of going to the oil fields on your own because there is too many tool dressers. I would not stand any show here if it was not for Mr. Wilkinson because there are too many applying and he told me that in the big oil fields they won't have a green hand unless they can't get anyone else These wells here are only small ones so I will not have it very hard while learning.

I get mixed up here on the time the time here is half an hour slower than our time& half an hour faster than railroad time I call it the middle time If I ask anybody what time it is and they tell me then I ask him if he keeps fast slow or middle time that is the only way I can keep track.

Mr. Wilkinson has a couple of fine sons here they are nice quiet boys one of the is married & the other is only about 17 yrs old everybody here speaks well of Mr. Wilkinson & I think I will have a nice man to work with If the well he is drilling now amounts to anything they will put a couple more down at once & I might be able to get Wells a job pumping I have talked to the stock holders & they seem like nice men I will do my best so that will make it easier for me to get Wells a job If they see that I am not lazy and will tend to my work they will judge him by me Everything depends on the well that he is drilling now if it is not a dry hole we will g on down the river that is the reason I would like to have the money as soon as possible so there will be nothing to hold me back If I get work with that tank builder two days this week it will pay my fare and what you will send will pay my bord and I can get a better boarding house I am well as ever with the exception of blistered hands and neck Hoping to find the rest of you in good health I remain wishing an early reply

Love to all
Your loving son
WCM (William Charles McConahy)

PS Lydia can give the order to Miss Sphere and she will bring the money up with her when she quits work Sat.

To Mary Phillips McConahy from her son, Wells, who went west when he was age seventeen.

St. Marys, Va.
March 30, 1900

Dear Mother,
    I arrived here yesterday and I have not got work yet. I am going up the river in about 1 hour – 12 o'clock to W_____
I will wright later. Don't worry.

Good-by,
Wells

Wells McConahy in New Mexico to his mother Mary Phillips McConahy in Pennsylvania.

Albuquerque, NM
Aug. 1900

Dear Mother,

I arrived here last night. I have struck for a job in every town that I stopped in but have not found one yet. I expect I will have to go to Los Angeles CAL & get a job of some kind you might as well put the wheel up for sale it is a $60 wheel, 1900 model, 24 inch frame, 81 gear, take off the bell and mile guide on the front wheel has that part came that I ordered? get Fred to put it on, the balls are in the bottle at the head of the longe and sell it about $40 or not much less as it cost over $30 put an ad in the paper I was in Denver but that town was dry I left the clock, night shirt and game board over at Fred's have you heard anything from Mead about that wheel I ordered for R. B. I seen their shop at Chicago it's a large firm you can write a letter to W.P.M. at Los Angeles, CAL and after 10 days return and give the news I will close

Your loving son,
Wells

P.S. Chal Grandy owes me 88 cents for 4 hr work have you seen him I did get that job in Kansas City that I told you in last letter

F.O. Engstrum
General Contractor and Builder
Oxnard, Cal

September, 1900

Dear Mother,

I am now working in the beet sugar factory here at $2.06 a day, as they laid me off at Bakersfield I worked 3 days and could not get another job I went to S.F. and could not find nothing their and came here and I could get mail or express and let them return Tell Will never to come to this state as the oil field is over washed with men now as the whole state is Drillers make $6 a day it is 6 miles from town on a desert They work all week then go to town and spend every sent the saloons make all the money out here they are busy all the time have you sold the wheel yet? Put an ad in the paper the west is no place for a person without money, not even Denver everything is deer your hay is 10 cents for a lb 5 cents for salt if I were you I never would go to Denver it's nothing but a desert all around it you can't get a job unless you are a native son if you tell them you are from another state they say no I am working on night turn can't say how long I will stay here I will close this time

Your loving son,
Wells

Be sure & tell Will not to come to this state for work it never rains out here – only in winter I haven't seen rain since I left Ohio and I seen and felt to last for a while

341 Collins Ave. EE
Pittsburgh, Pa.

Mrs. McConahy

Your letter received today. I am indeed sorry that you have been having such an unhappy time. No one can feel a mother's love like she who loves and to advise is like saying be "clothed or fed" without helping with the necessary means. I can assure you that all things work together for good to them that believe. I was never so much disappointed as when I went to find Wells. I could not stay with him as I wished to move here. I had intended to have him with me and he could have worked steady eversince as to him going away, other boys have left home and are none the worse. I know it is hard to be broken away from those we love. With respect to the best way to find him there is none except to get it through an agency, or advertising. You may be assured of this much that as long as he is in the west and is at all manly, he will have friends who will encourage him to do right. For myself I firmly believe he is either in or near Los Angeles or has gone north he knew your condition and after wished to make money to help you he may not have written because he could not get it to you he may even have forgotten to think of home, but sooner or later he will sight for "home and mother". I speak from experience. I will do as you request and trust that He in whom is all help and consolation will give you peace of mind and rest, and that all will be well with you all. I never said a word to Wells that would lead him away from the right way and I thought more of him than my own brother so I am only too willing to be on the look out for him.

Kindly yours,
J. M. Hoffman

D.D. Phillips in California to his sister Mary Phillips McConahy in Pennsylvania. He's referring to his job as a forest ranger.

Lotus
Dec 9th 1900

Dear Sister

Your letter is at hand I am located for the winter at Lotus and to try my luck mining once again and in the Spring I expect to go to the mountains at the same job I had last Summer -- there is five others after the place but I think I have the inside track it is easy work riding around all of the time -- I wrote to your son Wells as soon as I received your letter but have never had enny word from him where is he at present & I will rite again -- for I would like to see him

the rest of the folks are at Truckee Nevada for the winter

We are having a very warm winter here no frost as yet warm rains and lots of grass

I am well and like all miners I expect to make a rase this winter and then I will try and see you all once more.

Direct to Lotus Edorado Co Cal

DD Phillips

Office of
American Beet Sugar Company
Oxnard, Cal
December 13, 1900

Dear Madam:

We have your favor of December 4th and note your inquiry regarding your son Wells P. McConahy. In reply we beg to advise that your son has not been in our employ during the past year and we are unable to give you any information regarding his whereabouts.

Yours truly,
American Beet Sugar Company
Y. O. Cather,
For Manager

C.A. Phillips, Charles' son, in Colorado to his cousin William McConahy in Pennsylvania. William is Mary Phillips McConahy's son.

Victor, Colorado,
February 8, 1901

Wm. C. McConahy
Ellwood City, Pa.

My Dear Cousin,

I was very much surprised to hear from you. Glad to hear the folks are all well. We are all enjoying the same blessings at the present time. I can give you all the information I have with pleasure. There is all kinds of mining in this state. The wages here for common miners around the mine is $3.00 per 8 hours. Engineers $4 to 5 per 8 hours. Black smiths $4. Timbermen $3.50. Pump men $3.50. Leadville has nearly the same scales. Both camps are about 10,000 feet altitude. The climate here is 3 months late in the fall 6 months winter, and 3 months early in the spring. Have very little summer weather at any of the quarts mining camps. The coal miners are much lower. They are always boring for oil in the fields at Florence 35 miles south of here. There is quite an oil excitement at Steamboat Springs, Routt Co. this state. At Florence there is several large mills for treating Cripple Creek. They pay $2.00 to $3.00 an hour. Coal is all mined by contract. You can find all kinds of climate in this state and all kinds of employment imaginable. Nearly all kinds of farming & fruit growing. A large live stock industry and manufacturing. The best way is for one to come and see for himself if possible. This state is gorging ahead at a rapid rate. I am leasing on Ophim Cos. Dead Pine claim at present. Am doing first rate. Took out $4000 worth of ore last month. Hope to do better this month. Wishing you well and prosperous. I am your cousin,

C. A. Phillips
Box 503
Victor, Col.

D.D. Phillips in California to his sister Mary Phillips McConahy in Pennsylvania.

Lotus
Feb 22 1901

Dear Sister

Yours is at hand was glad to hear from you but sorry that you do not know where your boy [Wells] is but hope he will come out all right I will do all I can to hear from him

And hope you and Sister Maria are feeling better before this -- I think you had beter come out here next Summer and try this part of the world for a year & see if it will not do you good -- I have not maid enny money this winter yet my Pardner & I are goan to lease a place I think there is good times & I am in hope yet -- if not I expect to go to the mountains by the first of June to be on the reservation next Summer So if you come out we will try and make it pleasent for you

Vade Bryson (Phillips) & Mother are at Truckee Nevada Co this winter the last word I had from them they was all well

I have no news to write but I want to hear from you often so I thought I would let you hear from me

Yes the pictures came to hand all right -- thanks for them with kind regards to all I remain as ever your Brother

DD Phillips

D.D. Phillips in California to his nephew William McConahy.

Tahoe City May 30 1901

Dear Nephew

Yours received & contents noted -- I am goan on the government reservation again this Summer I go to work on the first of June -- I remember Wm Wilkeson well & you can tell him that I would be glad to hear from him & I will answer as best I can & as for the Fisher girls I remember them well & send my kind regards to them & tell Nan that if I was not so old I would come & see her there is lots of oil wells in the southern part of this state but I do not know what chance thare is to git work but I expect you would stand a good chance as enny one else there is lots of work here but it is in the lumber giting out logs & wood So if you should come out here be sure & come to Lake Tahoe & stop at the Tahoe Inn & let yourself be known for the landlady is my niece Mrs. Bryson who was before maried Vade Phillips & they can tell you where you can find me

When you write to me direct to McKinneys Placer Co Cal for I expect to be there all summer

With kind regards I am as ever your Uncle
DD Phillips

McKinneys
July 28th 1901

Miss Myrtle McConahy

Dear Niece

I ask your pardon for not answering yours long ago I am not mutch of a letter writer at best. And when thare is no news to write I am no good I am always glad to hear from you I have nothing to do but ride over the government reserve and look out for sheep and fires and see there is no one cuting timber -- there is no hard work only riding horse back I am giting used to that -- So it does not bother me mutch -- only I am giting old I was 62 years on the 24th of this month so you see I am one of the old boys -- we are having warm weather for the mountian jest right but in the valleys it is very warm that is one reason why I like the state -- as I set outside of my tent in shirt sleeves I can look up on the mountian peaks and see snow ten feet deep I have not had enny word from the rest of the folks for sometime they was well with lots of work they are ceeping Hotel at Tahoe City Placer Co. I have no time to go & see them although I am in sight of the house every week but it is nine miles off on the shore of the Lake Tahoe I am always glad to hear from you so write often and I will do the best I can to answer

DD Phillips

D.D. Phillips in California to his niece Myrtle McConahy in Pennsylvania.

Lotus

Dec 20 1901

Miss Myrtle McConahy

Dear Niece

I have come to the conclusion that you have forgoton your old Uncle Dan but he has not forgoten you So I will try and pen you a few lines. I am well with exception I feel as if I had the rheumatism or old age it may be both combined I am not doing mutch this year we have had rain but not enough to make water to mine with. I will enclose a piece of gold that I found last winter. So you will have some little token to remember me by -- the rest of the folks are well or was the last time I had word from them the middle of November they are at Tahoe City Placer Co. -- it is rumered Hettie Clark is Maried to a man by the name of Frank Sickels I do not know him he belongs at Stocton and is in the clothing business -- I wish you a happy Christmas & a happy New Year

DD Phillips

Samuel Pollock, Lydia Maria's son, in Colorado to his aunt, Mary Phillips McConahy in Pennsylvania. First letter was written by Lydia, but was not sent until it was included with this letter from Samuel.

Dr. Samuel H. Pollock, dentist

Jan. 11, 1902
Rocky Ford, Colo
New Year's Day

Sister Mary,

I am very sorry your health is so poor you will have to stop fretting or your nerves will break entirely down did you ever try Miles Nerve Cure if you do not quit fretting you cannot get any better come to Ill and visit around and see if that will help you I am going home in the spring my health is better than when I came If you take the gripp stay in until you get well but you must quit fretting or you will never get any better

Love to all
L. M. Pollock

January 10

Dear Aunt,

I have just discovered this letter in my packet. Ma handed it to mail without putting it in an envelope therefore I over looked it Since writing the above letter Ma has had the grip and was quite sick but is able to be up again. My wife has also been very sick but is able to sit up in bed and eat some

Your nephew
Samuel

Barbara Pollock, Lydia Maria's daughter, in Illinois to her aunt, Mary Phillips McConahy in Pennsylvania. Rebecca may have had tuberculosis.

Foosland Ill
July 12, 1902

Dear Aunt Mary,

You had us all guessing again what had happened when you did not either write or come. We were glad to hear that Rebecca was some better and hope that she keeps on improving.

Ma is still in Decatur and the last time she wrote she talked like she'll stay two months yet but if you folks will only come she'll come home. David doesn't know the first thing about the oil fields. Surely you are much nearer the majority of them than we are. They are getting up quite a boom in oil around Rocky Ford, Colo where Joseph, Samuel, and Robert are. Perhaps you'd better write out there and they'll tell you what the prospects are. I understand that all kinds of trades got good pay out there but common laborers are no better off than they are here because of the competition with Mexicans and Indians.

The climate is superb but it would be too far to go. However let Rebecca come along and you can make up your minds what to do when you know where you are going to settle.

There is an old Sunday school teacher of mine from Scotland who is coming to see me this summer. I had a letter from her yesterday and she thought she'd be here about the 15th of September. She is in Canada now and is going on a two months excursion to Vancouver and expects to get a stop off at Chicago on her return when she will visit me. Of course she may manage to get stop over privileges on her way out but it is hardly likely.

As to the best road to take I'd get the cheapest line from Pittsburgh to Chicago and after you are there you go to the Wabash depot at 2:15 pm any day but Sunday and buy a ticket for Foosland. Your train gets here a little after six o'clock in the evening. David's store is within 500 feet of the depot and the only store in the village so you can't miss it.

You'd better send a postal check ahead of you so I'll be at home. That train may be 2:30 pm but I'll send the newspaper notice in this letter. I may send a Rocky Ford paper if I can find one with oil booms.

Now just get Rebecca ready and let her come, it won't hurt her and may do her a lot of good.

Hoping to hear from you soon.

I still remain,
Yours sincerely,
Barbara Pollock

Robert Pollock, Lydia Maria's son, in Colorado to his aunt, Mary Phillips McConahy in Pennsylvania.

November 17, 1902

Dear Aunt Mary,

I hope you will pardon the delay in answering your letter. I have been away since receiving it, and busy when at home, and this, coupled with a little forgetfulness, accounts for the delay.

Now as regards the advisability of Cousin Rebecca coming to Colo for her health will say this: we have a great many coming here almost daily for tubercular trouble and ought to be able to advise intelligently, but it all depends on the stage of the disease and the complications. Patients should be seen before advise is given, as many come who receive no benefit whatever, but on the contrary do not do as well as at home. When they come early, and the organs of the body generally are in good condition, many do well, but late cases of tuberculosis, when they are not able to get out in the fresh air and sunshine, get discouraged and homesick, and gradually fail. Pulmonary cases do better than intestinal cases. Are you sure it is tuberculosis? Have you had any microscopical work done?

If you and your doctor think it is advisable for here to come we will make it as pleasant as possible for her, and take the best of care of her – you may be sure of that. The rule is that tubercular patients do best in a dry high climate. We stand ready to serve, and it will be a pleasure to help in any way possible. Awaiting your decision in the matter, I am

Your loving nephew,
Robert M. Pollock, M.D.
Rocky Ford, Colo

D.D. Phillips in California to his sister Mary Phillips McConahy in Pennsylvania.

Garden Valley
Dec 10th 1902

Dear Sister
I received your welcome letter but sorrow to hear of your trouble with sickness in the family but hope by this time they are at least better I am goan to try and git on the reserve next

summer and if I should will camp handy to the Rubicon Springs and would like for you to come out and camp with me for I know it would do you all good and I could be with you most every night would be gone about four nites in each month -- We are now having one rainey time and it looks as if we would have lots of it this winter

Jane is in Stocton and Vade is at Tahoe City but intends to go to her Mother about the first of January. let me hear from you soon and give regards to all I remain as ever your Brother

DD Phillips

From the Decatur Herald January 9, 1903. Milton DeWitt Pollock is Lydia Maria's son.

M. DeWitt Pollock, M.D.
A Medical Practitioner of Decatur, Ill., who has Fast Won a Successful Practice

For the past eight years Dr. DeWitt Pollock has been engaged in the practice of medicine in this city, and has met with unqualified success. Although a young man he quickly showed he was possessed with unusual talents as a general practitioner and is deserving of the marked popularity he has gained since taking up his residence in Decatur.

He was born and reared in Champaign County, Illinois, and attended the common schools of the county. In 1892 he entered Rush Medical College, in Chicago, and graduated from that institution in 1895, locating in this city immediately after.

Quietly and without ostentation the doctor has followed along the lines of work of general practitioner, and has been steadily winning to himself a large following and most lucrative practice. He is painstaking, careful, prompt, and efficient in all cases he undertakes, and has made many friends by reason of his very pleasing manner as he has in his methods.

Dr. Pollock is a modest man, he shrinks from notoriety, and it is with much diffidence that he consented to give the Herald even a limited amount of data concerning himself for publication in this issue.

Besides being thoroughly versed in his profession, he is a most agreeable gentleman to meet, and has been accorded attention from the people of the community to which he is justly entitled.

He occupies pleasant offices at 305 Powers Building, well equipped for his practice. Dr. Pollock is a member of the American Medical Association and of the Illinois State and Decatur Medical societies, being one of the censors of the latter society. He is medical examiner for several insurance companies, and owns a pleasant home on West Packard Street.

D.D. Phillips in California to his sister Mary Phillips McConahy in Pennsylvania.

Garden Valley
Feb 1st 1903

Dear Sister

Yours of Jan 20th is at hand and contents noted. Was glad to hear from you. but sorrow to hear that the sickness was no better -- I still think the place for Rebecca to come is the Rubicon Springs She can camp out and still have the use of the Springs -- in regards to wages in this state for picking fruit is from $1.00 to 1.50 and board per day -- in the mines and loggin camps about $2.50 I think the man that makes $5.00 per day had all the prunes he gathered (or you mite set it down as a not so) As for fruit lands in El Dorado Co it is all good with water but there is where the trouble come in not enough water to erigate with Sacramento Co is better Some parts of it they do not have to erigate -- I do not take mutch stock in enny thing that have to advertise so strong and ofer so much inducements to sell for thare is lots of folks out hear that would like sitch a place. I send you a map of land in Glen Co that I think is all right the old home of Dr Glen has always been cald the Garden Spot of the State and they are fetching water in to erigate with and some of it does not nead to watered -- I am aqainted with Mr Rideout and what he says I think you will find to be all right but I think it is best for you to come & see for your self before you sell out thare it will not do you enny harm to take a change If I had staid back thare I think I would have been dead long ago

Ester [Mehetible Jane's daughter] died in Petaluma on the 5th of Jan with newralga of the stomach Vade is in Tahoe City and her Mother is stoping with Hettie at Reno, Nevada they are all well -- I send you a paper with the map in it have Rebecca come out here by the first of June to go to the Springs or before but she can not git to the Springs for snow until then

DD Phillips

Vade Phillips Bryson in California to her Uncle Dan Phillips in California. Johnny was Ida Phillips' son. Vade raised him after Ida died.

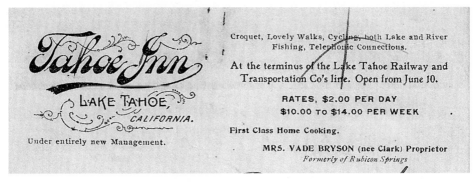

Tahoe Inn Letterhead

Dec. 27, 1903

Dear Dan

The Grim Reaper has taken our dear little John. Was taken so suddenly from us with an awful hemorrhage. Was just like pumping. I never saw any thing like it and never want to witness it again. I do not believe it was three minutes from the time the hemorrhage started until he was dead. Poor little soul was so scared. I said My God John shall I send for a Doctor and he says "I'm dieing mama." He was downtown that day and the day before. The Dr. said it was from over exertion but would not have lasted but a day or so longer as his bowels was running off terrible and was spitting up great white chunks. They say both these symptoms are the last. he had got so weak and had for the last two weeks talked about dieing a great deal.

His father came up and stood all the expenses. We kept Johnny from Wednesday night until Saturday at 2 P.M. He looked lovely. The day he died he went down to Tommy Kohler and got his hair cut and was shaved. Tommy said something struck him then. Dan -- he got awful bad. The cough was enough to kill him. That day after coming from town he says Mama I am going to die.

Grandma takes it pretty good. I talked to her every day and told her he would soon leave us so I had her prepared. But Dan we miss the little dear so much. Love from us all. Write soon.

Your loving niece,
Vade

Dec. 27, 1903

Truckee,
March 20th 1904

Dear Sister

 I received your letter the day I left Garden Valley -- but the papers and slipers came on the 18th all right and they are jest what I wanted up here for I am helping Bryson to git through the snow which is from four to five feet from here to Lake Tahoe which is 15 miles We have been at work for a week and have only 5 miles broke and it is snowing today about as fast as it can -- he has to carry the mail on snow shoes So you see it is a hard job and he is in a hury to git through with a team I am sorry to hear you are not feeling well I think by what you say your kidney is whare the trouble is

 I had to go up on the road to git the sled out of the snow so Vade will write you I remain as ever your Brother

DD Phillips

My Dear Aunt Mary,

 Will drop a line in Dan's letter. I have intended writing for a long time but something always came in the way.

 We are all well at present. Dan said he wrote you about losing our dear little Johnny. Was so sad at his age and so bright.

No one could beat him on any history, was a fine artist, was natural as never took a lesson. He has only gone before.

Mother was very sick for weeks after John's death. She will be 88 years Tuesday the 22nd. She is so smart for her age and has her mind good yet. Am going to have her picture taken as soon as I can.

We are having dreadful storms. has stormed continually since the 3rd of Feb. Dan came up about a week ago, he looks better than I have seen him in a long time. he told me how you felt and I think if you will get some of Munyons Kidney Cure it will help you so much. I think Munyons Medicines are all right. We have been taking Paw Paw, one of his last medicines.

Mother joins me in best love to all.

Your niece,
Vade

D.D. Phillips in California to his sister Mary Phillips McConahy in Pennsylvania. After Mary's husband died, she was unsure about her future and was looking for a place to go—Florida.

Placerville April 6

Dear Sister

When I rote to you some time ago I was feeling very bad but have been giting better ever since and at present I feel fine. there was lots of snow in the mountian this winter about 20 feet and it don some damage to the buildings but Bryson says not as mutch as was reported. there is about eight feet of snow at the present and it is like ice -- at the present time it looks as if there would be a big crop hay and grain in fact fruit & every thing I wish you could see California at the present time

have you still got the Florida feaver let me hear from you with regards to all

from your Brother Dan

William McConahy in Hookstown, Pennsylvania where he was drilling oil, to a sister in Ellwood City, Pennsylvania. Myrtle had typhoid fever.

Hookstown,
Pa Feb 4, 1906

Dear sister,

I rec'd your most welcome letter. Sorry to learn that you folks are in such a plight. I think you done a wise thing by getting a nurse. You don't want to all get down sick for the sake of a few dollars. I am just about as hard up as I can get at present but can make ends meet after a while. We have been fishing a month tomorrow & will have to quit & drill a new hole after all the expense we have gone to. I put off writing in hopes I could send you better news. I will try & go up next week some time if I possible can. I am afraid you & mamma will both be broke down. Had better keep the nurse till you get straightened at any price don't let the price bother you. Do you think Iseman is a good Dr? If Myrtle gets bad you had better send for Britton. I will close hoping this to find you all convalescing. Am well & hearty as ever. Love & best wishes to all

Your loving brother,
Wm

William McConahy in Hookstown, Pennsylvania to his sister Myrtle McConahy in Ellwood City, Pennsylvania.

Hookstown,
PA March 16, 06
Miss Myrtle McConahae

Dear Sister,

I re'cd yours & Rebecca's most welcome letter. Glad to learn that you are getting along so well & hope you will continue so till you are perfectly well. You have had quite a time of it. You seemed to have a good many friends by the amount of stuff they sent to you. We got the last well put to pumping & it is making about 5 bbl & is getting better. We are down about 400ft – with another one. Expect to finish it next week if nothing happens. I suppose Shaner will have you folks sold out by the time I get home. I had better stay away or he might get me too. Well Myrtle I guess I will go to bed. I can tell you more than I can write. (That is when I get home). I am as well as usual hoping this to find you all the same. I am with love to all you loving brother,

Wm.

J. P. Pollock, Lydia Maria's son, in Colorado to his aunt Mary Phillips McConahy in Pennsylvania.

THE POLLOCK RECORD

SYSTEMATIZE ∽ SAFEGUARD ∽ SIMPLIFY ∽ SHORTEN

The businesslike short cut in bookkeeping

1908 Colorado Avenue
Colorado Springs, Colo
June 24th, 1906
Mrs. Mary McConahae
Elwood City, Penn.

Dear Aunt,

Your letter to Robert was forwarded to me from Rocky Ford. I presume he will answer, but not being sure of it I will. Rocky Ford is on the Santa Fe Railroad. We live a hundred miles west of Rocky Ford also on the Santa Fe. You can come into Colorado Springs on the Denver and Rio Grande, Missouri Pacific Colorado and Southern and the Rock Island. You may not be able to get a stop over at Rocky Ford. I think if you visited at Rocky Ford you would have to pay car fare from Pueblo which is 54 miles west of Rocky Ford. Aunt Lizzie, her daughter, Evra, Joe Phillips and family are living in Denver now, 75 miles from Colorado Springs. All of the roads entering Colorado Springs go to Denver also. I think you will have to see about your stop over privileges at Colorado Springs and Denver. Aunt Lizzie writes me that she has not heard from you for a long time.

My brother David is living in Southern Colorado two
or three hundred miles from this, south of Durango. His
hometown is a very small place named Allison. You would have
to stop at Durango I feel sure. I do not know what road or roads
go through Durango.

If you can possibly arrange to stop at Rocky Ford, Colorado
Springs, Denver, and Durango, you would have to start pretty
early in the summer to get through into California before
winter, as we would expect you to give us all a good long visit.
George Phillips, one of Aunt Lizzie's boys is living at Cripple
Creek, the great mining camp.

We are glad to hear of your intentions to visit us and hope
you will carry the plans out.

Affectionately,
J. P. Pollock

Mary Phillips McConahy in Colorado to her children in Pennsylvania.

Colorado Springs
Aug 19, 07

My Dear Children,

I have received one letter since I arrived. Sorry to hear of
Willie having La Grippe. I hope he will come home and take
a good rest. I think he is working too hard. I think by your
handwriting you are about nervous enough to take a rest. I wish
you were having as good a time as we are, hardly have time to
write. Yesterday Dr. Robt and family were all here. Also Dr.
Samuel,[the Pollock boys] his wife is in Ill. Their son Carlyle

did not come. he is in business with his Father. I feel very proud of my relatives so far. We all had our pictures taken yesterday. I am afraid they will not be very good it rained after dinner and did not clear away until after four o clock and then the wind blew so hard. Robert his wife and daughter expect to stay for awhile. Samuel went home on the Ten train. We all went to Manitoew in the evening to the Soda Springs. Samuel paid the way & Robert treated us all to a big sack of popcorn just freshly popped with butter and salt, it was fine. Samuel wanted to treat to ice cream but we had no room for that. We came home had supper and the boys gave us remenience of their boyhood days I laughed until my sides hurt they are sore yet this morning Last Thursday pm Myrtle & I went in a buggy about five miles to see a Polo game played on horseback. A very exciting game. Friday Wayne Myrtle & I walked up Pikes Peak to the Half-Way house. Myrtle wanted to walk to the top but I thought that far enough. Leland walked clear to the top. Saturday night I went to choir practice in the evening and started up about ten oclock got there at Half past two in the morning Went up to see the sunrise. Came back and went to Sabbath and church in the morning and Endeavor and church in the evening.

Lovingly,
Mama

4 pocket for lunch The rest of
stuff we give the dog and
started them on ahead told
him as soon as we hitched up
we would come after him.
I harnessed the horse and went
to put the bridle on him but could
not get the bit in his mouth
Dale come and we both tryed.
as we give him some hay thought
when he had his mouth open
we could then we tryed barley
but he shut his mouth Even
him _____ to give it to
It was raining all the time so we
hitched him in the rain because
he was so contrary. We kept the
campfire going and waited for
Dan & Henry They came at noon.
We had lunch. but it kept on raining
so we concluded to stay there all
night, as it was Seventeen miles
to the next stopping place could
not get there before dark over
the rough roads. They set up
a stove that was left in the house
So we had it very comfortable

Jergens, Nov. 5, 1907

Mary Phillips McConahy returning from Rubicon Springs, California to her children in Ellwood City PA

Jergens
Nov. 5, 1907

My dear children,

We left this land of sleet and snow Friday the twenty-fifth of October and arrived at the land of sunshine and flowers on Tuesday the twenty-ninth, had made calculations to start on Thursday and expected to get to our journey's end on Saturday, but was raining. And on Friday morning we started a little boy about 18 years (who had been with them all summer) went on ahead with the cattle. The rest of us expected to go after him in a few hours. But a hail storm came up and we could not all get ready. So about half past two PM Vade, Alice and I started in a one-horse buggy. Expected to overtake him at the eight-mile house where our folks had taken some hay and barley a few days before. Also their stuff for the valley. The folks who had been there for the summer had gone below, so the house was vacated. By the time we got there and had the harness off the horse, it was pitch dark. The boy took the horse to the stable. Vade went outside to build a campfire and I went into the dark house to open up a bale of hay with a little dull sledgehammer. I finally got it opened up and Lewy, the boy, took a little armful into the barn to the two horses. They did not get any barley.

We started in such a hurry we forgot our candles and provisions, except for a few baked beans and some fried bear meat that was left from breakfast. In a strange place in the dark and trying to get something to eat, you can just imagine how we looked. Vade would light a stick from the fire outside, by the time she got in, it would be out. I stumbled on something, asked her what was in that can, she said it was lard. I told her I would soon have a light. I took a piece off an old apron I had on and tied a stone in and put it in a pan of lard and set fire to it. And Vade said the light of it would make an electric light shamed of itself. She never saw a light made that way before. We had a fifty-pound can of lard so we had all the grease we wanted -- kept a light going all night.

When we got a light we sat down to eat baked beans and bear meat and hot water. We did not eat much for we wanted to leave something for Lewy in the morning. For breakfast we had baked beans, bear meat, and

We told Lewy to eat all he could for he had a long day ahead of him. The meat that was left we put in his pocket for lunch. The rest of the stuff we gave to the dog and started them on ahead. Told him as soon as we hitched up we would come after him.

I harnessed the horse and went to put the bridle on him but could not get the bit in his mouth. Vade came and we both tried; so we gave him some hay, thought when he had his mouth open we could. Then we tried barley, but he shut his mouth every time, so we had to give it up.

It was raining all the time. Vade hitched him in the rain because he was so contrary. We kept the campfire going and waited for Dan and Jim. They came at noon. We had lunch but it kept raining so we concluded to stay there all night as it was seventeen miles to the next stopping place and we could not get there before dark over the rough roads. They set up the straw that was left in the house. So we had it very comfortable. Next morning, (Sunday) was pleasant when we started but soon it began to rain and rained all day. Sometimes we were below the clouds, in the clouds, and above the clouds. It was a grand sight -- to be above the clouds. I will never forget our trip across the mountains. Our next stopping place was Uncle

Tom's. Expected Lewy to go on Sunday morning and not wait for us, but one of the cows had a calf Saturday night, so he waited for the rest of us.

We could have gone further but it was raining so hard concluded to stay until Monday morning. That stop cost $13.00. The calf ran along with the cow for quite a way. Then it gave out. Jim was driving a spring wagon with a box hitched on behind with a black pig in it weighing 150 lbs. Above that was a coop of chickens, on top of that was our can of lard, packed meat, carpets, rugs, and a little of everything in his wagon. So they put the calf in with the pig. Dan was on ahead driving the stage piled full, drawn by four horses.

Monday night Vade and I put up at Georgetwon, a distance of 25 miles from Uncle Tom's. The rest stopped five miles the other side. We waited there Tuesday morning until they came. From then on we drove behind Jim to watch the calf and the pig. Sometimes the calf would be under the pig. Then we would call Jim and he would get out and fix them up. He wanted us to drive ahead -- but we were too much concerned about the livestock to do that.

We arrived at the ranch about four o'clock Tuesday evening. Lewy and the cattle got there about dusk all safe and sound. I told Uncle Dan I never wanted to see him drive the stage over that road again. Some places the road is so sidling right on the steep mountain side. he is getting too old for that kind of work. That was what worried me. I was afraid something could happen to him so high on the stage. Vade said she rode behind him once. It made her so nervous she said she never would again.

He is not feeling very well since he came to the ranch. Vade says she never enjoyed herself so much in her life as she did that trip. We laughed until our sides were sore. The whole distance was 66 miles.

It is very warm and dry here yet. They do the plowing in the spring and sow the seed in the fall. They are trying to get the seed in now before it commences to rain. We have been very busy since we came. Alice and I picked the grapes on the place. What was left -- have made some marmalade. Want to bottle some grape juice tomorrow. There is quite a vineyard here, some quinces. The apples have been taken. The house is an old timer, a story and a half, three rooms down and two up.

Murphy's would have Myrtle go with them via Truckee. That place is about as large as Wampum. From there to Sacramento, then Auburn home. She has not arrived yet. Glad she was not with us in the rain. Murphy's men were here Sunday for supper. They came down with their cattle. They said Myrtle had a letter from Joe Phillips that he is coming soon and is going to take her home with him. I don't like to see her go so far away. I like it here. XXX for Charles.

Love,
Mama

[Ed. note: Charles Hartung was born April 4, 1904.]

Jurgens
Feb. 27/08

Dear Relief,

I received your letter yesterday dated Feb 10. Glad to hear you are all well and enjoying yourselves. I think the Grippe has full sway there.

How thankful I am that I am in the land of sunshine and flowers. And no sign of Grippe, cough or cold. This is certainly an ideal climate. Jim, Vade and Alice have gone to Placerville today.

I think I told you about Vade getting her teeth extracted. There was three pieces of roots of an eye tooth left in, caused an abscess on her cheek. And has never healed up. She will have Jim and her Dr with her at the Dentists.

I sent you two little dresses and a robe with Vade to mail at Placerville. The first dress I made a failure of. I did not think the old machine would stitch. So I gathered it around the neck. It will be easy to make it larger, just let the pleats out on the shoulder and the neckband is long enough to let out. The robe is for dear little Charles when he goes to bed early to throw over him. I sent Cecil one. I tried to get white but could not get the goods in white. Myrtle is going to hemstitch a little dress for you.

It would be comic to see Mr. & Mrs. Wright go to bed in the rain. Uncle Dan & I talk some of going down there before we go to the mountains.

You and Mabel were pretty slick letting your Mothers get away just when we did. I can almost hear Mame making fun of Mabel. Pour Mabel. Hope you will all get along well.

Did you ever find that first quilt you pieced and I set together?

Will close wishing you all good health & success. Tell Charles to send me word when he is coming and I will meet him at the station with some oranges. Kiss him for Grandma. Write soon. Love to all.

Lovingly
Mama

A thank you note from Mary Phillips McConahy to her daughter Myrtle.

My dearest Myrtle,
It is sweet to be remembered.
And in so nice a way
I cannot find words to express
The thanks I would like to say
Showers of blessings I pray
Love,
Mother

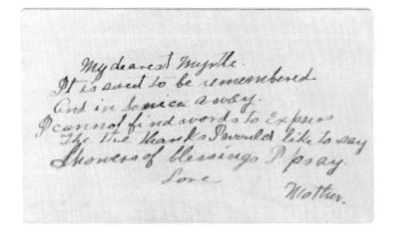

Dear Sister Relief,

You didn't answer my last letter but will write a few lines to you anyhow. Mama, Uncle Dan and I are alone. The rest went to Placerville. A week ago last Saturday Vade, Mama, Dan & I went to Zimmerman's. The rest came back Sunday but I stayed until last Friday. I had a great time. Last Sunday Alice & I went calling on the two Jurgen girls. They have the post office.

I turned my blue skirt and it looks as good as new with the exception of a few patches. I made a skirt box out of an old trunk. Lined it with wallpaper and painted it red. I painted a big square box white on the inside and green on the outside. I am going to put my shirtwaists there. I am very busy.

We will go to the mountains before long. Wish you were here to go along. Mama is talking of buying a few acres near Galt. Galt isn't near as large as Ellwood. I will die if I go but I don't think I will go.

I have to fix all of my waists larger as I am getting so fat. I like Sacramento. I would like to live there. I am going to make you a little baby dress. Taking lessons.

Vade sent for a phonograph Edison today. Vade, Jim, Alice & I went over to Orillas last Sunday evening. They have an Edison they played for us. They have the same whistling song like the one we have. Well, Dearie, I must close as space is limited. Write me once in awhile. Kiss Charles for me, also yourself and Bert. Love to all,

Sisterly,
Myrtle

Lotus Eldorado Co
April 24 1908

My Dear Children

I received your ever welcome letter Glad to learn of your all getting along so well. You must be careful and not get to smart. 26"A.M. This is the third time I have attempted to write this letter. We have had so much company and getting ready to go to the mountains that everything seems to be in commotion. Last Tuesday Joe Zimmerman and his mother came Wednesday Miss Orelli and Mrs. Boyer of Sacramento came and Thursday, Mr. Zimmerman came again his mother lost her pocket book the day they were up (We found it, She lost it near a house) they found it and kept it for her. And before we had lunch Old Mrs. Orelli, her daughter, daughter in law, Mr. and Mrs. Boyer and Charley Leanarty came. We had music and a very pleasant time generally. Friday Charley was here in the forenoon. And he and Myrtle went to Georgetown for a dance. Expected to be a swell affair. They started at Two o clock P.M. was going to "Mrs. Orelli's" sisters folks and go with them.

This Charley is a very nice young man. Born and raised here, his father died when he was fourteen years old. He is the oldest of five children, has always had the family to take care of. His mother died two years ago. So you may know he is a steady young man. He is twenty-nine years old, pretty as a picture, dark eyes and hair. Tell Rebecca she will have to come and help Myrtle out. There is other nice young men here (honest ranchers) Orellis own fifteen hundred acres of land, five hundred head of cattle. They come to the foothills in the fall and mountains in the summer. Mike Orelli came to see Alice

Blair Thursday evening but she had retired early and did not see him, she said there is only one she would get up to see.

Last winter has been exceptionally dry and the hay harvest is almost a failure. Some will not harvest their grain at all. From appearances there will be plenty of fruit. Uncle Dan did not go to the mountains as expected as it was rainy all week. He and Mr. Bryson intend going next Monday. And if the snow is off the mountains enough Vade will go up next. They will take a load up and Mr. Bryson will come back.

Take good care of that nice little family. Would like to see you all. Write soon with Love to all with xxxxxxx for all

Lovingly
Mama

Mary Phillips McConahy in California to her children in Pennsylvania.

Lotus El Dorado Co
No date (May 1908?)

My Dear Children

I will send you a box containing Passion flowers. Vade brought them from Placerville yesterday so I could see them. They are so pretty, I hope they will keep nice so you can see the "Halo, the Cross, the Hammer and nails." All in the flower. It is a vine. Vade intends to get a root of it next fall. Vade is sending a box of flowers to Truckee for her sisters grave for Decoration day, her nephew is buried there too.

We all expect to go to Placerville Saturday. Vade's Father, Mother and little boy are buried there also her uncle Joe Ball.

My brother Alden is buried on the shores of Lake Tahoe. I want to go to his grave next summer.

Uncle Dan has had a great time with his foot. I believe I have been the means of saving his life. His foot was about well and he worked so hard in the hay field and got so very warm and his foot commenced to swell and turn black and purple. I have been keeping warm poultices on it ever since last Saturday morning. I treated it about as I treated my hand when it was so sore, did not have much effect on it. So yesterday I made a poultice of wormwood that helped it some. This morning Vade & I went to the woods and got some pine pitch and put some in the poultice too. This evening looks as though it would get well, but will be sometime before he works much. Vade wants me to go in partners with her and will hire a man to take Dan's place. Mr. Bryson intends to mine this summer. I think if Rebecca comes out this summer and keeps books she will be the right one in the right place.

Mr. Orelli and Charley Leonarty have been here all evening. As it is late will close. Myrtle is visiting Miss Myrtle Jurgens. We intend starting for the lake the 8th of June. Would like to see you all. Goodnight

xxxxxx Lovingly,
Mama
Take good care of your little babies

Jan 2, 1909

Dear Aunt Mary,

We received your welcome letter day before yesterday but I had company and could not get it answered till tonight. We would like so much to have you come and visit us on your way home and bring Uncle Dan to visit us and see the country for himself. It is a newly irrigated district and there are always so many drawbacks to a new country. My husband does not like it here and wants to go to California if he could find a place to suit him. The altitude here is 6200 feet and he doesn't feel good. However we are on a homestead and it has about 2 ½ years to run. There is 80 acres belonging to Dr. S. H. lying next to us which he would sell I think for $2000. It has water and can almost all be watered. Some bad arroya's at the south end and pinon and cedar on the highest part. All in sage brush. We are setting out lots of fruit trees and have 35 acres in alfalfa. The soil is rather adobe. I like the climate as it is nearly always pleasant thru the day but the nights are always cold. We have had 6 degrees below zero this winter and considerable snow. Last winter it got down to 10 degrees below once. We have a nice community, organized a Presbyterian church last summer and have preaching ever two weeks and a good Sunday School. We are three miles from Allison.

As for Uncle Dan staying with us you know anyone that is like mother Pollock will be welcome in our home. I often wish I had some one to cheer up my husband. He so often feels badly since his health gave way.

About chickens, I'm afraid the coyotes have run away with more than any profits so far, and woven wire is expensive.

We are on the Denver and Rio Grande, 40 miles east of Durango. The place used to be called Vallejo. They charge 5 cents a mile on this road and the best way is to by a 1000 mile ticket at 3 cents a mile (except on the most mountainous parts). You might get excursion rates but I couldn't promise them. It is a narrow gage around here.

Now we <u>do</u> enjoy having our friends visit us and would all like to have you come so much. The children go to Allison to school every day in the buggy so if you did not send us word in time you'd soon find us after landing.

Now I told you all the bad things about the country as we don't want Uncle Dan to be disappointed in it as my husband has been somewhat. As for me I like it all right if only it agreed with him. With love from us all to you both I remain,

Your loving grand niece,
Barbara L. Pollock

Mary Phillips McConahy in California to her daughter Rebecca McConahy in Ellwood City, Pennsylvania.

Lotus Jan 10 1909

After received your letter I sent to Sacramento for a ticket to Denver. I rec'd word that I would have to come there for it, and that would cost One dollar and seventy cts extra. Since then I have received word twice from Myrtle not to come there now for it is so cold. Almost as cold as Pa., and I had better wait until spring. I am afraid myself for it is like spring here all the time. Just lovely and Dan & Vade will not let me think of going this time of year. There has been great rains here and danger of washout and snow on the mountains. And danger of a blockade and great suffering crossing the Rockies. So I have about given up the trip at present.

If you get a position in Denver you can board with Aunt Lizzie cheaper than we could keep house in winter. They are all as good to me here as can be. And Bryson was too when he was home. They just wont let me go.

I am sewing for myself this winter. Made a shirt waist And we have commenced on battenburg work. The collar you sent put us in that notion, it is so nice. I sent Cecil his mittens am knitting Charles'. My yarn run short the reason his are not done.

I received a letter from Mrs. Wright yesterday. She said there was no snow there but could see it on the mountains. Is colder there than it has been for eighteen years.
I only wish you could see that part of the country. And down by Galt land is coming up so fast. They think here I am very foolish if I sell that land.

If I am here in the Spring will get Uncle Dan to go with me and set it out to something. The poorest kind of land there cannot be bought now for less than $100 to $125 per acre. I am a walking advertisement for this country (or county) for I weigh more than I have for 30 years.

Lotus February 17, 1909

My dear children,

I received you lovely presents also the magazines. Many thanks. The presents landed in Lotus on the 13. A lovely remembrance.

Glad the children are all better and are all prospering.

Glad to hear the old hen faired so well. Who in the world took her head off?

It almost makes me shiver to read of the cold in that part of the country. I don't believe I can ever get used to such cold weather, for when it is a little frosty it seems so cold. I want you to be sure and watch the children from the streetcar.

How is Florence Dreads getting along since she cam back to Ellwood?

I will have to hasten as Dan and Vade are going to Murphy's and will take the mail.

I sent you a letter last week. Will write to Myrtle next. Glad she isn't a night operator any longer. Received your lovely card also Charles'. Dear little dear. Love to all. Write soon. Love and kisses for all.

Lovingly,
Mama

Colorado Springs
May 9, 1909

Dear Aunt Mary,

Your letter rec. We were all glad to get the pictures. They are both fine. Uncle Dan is a good looking man. He looks very much like Uncle Charles the last time I saw him some 12 or 13 years ago. Tell Uncle I hope he is as good as he looks. I would like to see him. Tell him to come and make us a visit. My mind goes back to old Penna where I first remember seeing Uncle. Then to Illinois when he staid with us for a time and still we both live. My life since that time has been a reasonably happy one and I believe his has been also. Since that time many of our dear ones have gone to the better land. I hope we will both be prepared to meet them there. There are Aunt Lizzie, Uncle Dan, and Aunt Mary left. I feel that I ought to honor them for the sake of or in remembrance of dear Mother.

Our men's Bible Class were given white carnations each member a flower which we were to wear in honor of our Mothers. It made the day seem hallowed. My heart has been tender all day. How little a boy really appreciates a mother and her sacrifices for her children till she has gone. It will not be many years till I will tell her so myself. She certainly did her part in the battle of life with a large family. Heaven only is sufficient reward and this I know is her's.

A short time ago I wrote Uncle Daniel Pollock for a history of the Pollock family going back as far as knows giving the names of each and coming on down and giving his brothers and sisters who they married, their children, where they are, if he knows and then his own children and families.

I wish you and Uncle would set down some time and give the history of the Phillips family commencing as far back as you know anything of them giving their names. I would like to get it on both sides of the house and complete as possible.

My family is in usual health. Ruth is not as strong as we would like. Robert is taking up her case to advise us which treatment is best for her so far as he thinks it is called for. Leiland will soon finish his third year in Colorado College and is holding his health very well. He ran 10 ½ miles the other day in an endurance race. He was 4 in a group of 10 who ran. Avery who is 16 is doing well. Stands high in his classes and the estimation of his teachers. His voice is just changing. So far the boys are boys of good habits and both members of the Pres. Church.

Emma Hinton Pollock is at Rocky Ford under Robert's care for lung trouble and we are afraid she will not live long. She has been in delicate health for a long time in fact never very strong. So there is not much to build on. (Jeanne Sorrel) Pollock is at Phoenix

Arizona. Her husband is with her. She is no better we hear poor woman. She has been a sufferer for so long. We hear that Milton is better and practicing medicine. David is in usual health. Wells, his boy staed in Colorado Springs and went to school during the winter. He is a good boy 19 years old. Helen, their daughter staid in Rocky Ford and went to school. She has gone home. She is in good flesh but her nerves trouble. She is a fine girl and we hope she will get over her nervous troubles.

We got a letter from Rebecca saying that she in contemplating visiting the west – with staying if she likes a time out here. We will do all we can to help her in any way we can. I suppose she will not get as far west as California. We have written her and hope we will have the pleasure of a visit from her.

I must close and go to church. It is now in the evening.

Affectionately,
J. P. Pollock

Mary Phillips McConahy in California to her daughter Rebecca in Ellwood City, Pennsylvania.

Jurgens
May 16, 1909

Dear Rebecca,

I received your ever welcome letter. Was so glad to hear you were all well.

Wonder you are all not sick with such weather. I read so much about it in the papers. As for this part of the country it has been very warm and dry and has been very pleasant and dry since sometime in March.

Vade and Jim came down last Monday to help make hay and will be here until the last of the week. hay is so very poor. If it had been a good year they would not have touched this poor dry stuff.

I sent Uncle Dan and my picture to Joe Pollock also a pillow top to Ida. she did not answer my letter and Joe never said a word about it. It will soon be their harvest time for them. The busiest season.

They were so crowded when we were there If you could arrange it so you could be there after the harvest season is over I know it would suit them better. You will get to see Emma Pollock at Rocky Ford. I think you would enjoy yourself there they are so friendly and nice. If you could only come out to that CE Convention you would get to see some of the beautiful mountain scenery.

I suppose you would have a chance to sell your ticket and come on or go back to Col and sell it there if you wanted to And might not cost you much more than a straight ticket. Then you would see something worthwhile. Be sure and put your initial on your ticket instead of your name.

My ear is better. Send your letters to Jurgens I have a chance to send this to the office. All well as usual. Good bye and love to all

Lovingly Mama

Myrtle McConahy in Colorado to her sister Relief Hartung in Ellwood City, Pennsylvania.

Denver, Colo
June 21, 1909

Dear Sister,

I received your very pretty Xmas presents. Thank you very much. The candy tastes like more. I received some very nice presents. Also had a nice time. I went to the theater twice this week. Had an auto ride last night. I am going to the auditorium tomorrow night to a concert. Have had a vacation since Wednesday. Expect to go to work Monday. Rebecca and

Effie are coming West at last. Me for the East. I can hardly wait. Bertha White is back in Ellwood again. I wrote for a position in the telephone office and can have one as soon as I return. Isn't that great? We are having spring weather now. Had skating for Xmas. My but I was homesick when I saw them. Mary Steinberger wants me to stay with her in New Castle. I was sewing tonight and run the needle of the machine thru my finger. It is alright now. George and Flo's married life don't seem to be very happy. Poor Flo I feel sorry for her.

I received some very nice presents for Xmas. I have one on the way yet. A pincushion, an apron, several handkerchiefs, a box of candy, a picture, a scarf, three cushion tops. Some money from Willie and Coz Joe. A hatpin holder, several pretty post cards and I forgot what else. Had a letter from Mother Vath. She is staying with Mrs. Keeth until March. I would love to see you all. Hope to soon.

Will close with lots of love to you Dear. I have a book for Charles, and one for Florence. Will bring them with me.

Wishing you all many happy and prosperous years.

Lovingly,
Myrtle
1130 Humbolt St.
Denver, Colo

Jurgens, June 28/09

My Dear Myrtle,

I received your ever welcome letter of June 12". Answered it the next day. Never heard what you thought of your birthday present. When you wrote you was not feeling very well. So I have been just imagining you are both sick. If you are let me know and I will try and work my way Eastward.

I had a little too much excitement for me a few days after Uncle Dan went away. Mrs. Lunamen and little girls were here and all at once Anna said Oh! there is an adder [snake] in the house. I looked and he was over by the kitchen table. Well I was never so frightened in my life. I supposed it was as poisonous as a Rattlesnake. I just went after it with a sharp stick jabbed at it and took five inches of its tail. If it had been at the other end of the critter it would have put an end to it. As it was it made its escape. In the fracas everything in the kitchen got a move on, Tables, cupboards, rugs, flour barrel. And the wood box I put on the porch so I could have a better chance to see snakes, not very pretty things to look at. Although these are a little out of the ordinary for they have four feet. There has been two in since. Pearley killed one and I killed the other. I think I have all the holes shut up now in the kitchen. Everybody says they are perfectly harmless, that they come in to catch flies. I'll take flies every time in preference to snakes. Now don't dream of snakes. I was afraid I would but I don't.

I received a postal yesterday from Lizzie Swick. Said she would answer my letter later. I hope she does I would love to hear from her. What do you think! They say Ray Clawson is going to be married next month to a lady in Ill, got acquainted with her through correspondence. Says he has enough of the Calif girls. Mrs. Lunamen and family are invited to the wedding. She is coming out here and be married. I would like to know what kind of a breath he has before I would come all that distance to marry him.

I expect Uncle Dan home any day now then I will know more. Orellis started for the mountains yesterday. Maggie says she will write to you when she gets there. I was over twice last week to see them.

I am sending you the tapestry catalog that rose pillow top you have. I sent for in your name and they sent you the offer for those free lessons. No difference if it is dated back The outfit I sent for was long after they sent it. I have several packages of paint here never opened. If you want them will send them. Thought you and Lydia would like to do some painting. The magazine has some such nice reading in it. You and Lydia notice what it says about taking things moderate and resting. I enclose a prescription you had better get filled.

Love and xxxxxx
Ever your loving Mama

Jurgens,
July 5/09

Dear Rebecca.

Received your ever welcome letter the 2nd of this month. As Uncle Dan has not arrived thought I would not answer until I would see what he had to say. He came home Saturday afternoon. Almost four weeks would have passed had he stayed until Monday and working hard all the time. He hauled eight loads of household goods from the lake, one load a day. He got up this morning sick, sick at his stomach trembling and his back pained him so. His stomach is better but his back still pains him. He is sorry now he did not take that job of working for Mr. Calwell, said he would have something in the fall. Vade talked him out of that. That is hard work but some encouragement when you think you are going to get paid for it. They want him to come back and help. He would not go if there was anything doing here. He wants me to go to Rubicon. Says he will pay my way and when I leave there I can get rates so I will not be out of pocket any. Mrs. Lewis is talking of going and wants me to be sure and go. we will camp out and board ourselves. Think I can make money painting pillow tops. My liver has been on the warpath ever since I had that spell of grippe. I caught at Humphreys only while I was at Rubicon that short time. Then I never felt better in my life. Now I have to be taking something all the time for it. I may never have such a good chance again. So I concluded to go, that is one reason. I am so afraid to go where it is so changeable and cold. I know I could not stand another siege like I had. Vade is better and on the jump. Expected several there for the 4th.

Dan says everything is topsy turvey he thinks she will surly sell her place by fall. Such a beautiful location, nicest on the road. Wish some of the rest of you could come to Rubicon. I think Lydia will have to make a change soon. Myrtle must be busy, never written since I sent her the pillow top. Did she send one to Joe Phillips. If not I have one to send to him. I am sure you will have a nice time in Col. Glad you come while Aunt Lizzie is living, she is so lovely as well as all the rest of the friends that I ever met. Find out what is the matter with David Pollock. He wrote that he was coming out the 1st of June. That is the last I heard.

Hope Myrtle and Keif have made up again. I don't see the use of them spatting so much. We have a very quiet 4th here. Are having quite a time at Placerville. Will close with love to you and all the friends. Write soon. Good-bye.

Your loving Mama

Part of a letter from Mary P. McConahy to her daughter Rebecca in Ellwood City, PA

Aug. 2, 1909

One reason I insist on you coming West is I think it could do you so much good. And I think it will pay for us to look after poor old Uncle Dan for a little while. He often wishes he was dead. And I don't wonder at that. I know I would if I had to live the way he does. Sometimes he wishes he was off in a little cabin by himself. If he once gets located down there he could stay by himself. I will not be much help to him and stay here.

I would like to stay until I make some money as long as it is easy work & if I got sick I would be cared for.

As for Myrtle she wrote some time ago that she expected she and Keef would be married sometime. Don't tell her I said anything about it. I think it is the best thing she could do. I don't think she will ever find a nicer or truer young man than he. I will gladly send you the twenty if you will only come. There is a chance for you to make money with the fruit. That is what I came to Gilroy for. I would love to see you all but if I stay a little longer I may have enough to buy us a home. That place at Galt will certainly come up in value.

Lovingly
Mama

Part of a letter from Mary Phillips McConahy in California to her daughter Rebecca in Ellwood City, Pennsylvania.

Aug 1909

… be a good place for Wm to rest up come out and help Uncle Dan get fixed up. He has a horse & buggy. He would have a good chance to ride around and see the country. It is nice to have a stopping place when so far away that you can call home. I wrote to Mary Cowden and sent her some garden seeds but have not heard from her since. Wrote to Mrs. Falmeth and she never answered. If Joe Pollock would write to Joe Fields, he could give him more information about the family tree than anyone else. He was going to have it printed. I want to get one. I wrote to Mary for Joes address. My Father had three brothers and two sisters that I know of. Uncle Stephen Phillips is the only one I ever saw. Aunt Lizzie certainly remembers him. Was drowned in the Ohio River, was on a steamboat. As he was a very early riser it was supposed he got up before quite daylight and stepped overboard. His body was never recovered. And dear old Aunt Polly Phillips Bard must be over thirty years since she died. Uncle Elijah P I think and Michel the other brothers. I saw his wife when I was in Vermont (Aunt Sylvia). Then there was Aunt Laura Phillips Pangborn. She moved to Iowa. It was through her daughter that Joe Fields got most of his information regarding the Phillips family.

I think we are of old Puritan stock for brother Alden was named for one of the Pilgrims. Alden Church that was my brother's name. And Father was a drummer boy in the war of 1812.

The best way is to get what Joe Fields has collected. He may have it printed by this time. I would like to buy the history from him. He could tell more about the family that ever knew. My mind is not settled enough now to think. If I get Joe Fields address I will send it to Joe Pollock.

I intended to finish this letter last night but the lights were too dim to write. Relief sent me a clipping from the paper in regards to Mrs. Blats death. I will send it to you.

Oh why should the spirit of mortal be proud
Like a fast falling meteor a fast flying cloud.
A flash of the lighting, a brick of the road
He passes from life to rest in the grave.
This the wink of an eye, tis the drought of a breath
From the blossom of health to the paleness of death
From the gilded saloon to the bier & the shroud
Oh, why should the spirit of mortal be proud?

Aug 10, 1909

I just received a letter from Lydia. She is not so well, her nerves are bad, eyes and head pain her and her arms. The same as she was two years ago. Said she has been feeling better but the warm weather knocks her out. Do you think she could stand to come out here? I don't believe she will live long there. Ralph gets a months vacation on pay. There is a nice house at Galt and Dan would bring his share could have fresh milk and eggs and fresh air. Says she feels like crawling off and taking a complete rest. If they could come to Col you come along if she don't come & keeps sick I will have to give up my position I don't like to for it just suits me.

To Vade from Mary Phillips McConahy. Mary is with Lydia and Cecil in Santa Cruz.

Monday morning Oct. 31

This is a lovely warm morning. The sun is shining. The first we have seen since we came here. Yesterday there was a fine mist. Lydia thinks this would be a nice place to spend the winter. If I go to Galt which I intend to do if there is any chance at all for I do not want to disappoint Uncle Dan again. She will be wanting somebody for company too.

That chicken you gave me was about the finest I ever tasted. And the Prince of Wales cake kept so nice and moist. We kept it for a little treat all the way. You ought to see Mr. Robb

Stewarts house. I think it the most convenient one I ever saw. Three years ago there was only one house on that street. Now it is built up almost solid. There is one vacant lot next to them. The price of it now is one thousand dollars. One orange tree on it, that is all. The girls ride five miles to their work in the department store. Have worked five years for the same man and each receive fifteen dollars a week. Would not go back East to stay under any circumstances. Cecil is wanting to go to the beach so will close. Good bye. x

Aunt Lizzie Phillips (Charles Phillips' wife) to her niece Rebecca McConahy. Mary returned to Pennsylvania because Lydia was ill and didn't visit Aunt Lizzie.

Denver, Colo
November 13, 1909

My Dear Rebecca,

Will try to answer your welcome letter. Evra is so busy all the time that she can't get time for anything only work. She has been sewing at night so you know what that means but she has got to quit it soon as she gets what she has done.

Well we are all well. Dollie is in Kansas visiting her folks. Had a letter from Irma a day or 2 ago she is very busy housekeeping they are by themselves now & she thinks it much nicer. Well I suppose you was very much pleased to see that mother of yours. Hope she is well but you can tell her that I never will forgive her for her smartness for going home and not stopping here. I was counting so much on seeing her. When she was here before I wasn't a bit well & then there was so many here that it was hurly burly all the time. Now am so much better & all alone all day & I thought we would just have a fine time here all alone & to think she would do that way. I can't get over it. Tell her to please answer my last letter anyway.

We have had the nicest weather all fall we are just having our first snow storm its been at it since yesterday morn. Haven't had any freezing weather yet its so nice & warm the grass is green and nice as it can be but is covered with snow now but it is not cold enough to freeze

I must thank you for your recipes the tail end of the garden is certainly wrong names for it is the whole of the garden. I just made a lot of chow chow before I would of tried it but it will keep another year. Jack & Molie sent us enough of apples to do us all winter & plums & prunes besides.

Mollie is coming here to spend the holidays expect we will have a time with her 3 big boys such fellows make quite a stir around

Now tell your Mother that I haven't got over it yet & don't know when I will give her my love at any rate to Myrtle and all the rest hope this will find you all well & enjoying yourselves.

Your loving Aunt Lizzie

PS I always thought Sunday was a day of rest but I think you make it the hardest any of the seven the way you put it in.

Lydia McConahy Brown to her sisters in Pennsylvania.

Gilroy, Cal
October 29, 1910

My Dear Sisters:

Well here I am again. I received Rebecca's welcome letter but I am sorry to disappoint you all as I am myself. Too bad

Florence won't have Cecil to play with as I think they would make a pretty good pair. I am anxious to hear whether Mother will come or not. I got a letter from her the same day I got yours, they sent me Nellie's [Nellie Brown] picture on the postal she is a dear little thing I would like to see her. Cecil's throat is a good bit better but still has a hacking cough but the Dr. says he will be alright but that I had better stay here a year. My new glasses suit my eyes alright haven't had any headache, and I have been sewing and doing some crocheting making a collar and cuffs for my coat. Alex and Vira are going to the fiar next week. I have had a good time this week. Phoebe, Sylvia, Cecil and I all went to church this morning. Edward & Russell went in on their wheels. Well I will close hoping to hear from you soon. I was in hopes I would be home for Halloween but instead will make a cake and candy for the folks here. I want to give Cecil a bath so good night.

With love to you all, I am as ever

Your loving sister
Lydia

D.D. Phillips in California to his sister Mary Phillips McConahy in Galt, CA.

Michigan Bar
April 23, 1911

Dear Sister

I cam down here on the 17th and intended to stay a week with Hettie and then go to Galt to see you. I was here only one day when Mr. Sickles went crazy and tride to kill every one in sight I sent little Wells to git help and send after the constable and we took him to Jackson the county seat of Amador Co -- the Juge will not be home until the first of May -- and then he will hafter to go to Jackson to see what they do with him.

I expect Vade down today Bryson I think has gone to the mountians So at present I cannot say when I will be at Galt I cannot git enny one to stay here wile I am gon -- and Hetty cannot tend to everything here

Yours of the 12th came to hand on the 21 so that accounts for me not answern sooner.

DD Phillips
Direct Michigan Bar
Amadore Co
California

D.D. Phillips in California to his sister Mary Phillips McConahy in Galt, California.

Michigan Bar
May 7 11

Dear Sister

When I came down here I expected to see you before this but Sickles went crazy & is in the insane asylem at Stockton & I am with Hettie looking after the stock and I can not leave her by herself and I will hafter to see them to the mountian I am afraid the season is goan to late

So I think you & Lydia had better come & camp on the Summit this Summer I am sorry that things has turned out as it has but I can not help it and I think it best to go to Summit once more and as I could not do enny thing in Galt this Summer. So I think it best for you to come to the high range and have a good time

DD Phillips

D.D. Phillips in California to his sister Mary Phillips McConahy in Pennsylvania.

Phillips' Station Sept 7 1911

Dear Sister

The weather has been cold & windy but at present it is warm in fact it is as nice as it can be -- I was over to Lake yesterday

12000 fish to stock the head of the American River and I expect to take the empty cans back in the morning the trouble is about over for the Summer and will have it easy from this out -- We are having a mining excitement about five miles from here on the head of the Rubicon River. I would like to be at the Rubicon spring and see what I could find out but I hear that it is all take up they are giting ready to build some next Summer I will have some timbers in this fall -- and then it will be pack up and git out.

Dan

Hetty Sickles in California to her aunt Mary Phillips McConahy in Pennsylvania.

Dear Aunt Mary

Some time past I sent you some postals of this place, am wondering if you received them. Had some prettier ones early in the season but they did not last and have not been able to get any since. Am so glad your daughter is so well now. Mr. Orr was telling us when here.

How is Myrtle, and where is she, you never say when you write.

Have had a busy season, but now is about ended, so we will have a little time. And as the season is so short do not mind the hard work.

Have more letters to write so will close. Let me know if you received the postals.

Love to yourself and daughter
Hetty J. Sickles

A copy of the following song was given to Cecil Phillips, Lydia's son, by his grandmother, Mary Phillips with the inscription: "A happy new year, Cecil dear." The song was published by the Pennsylvania State Sunday School Association, 1913. Words by Samuel Gill.

BATTLE HYMN OF TEMPERANCE
Tune: John Brown

We're a host of earnest people who have heard the trumpet call,
That the Lord of Hosts has sounded to dethrone King Alcohol,
And they're rising in the country, in the cities, great and small;
Our host is marching on.

(Chorus)
Rise, then, rally'round our banner,
Jesus Christ is our commander,
Alcohol must soon surrender,
For now the battle's on,

There are cries and groans arising, calls for help on every hand,
As our fellows bend beneath this curse, this blight
on our fair land,
So we've sworn to fight their battles, lift their burders,
lend a hand
To dethrone King Alcohol.

(Chorus)

We had uttered much entreaty, and full many prayers had said,
That from the curse and burden of this king we might be led,
But now we join in battle under Jesus Christ our head;
King Alcohol must go.

(Chorus)

King Alcohol's a tyrant, full of bloodshed, crime and lies,
Who has filled the world with sorrow, all unheeding
mankind's cries;
So now the battle's raging, and will rage until he dies,
And right has been enthroned.

(Chorus)
Old Alcohol, the tyrant, might become a servant true,
He might drive our motor wagons, light our house, plough the
blue;
But if he won't be useful, he must take his rightful due,

Since God is marching on.

(Chorus)
The Lord of Hosts is with us and will never sound retreat,
Until Satan and King Alcohol are humbled in defeat;
And then our trophies bringing we will lay at Jesus' feet
And crown HIM LORD OF ALL.

(Chorus)

Partial letter from Mary Phillips Mc Conahy in California.

Pages 3 & 4

Mr. Wright's yet. Will be glad when I get what few things I have in this part of the country together again. My box of bedclothes and rugs are at McJunkins apt. Suppose after Ralph gets to Galt we will get there sometime.

Hope we can live cheaper there than here. This is such a lovely place for anyone that is ready to live a retired life. Commenced raining Sunday night – been raining ever since except Tuesday. That is the day we moved back into the house we first lived in. Just lived in the other house one week. Soon made up our minds to move when it commenced to rain for we had to go out in the rain much more than in this house. We got word form another party which is much better and we are very comfortable now. Lydia is taking the viaba treatment now and (she's a good ways from well yet) I do the rubbing act.

Mama Acker looks well, has that hacking cough yet. Harry is not very well yet. He and Mame don't either of them take any care of themselves. Maud looks well cough much better.

Maggie would rather live in this part of the country. Did Mr. and Mrs. Pool join the church? Would love to see you all, makes me shiver to read of the cold weather back there.

Take care of yourselves.

Lydia McConahy Brown in California to her mother Mary Phillips McConahy and her sisters Rebecca and Myrtle McConahy in Pennsylvania. Ralph Brown has tuberculosis and is undergoing treatment.

Bakersfield, California
Aug. 13, 1913

Dear Mother & Sisters,

Well here I am at last. I have not forgotten you, no never, for I think of you every day. I received Rebecca's welcome letter today also the cards she sent. It is so nice you had a nice trip with such nice girls too. Well we are having very nice summer days; another hot spell has passed and we are having a few days of cooler weather.

Ralph helped to unload a car of engines for the Bessemer, they finished it Sunday. Sunday morning a couple of large wheels fell over and caught a man around the waist and to save the man Ralph and another man held the wheels up for a couple seconds and put Ralph on the bums. One wheel weighed 2500 pounds and the other one 2100 pounds. Ralph almost fainted when they got them propped up he couldn't of held it any longer he has been stiff and sore – feels some better today. He is slowly improving. No steady work yet. I am still sewing on the baby wardrobe for my neighbor. Got $1.50 for what I have finished. I want to get it done so I can make Cecil a couple of suits for school. The Eastern scenes on post cards look better to me than California ones.

Ralph weighs almost 112 pounds with coat off. So you see is not a very large man at present. Wish he could get some light work to do until he gets stronger or I could get to do something with some money in it. We have enough for about another months rent and that is about all. Will have to do something soon. Cecil is growing and is as brown as a berry.

Mr. Brown has been canvassing this summer but has not made much beside his expenses. I wish Mother would do and see Pearl and see if she and Arthur can't do something for Nellie. Father has not sent a cent since the first of the year. Aunt Emma wrote and said Nellie has not been well at all the Dr. says it is her age. She said two weeks out of every month she is hardly able to drag around. Aunt Emma is willing to give her a home but thinks the rest might help her and keep her in medicine. As we are at present it is impossible for us to send back any money to help her. Father has been up against it ever since he lost his position here. Mrs. Brown told me that another cent was not going back to her. So you see it is up to her sisters & brothers to do something. It is a shame to impose on Aunt Emma to just keep her. If Arthur can afford an auto he might help Nellie some. I just feel like flying sometimes but try to be content and do the best I can and trust God will help us out. If we can make expenses while Ralph is taking the treatments and he can give them a fair trial and get his rest I think they are doing him good. The Dr. says he is doing well to hold his own during hot weather. His bowels are better and he has a better appetite than he has had for a while. Watermelons are five and ten cents apiece now if they had the food value he could get along fine for he likes them so well. My hens are not laying much now. Some days I don't get an egg and then I get three or four eggs. Ralph is tired of eggs it is hard to get something to take their place. I have killed a couple of cockerels but they are not very large yet. I just have five pullets. Well I will close as I want to sew. Take good care of yourselves and enjoy your eastern weather. Love to all and XXXX to Charles and Florence.

Your loving daughter and sister,
Lydia

Lydia McConahy Brown in California to her mother Mary Phillips McConahy and her sisters Rebecca and Myrtle McConahy in Pennsylvania.

Bakersfield, Cal
December 19, 1913

Dear Mother and Sisters:

I received your welcome letters so glad to get them do not know what I would do without them. Things are moving along as usual. Ralph is about the same he stays so weak but I think if it would come nice weather he would gain faster. He has finished all of the serum he had sent for. We have been thinking and wondering if it would not be a good thing to send him to the Pisgah Home near Los Angeles. It is run by Dr. Yokum. Mother heard about him up at Mr. Wrights. A lady here told me about it last summer after he began the serum. If don't cost anything and is among the foothill and I think the high altitude would do him good and would be a change of climate. He wants to get away from the malaria as he has had a few shakes and one real hard one. the first time I ever saw any one shake. He has been taking quinine for that. We have not heard from the lodge yet. Mr. Burk here wrote to them two weeks ago and has not heard so I wrote a letter this morning to them and told them how had we needed the loan so am anxiously waiting a reply.

I got a letter from Vade yesterday telling about a foreman on Judge Shields ranch wanting someone to cook for four men. He wanted Hetty but she did not want to go so far from home & children. Wages $30 a month I would like to take that and wrote her but can't say what I can do yet until we know what the lodge intends to do. I have been busy writing all day this is the fifth letter and eight postals Cecil wrote three postals. He got Charles' card today. Charles can write very good. I can't realize he is getting so big. Cecil is coughing pretty hard this is his third week of whooping cough. I hope he does not have it hard.

There is a small pox scare here now about seven or eight cases. They won't leave Cecil go because he is not vaccinated and Ralph won't have him so now I am glad he didn't since he began to cough. He has missed two weeks of school. Good many of the children are staying at home because of not being vaccinated. Also have diphtheria and scarlet fever. Good bit of sickness just now. I will send you some of the California mistletoe. We cannot send my gifts this year I had not time to make any or money to buy. Too bad about Pearl's baby. It is about seven she has had.

You didn't say what color your bonnet is or if it had a feather in it about one yard long. What new thing did Relief get she might say hello once in a while. Well I guess I had better stop so a Merry Xmas to you all.

Your loving daughter and sister,
Lydia

Placerville, Calif.
March 22, 1914

My Dearest Aunt Mary,

I am ashamed of myself for not writing but I have been very busy in school. We have just finished one set of examinations and are preparing for finals sometime next month and then again in May and June.

We were all very sorry to hear about the death of Lydia's husband. I expect she will go East again now.

At present we are having lovely weather. We have had the hottest March weather this year for eight or nine years. Dan is feeling considerable better now. He looks so much better. He wishes to write a few lines so I will close. Give my love to Myrtle.

Lovingly,
Alice Bryson

Lydia McConahy Brown in California to her mother Mary Phillips McConahy and her sisters Rebecca and Myrtle McConahy in Pennsylvania.

November 8, 1914

Dear Mother and Sisters,

Well here I am this lovely Sunday afternoon keeping house all by myself. The rest have all gone to Sunday School over in the Rochester school house. I went to church this morning with Mabel in to the M. E. at Gilroy. I saw Alex McJunkin he goes to the M. E. South. He ___ in on this bible. Two weeks ago when I was at church I saw Edward Russe and Phebe . They have grown and Phebe is big and fat going to be like her aunt Mary the boys are fine looking young men. We have not been over to Alex yet may go this week some day. Ruth & Martin are growing Martin is the age Cecil was when we came out here. He has about as many freckles as Cecil has. Mr. & Mrs. Wright look natural and as of old also Mame & Frank. I have been having a nice time. Maud is better I got such a cold so came home to Dr. I still have the cough and taking Pinex for it. Even baby has the cold. Mrs. ___ had pneumonia when I came but is able to be up and around now. Her brother Mr. Branden is sick in bed now with the cold. It starts in head & throat and then mine went to my chest. So I will have to get rid of it before I start East. They want me to stay here until after Thanksgiving. Mrs. John Wright of Sheep Hill is coming here this winter. I have been in the look out for something to do but haven't struck anything yet. Harry Wright's lady came 6 weeks too soon and was very delicate at first but is a nice big fat baby now weighs 15 pounds has big blue eyes and is fair & sandy hair. Lucile is a fine big girl and nice looking. The fruit here has been very scarce the last three years on account of it being so dry and everybody has sold all their fruit so guess I'll not have any to take back. Last year Wright only got $138 for their crop this year a little over $600 so you see they are not very flush with money.

I will have to write to Aunt Lizzie and tell her I have not started back yet. Cecil has been going to school here ever since we landed here he likes it here. I had a very nice time in Oakland saw the fair buildings they are very pretty especially the jewel tower and its glass dome some of the buildings are immense. Was out to the Cliff House several times. It will take some money to see everything during the fair time. Mrs.

Brown has got a rooming house in Oakland since I came here. She wrote and told me if I would go and live with them I could have the best they had. It is a small house and it pays $36 over all expenses. But I don't think it would be the place for Cecil. If I would work for her she would not pay me and I would use up all my own money. I would like to earn enough to pay Cecil's board and leave him here and go to school. I don't know what to do for the best. Only I won't start home until I cure my cold. It was nice warm weather when I took cold and don't know how I did get it. Cecil is well. My insurance is due the 27th of this month so I'll send the statement and Rebecca can send it out of my money there with her insurance. No, I'll keep it and send it from here out of the money I have here and then let you send enough for me to go home in here. I was in hopes I could earn more and not draw on what I have there. Well I suppose you see by the paper that Cal voted but they also voted out the Sunday law. They undertook too much and didn't gain anything only the alvterrment (?) of the red light districts. They gained it. They can't vote on temperance again for eight years. I am glad you enjoyed the peaches.

Cecil is anxious to go east and I will be glad when I get settled and can call a place home and get out of my suitcase and trunk. We had some rain last week. Well it is most time for the folks to be home so I'll close. The sun is going down.

Tell Charles and Florence I would like to see them and will some of these bright days.

Love to you all I am as ever,
Your loving daughter and & sister,
Lydia

Sunday night – when we were at the supper table this evening at 6:45 o'clock, we had the hardest earth quake shock I ever felt. I feared the worst and thought some one knocked at the front door. Mame said it was an earthquake and then we felt the shock. It made a queer feeling go over me and brought the tears. Mame says to tell you that if there should be another quake before morning to look for me next Saturday morning. Well I don't care for many quakes like that. I am gong to Mrs. Branden's tomorrow to stay a while he is not any better and am putting hot poultices on him.

Lydia McConahy Brown in California to her mother Mary Phillips McConahy and her sisters Rebecca and Myrtle McConahy in Pennsylvania.

San Juan, Cal

February 28, 1915

Dear Mother and Sisters:

I received Mother's note yesterday, also the papers many thanks. I saw about Uncle Charles birthday he is certainly getting up in years. Does he look any older in it than he used to. It makes me homesick to think I am missing meeting with the friends.

You certainly had a good time on your birthday would like to have been there with you all. Well we are still having about as near getting up to see Cecil as I was six weeks ago. Just 6 weeks today since I came

Did you get the letter I sent with the valentines and poppy seed and also some parsley? We haven't had such a walk since. Had several pretty days last week. It rained last night and some this afternoon. The hills are getting and green the weeds are growing fast and it is so wet they can't work. They worked all day yesterday. Twelve jap women went out to work and a lot of jap men. The women all wear large sunbonnets with lots of curtains to them to keep the sun off. The sun was real warm yesterday is cooler today. You and Rebecca better not come out until I get a trip home anyway. Wish it was not so far. Cecil is alright I am so homesick to see him. Florence must be a big girl by this time would like to see her. Well I want to write to Cecil so will close.

Your loving daughter and sister,
Lydia

Lydia McConahy Brown in California to her mother Mary Phillips McConahy and her sisters Rebecca and Myrtle McConahy in Pennsylvania.

San Juan, Cal
May 7, 1915

Dear Mother and Sisters,

Well here I am again enjoying Cal at its best. I wish you all could see the fields of lovely sweet peas. They are beautiful the lettuce is shooting up into pyramids and are beautiful now. We were up to Rucher yesterday and last Sunday. I did not get a letter written last week as it was my sick time and the ride last Sunday almost laid me up. We had to go around the 30 mile route that made 60 miles ride and part of the road was very rough. Harry Wright and I both hit the top going over one place. Yesterday we went the 12 mile route and it was very rough between here and Sargeant but good road from Sargeant to Gilroy. They have 48 different kinds of sweet peas on this ranch over at the other place the poppies are in full bloom. They have a field of the single poppies also one of Cal poppies the _____ are not out yet. They are beautiful. They have acres of onions which are pretty now. It is only eight miles from here to the coast over the hills. The fog comes rolling in over the hills every night and makes it very cool here it is hot during the day. Every afternoon the wind blows and then the fog comes. No need to go to the mountains and coast when living here. It is two miles from here to San Juan by the road we can see all the town from here it lies next to the hills and is a small country place with a couple of stores catholic church a small congregational church and a good 3 _____ school. It has a mission which I am going to see some day they charge 25 cents to go into it. I went with Mr. Allamand to Hollisten today to get a tooth treated that is hurting. My face is swollen on one side. Cecil's school is on in two weeks. My white dress is done. The skirt has four shimings around the top & waist made plain gathered on the shoulder long sleeves with cuffs will wear collar Myrtle sent with it and a little black velvet bow a card Mother sent got a black velvet ribbon belt with tailored bow in the back. Will get black skirt fixed this week. If everything goes alright I think I'll stay here until August. My task is to save some money now. Well it is late so good night. With love to you all

Your loving daughter and sister
Lydia

Vade Phillips Bryson in California to her aunt Mary Phillips McConahy in Pennsylvania.

Sept. 16, 1915

My Dear Aunt Mary,

It has been so long since any of us has heard from you. I have tried so many times to have Dan write you. I told him you would rather have one line from him, than a long letter from any of us. He said he didn't like to write you know how he felt. He now is very poorly, quite weak a general breaking down and his kidneys. Hetty will take him to Placerville in a day or so. He said today he didn't think he could stand the trip. So you see how very weak he is. (Excuse these ink blots, I didn't know how soiled this paper was.) Hetty is giving him tablets which is a tonic. I make him egg nogs which seems to strengthen him for a while. Will have Dr. Reckers as soon as she gets him to town.

Will write you again in a few days. Hope you will answer. We would love to hear from you.

This is Alice's second year in high school. She is with Wells & Louise [Hetty's children] -- are all in school. They are keeping house. I send them twice a week 2 roasted chickens, a big cake and bread. I have worked very hard this summer.

Did you get some pictures this summer from us, and was there one where Dan was in the wagon, where the tents are. Now be sure to answer this. With best love and a big kiss

Your loving niece,
Vade

Lydia McConahy Brown in California to her mother Mary Phillips McConahy, her brother William and sister Myrtle in Pennsylvania. Lydia is keeping house for a family in Gilroy.

Gilroy, Calif.
Dec. 2, 1915

My Dear Mother, Bro & Sister,

Well here I am again in my new home. I came here with Alex Sunday night. We were over at Mabel's in the afternoon. Carl and Mary were there also. Mr. Wright, Mrs. Wright has not come home yet. Mr. Wright looks well. Cecil likes to go to Gilroy school. He rides with George Wolf's children in the rig. It is 2 ½ miles from here. We haven't had much cold weather yet. It is raining tonight. I am sorry I did not get home but will make the best of it and do the best I can. I like it very well here, getting along all right. It is not a hard place. I have to get up at 5 o'clock so as to have breakfast by six or little after. Well I am sleepy. I am so thankful to get settled once again. I am tired moving around. Cecil likes the men here. How is little Nellie [McConahy] – how I would like to see her. Her picture was fine. I put the money Wm. sent to me in the bank. I'll keep it to draw on if I run short. I am almost broke so it was time for me to get busy at something. I have to have enough to get Cecil medicine. He is getting better. Well, good night or I'll not get up in the morning. Love to all. My address is Box 5139 Albert Goodrich, Gilroy, Cal

Your loving daughter and sister,
Lydia

Pittsburgh, January 26, 1916
Mr. William McConahy

Dear Friend,

I happened to think it was my turn to write. I got your letter dated Jan. 5 it made me kinder laugh to think that we both wrote on the same day. Will Bretton wrote me a letter on the same day and I wrote him one on the same day. I am not having much fun now, it is too muddy but good weather for ducks. I suppose you remember where you was on the fourth of July, the time we walked up the hill. I walk up & down that hill twice a day. I know about how long it is now. I am glad to hear you got work so soon. Does the gang from Moravia ever say any about me let me know. It was about time Pitzers boys were getting to work what do you think Will How is old Tom Platt, I thought I saw Tom up in town the other week but I guess I was mistaken.

If you want to see any pretty girls come and I will show you some. I am having lots of fun over at school well I guess this is all I might as well cut it off.

Give my best respects to the rest.

Yours as ever,
G. L. Felmeth
Duff College
#48 Fifth Ave.
Pittsburgh, Pa

Placerville, Calif
March 10th 1918

My Dear Aunt Mary,

Guess you think I'm a long time getting ready to write, so here I am at last. I've tried to get Dan down to write, but you know how he is. Well he has not changed a bit in that respect, and is about the same in health. Looks well. Every body speaks of how well he looks. Say Aunt can't you come out this summer or spring and have a good summer in the mountians with us. It's simply beautiful up there, and I know you would enjoy the beautiful flowers. All kinds. Now don't say no.

We have had such a lovely winter -- not even a shower until last month. I was up home for Thanksgiving and also Christmas dinner. No snow to amount to anything until along the last of February. No Northwinds -- was simply perfect and the spring is going to bring forth big crops. But what is this war going to bring forth? Now Aunt Mary you ought to be able to enlighten us on why the good Lord don't put a top to all the brutal treatment and especially to dear little innocent children. I can't for the life of me see where it all is "for the best." I do hope it will cease soon. All our best young men are gone. So many have died at the camps.

Write real soon and give our love to all the folks. And tell me how Lydia's health is. Would like to see her so much. Tell her to come with you. With best love

Vade

After November, 1918

My Dear Aunt Mary and Myrtle,

After a long spell of weather I am here at last writing to you, and I want to thank you for the lovely Christmas presents and also the paper. I have received two numbers, I enjoy reading the stories so much. Did you get our Xmas box we sent you both. I sent to the office by Wells and he forgot to insure it. I am always particular to insure it. I was so disappointed and am afraid you did not get it.

We are having the storm of the season. Have has such a dry winter. What a glorious winter in one way. The boys that escaped the Kiser is coming home. Such a blessing too, we had the President we have who is not in the chair to fill his pocket but for humanity's sake & the dear man I hope receives his reward.

Lovingly,
Vade

Part of a letter from Vade Phillips Bryson to her Aunt Mary Phillips McConahy in Pennsylvania. The top part is missing.

1920

Hope you will forgive me for my long silence. I am getting as bad as Dan about writing. The enclosed letter will show

I started to write you a month ago. I received the beautiful grape cut work which is wonderful. Have had it on exhibition ever since it arrived. And dear Myrtle I guess thinks I am very negligent. I don't mean to be. ...if I sell my place Dan, Alice and I are surely coming back east.

And have I sent Myrtle any? You know I am always so busy which does not cease with age that I forget sometimes.

Fanny and Alice Blair ask for you and Myrtle often. Now tell me if you will come out this spring? You will never know the difference in a hundred years from now – do come. With best love from us all to you and all your family.

Lovingly,
Vade

Vade Phillips Bryson in California to her aunt Mary Phillips McConahy in Pennsylvania.

Vade PO
El Dorado Co Calif

June 9, 1920

My Dear Aunt Mary,

I am now at our dear old mountian home (Phillips) and am looking forward to your visit with us. Dan has been quite miserable but Alice writes me is feeling some better. You get off the train at Truckee and stay there all night, then take the Lake Tahoe train in the morning and go to the Lake Boat to Tallac Stage from there to Phillips. This will save you going away to Sacramento. Now don't disappoint us. We are looking for you and have a tent right by Dan's.

I have been quite sick. Was in bed five weeks. Was my heart. Too much hard work. But am feeling fine now. Is just grand up here. I know you will love it here, so many beautiful wildflowers, from July on.

How is Myrtle and the dear little baby [Mary]? I want to send it something, will wait until you come out, then we will talk it over. All our family is quite well. Give my love to all your families and so much for yourself. Maybe you can't read this -- I am writing without my glasses as they are up to my tent.

Your loving niece.
Vade

PS. Write when we may expect you.

Vade Phillips Bryson in California to her aunt Mary Phillips McConahy in Pennsylvania.

August 3rd 1920

My Dear Aunt Mary,

Rec'd your letter in place of yourself and was very much disappointed as was Dan who is failing fast. If you and Rebecca can come out it would be so nice for us all and especially Dan so hope to see you both. I think the change here will be a great benefit to Rebecca. Is delightful now. We are awfully busy and have been all summer. Never less than 75 and the weekends as high as 111. I am standing the hard work alright. I must go now and mix hot rolls. With best love to you all.

Vade

Barbara Pollock in Colorado to her aunt Mary Phillips McConahy in Pennsylvania. Barbara was married to David Pollock, Lydia Maria's son.

Monday morning

Dear Aunt Mary:

I did not get your letter off yesterday so of course I've thot of something more to say.

S.W. says to tell Uncle Dan about the markets. We are on the Western slope of the beautiful Continental Divide so we cant reach the eastern markets without paying that high freight rate over the range and the local markets are easily supplied although they do pay good prices whenever they condescend to buy anything.

Monday's letter

DW was going to write to Uncle Dan himself but he is suffering from a nervous spell just now and I thot it wasn't best to write. He was in California seeing the Imperial Valley last summer but the water hurt him and he could not stay but he is interested in the Gridley colonies and might go to see them. I hate to think of letting him go so long but when the two older children come home from school he could go there and stay with Uncle Dan from June to Sept.

Monday, letter 3

I wish Uncle Dan would write and tell him all about the Gridley colonies and the climate there. Of course Uncle Dan will only come with you and stay here till then that would be the nicest way.

Now DW is nervous and often very miserable but is never irritable and I just can't spare him now from me and the little children, girls at that. Hoping to hear from you soon I remain

Your loving niece
Barbara Pollock

Emma Pollock (Lydia Maria's daughter) in Illinois to her aunt Mary Phillips McConahy in Pennsylvania.

Foosland, IL (winter)

Dear Aunt,

I send you an invitation card & will scribble you a few lines We are all well as common Mother is feeling better she occupies a good part of her time out doors. The weather is so nice for her to be out we have had only one shower since she came home it hardly seems like winter we have no snow

Pa has come home from Col he liked it very well out there Bro Rob & family and also Milton are gong to start for there next week. They are going to live a quarter of mile from Samuel and Rob's wife's sister and family is going so there will be quite a number of families from here in one neighborhood.

Mother received a nice embroidered handkerchief as a present from Willie Morrow when there and she appreciates it very highly as a present she can not find it since she came home thinks it fell out of her sachel in the hallway if it can be found would be pleased to get it as it is a present.

This invitation is for Grandma McConahy and the family. Well I must close as it is getting time for me to get dinner

Good by

Your niece,
Emma Pollock

Notes
Phillips Chronology
1900-1919

1900   Wells McConahy worked his way across the country and disappeared in California. It is not known what happened to him.

Vade sold Rubicon Springs Resort to Daniel Abbott.

1901   Vade operated the Inn at Tahoe City.

Hettie Clark (Vade's daughter) married Frank Sickles.

1902   Wells Sickles was born.

Relief McConahy married S. A. (Bert) Hartung of Beaver Falls, PA.

1903   Lydia Maria Pollock died in Foosland, Illinois.

Jurgens post office established.

Esther Doss (Vade's half-sister) died in Petaluma, CA.

John Meloche (Ida Phillips' son, raised by Vade) died of tuberculosis.

1904   Vade leased Rubicon Springs from Daniel Abbott and ran the resort until 1908.

Charles Hartung was born.

1905   Lydia McConahy married Ralph Brown and moved to Swissvale, PA.

Myrtle McConahy contracted typhoid fever.

Louise Sickles was born.

1906   Mehitable Jane Phillips died in Sparks, Nevada.

Late summer, Vade, Dan, and all at Rubicon Springs.

**1907
-08**   Winter: the family (Vade, Myrtle McConahy, Mary Phillips McConahy, Dan Phillips) stayed at the ranch at Garden Valley.

1908   Summer at Meeks Bay.

Myrtle in Denver where she worked at the Denver Dry Goods to earn money for her return to Pennsylvania. She stayed with Elizabeth Lutton (Charles Phillips' wife).

Florence Hartung was born.
Vade returned to Phillips Station and rebuilt the resort.

Mary Phillips McConahy returned to Western Pennsylvania in the fall because her daughter Lydia was ill.

Ralph Cowell of Moana Villa purchased Rubicon Springs Hotel.

1909   October – Mary Phillips McConahy returned to California with Lydia and her son, Cecil. They stayed at Sea Bright, Santa Cruz, and Galt.

Myrtle returned to Western Pennsylvania

1910   Mary Phillips McConahy and Lydia at Galt.

1912   Phillips Station burned again.

Myrtle McConahy married Norman Keefer and moved to New Castle, PA.

Mary Phillips McConahy returned from Denver to Western Pennsylvania for Myrtle's wedding.

"Vade" post office named after its postmaster, Mrs. Vade Bryson.

Lydia at Bakersfield with her husband Ralph and son Cecil.

1914   Ralph Brown died in Bakersfield, CA.

Lydia at Bakersfield, CA until 1916 when she returned to Western Pennsylvania.

Jurgens post office dissolved.

1916   Grace Hartung was born.

1918   Lydia McConahy Brown married D.D. Dowds of Beaver Falls.

1919   Alice Bryson married Henry Lyon and had a daughter Betty.

Old Phillips Station
1920 - 1935

I (Mary K. Sonntag) was born on March 18, 1920, in New Castle, PA. That same year, Mary Phillips McConahy planned a trip from Ellwood City, PA to join Vade in California. Her plans were somehow postponed for a year, but before she could leave, Vade got sick and died in May 1921. Mary and her daughter, Rebecca arrived in California later that summer.

Vade's two daughters, Hettie Clark Sickles and Alice Bryson Lyon, inherited Phillips Station from their mother. Hettie was appointed postmaster of Vade Post Office. These two continued to operate Phillips Station until 1929, when the cabins were converted into housekeeping summer cabins and lots sold off. Louise Sickles Day, Hettie's daughter, has written the story of Phillips Tract, as the old Phillips Station was then known.

Everything wound down. In 1930 Rubicon Springs was sold to the Sierra

> The 107 acres we still own includes about 20 acres of the meadow. In memory of the five women who worked their whole lives to save Phillips Station, I have established a trust fund in their memory to pay the taxes and any upkeep. The Phillips heirs will be able to maintain the Phillips property into perpetuity.
>
> —Louise Sickles Day, 1994

Power Company. In 1932, Mary Phillips McConahy died at the age of 86. Great Uncle Dan, himself in failing health, was never told of her death. He died the following year when he was 93. Alice Bryson Lyon's father, Jim, remarried but in 1934 died in an automobile accident.

Today, there is a family cemetery at Phillips Station. Here are the family members and some pets who are buried there:

> Louise Sickles Day
> Her mother, Hettie Sickles
> Her sister, Babe Sickles (died of Huntington's disease)
> Her brother, Wells Sickles (also died of Huntington's disease)
> Louise's husband, Ted Day
> Rod Lumley, Sally Lyon Lumley Myers' son
> Richard Clarke, Betty Lyon Clarke's son
> Harry Oakly, the Phillips' caretaker
> Mr. Brown, the family's trusted dog
> Pal, another family dog

Other family members are buried in Union Cemetery in Placerville, California including:

> JWD and Mehitable Jane Phillips
> Mehitable Jane Phillips' brother Joe
> Great Uncle Dan Phillips
> Vade Phillips Bryson and her son John Clark

The following are buried in a second plot:

> Alice Bryson Lyon and her husband Henry
> Alice's father, James Bryson

> Charles Lumley, Sally's first husband, is buried in a third plot.

Alice Bryson in California to her aunt Mary Phillips McConahy and cousin Myrtle McConahy in Pennsylvania.

May 1921

My Dear Aunt Mary and Myrtle:

Just a line to let you know Mother [Vade] is very low with bronchial pneumonia. She has been in bed over three weeks but had a relapse last Friday & has been at Death's door since. It is very uncertain and the Dr. gives us very little hope, but that change will be soon.

She has just returned from a trip to Petaluma and was feeling fine when she took cold and this set in. Will let you know as soon as there is a change.

Dan feels very badly and naturally he would miss her very much -- we all would. Dan has been very well this winter. Will write later.

With much love to you both
Alice

P.S. Myrtle, will send to you as Aunt Mary may have started so you can let her know -- if not --

Dear Mother -- Just received this today (Monday) it was mailed May 19 6 A.M. Alice's name is Lyon. I am going to write to her tomorrow but will send this on to you. All well -- went to the circus this afternoon. Come up and see us.

Lots of love,
Myrtle

Alice Bryson in California to her aunt Mary Phillips McConahy and cousin Myrtle McConahy Keefer in Pennsylvania. Myrtle forwarded the letter to her mother in Ellwood City, PA.

May 31, 1921

My Dearest Myrtle and Aunt Mary:

I was somewhat surprised today when I received your letter to know that you had not heard of Mother's death [Vade] as I was sure Henry sent you a telegram, but you know there is such confusion at such a time that it may have been forgotten altho' I still am very positive one was sent to you. I thought probably Aunt Mary may have started or in California and if so you could let her know she could come up there.

Mother was sick almost four weeks, just lacked two days. She had been in Petaluma for four weeks with her nephew and had a most wonderful trip. She came home on a Monday and the next Friday and Saturday she stayed in bed, apparently not very sick, but she didn't get any better so thought it was because she was in bed so much that it was causing her to loose her strength and on Thursday evening three weeks later she sat up for three quarters of an hour, which proved to be too much for her. She was worse the next day (Friday) so called the Dr. again and he said she was very much worse so Hetty came home that night and Mother immediately developed acute bronchial pneumonia and she just sank more and more each day, in spite of everything the nurses and Dr. could do, until death came at 12:20 on Saturday the 21st. The last week was terrible as she must have been in awful pain so they kept her under morphine and heroin after Thursday as the Dr. said there was absolutely no hope so we thought it was better to keep her as comfortable as we could.

Poor Mother, I can't imagine yet that she is gone from us forever. It just seems too terrible to be true. She was always so kind and too generous to us all and was only sixty six and still seemed to be in fairly good health. Of course her heart has never been as good since her bad attack a year ago, but she has been taking care of Hetty's children all winter and has done an abundance for us all this spring.

It seemed a double pity as Mother was just beginning to thoroughly enjoy life. She has built Phillips up until it has become one of the leading resorts in the lake region and she was just beginning to make money there as it has taken a lot of time to rebuild since the fire.

Then for the last two winters she has been going to Petaluma where she has been having the best time of her life. On her way home this time went to the city and met friends she had not seen for years, also took in the season of Grand Opera which she thoroughly loved. And next fall she was planning on taking Dan and going East to see all you people.

Our Dan is taking her death very hard. Of course it was a terrible shock to us all as no one ever thought for a minute Dan would outlive her.

Dan has decided he will be here with me now, and I only hope I can make it half as pleasant for him as Mother did. He adores Betty and takes most of the care of her so I think it is the best thing for him to be with her as it will keep his mind occupied most of the time.

Now, Aunt Mary, to be sure and feel just as welcome to come as if Mother were here. We are going to Phillips as usual for the summer and will be back here in the fall.

Myrtle, I do hope you can manage to come and see me some day too as I would love to see you both again. I will never forget the winter we spent together down on the ranch. I was just looking at the picture of Aunt Mary and Dan out in the yard down there today. Mother still had the basket Aunt Mary crocheted for her so we packed them all away today.

We are getting ready for the mountians so are busy packing. It is very late so I must go to bed as tomorrow is to be another busy day. Be sure and write me once in awhile as I love to hear from you both.

Much love,
Alice

Note written on the above letter.

Dearest Mother,

I received this letter this A.M. So sorry to hear of Vade's death when it would be so soon for you to see her. I would go this summer anyhow. It may be the last chance. Alice and Dan may be there and it may help them some. We are all well. Come up and see us. You will get a chance to spend the summer in the mts.

Lots of love to you
Myrtle

Alice Bryson in California to her aunt Mary Phillips McConahy in Pennsylvania.

Phillips
June 25, 1921

My Dear Aunt Mary,

    We received your letter yesterday. We were very glad to know you have not changed your mind about coming to see us. You can come anytime but thought it best to tell you that you need not rush your trip or shorten your stay at Seattle as August is the nicest month we have here and September is lovely too. We will be so glad to see you and wish you could bring Myrtle and little Mary along with you.

    Must close as Dan wants to write a line and it is almost mail time.

Much love,
Alice

Dear Sister,

    I am still on top of the ground. I feel well for me. Vade is gon   We all feel the loss but will do the best we can.

    We all long for you to come and will do all we can to make it pleasant.

Yours
DDP

Mary Phillips McConahy in California to her daughter Myrtle in Pennsylvania.

Phillips, Vade P.O.
August 20, 1921

Dearest Myrtle and All,

I know you will wonder why I never write. I think every day before another day passes I will have a letter to send. Myrtle, everything has changed since you and I landed at Rubicon. Then all was lovely. Vade was there. O how I do miss her. Uncle Dan and Jim were on the job and all went well. Uncle Dan is not able (he is now 82 years old) to do much – looks after Alice's babes and walks around so slow & so stooped then takes a rest. I told him I was going to write to you. Would I tell you that he was going home with us. He said "Don't tell her that." And Jim – glad he is not here after the way he finally acted. Hetty told me that her Mother made a will about seven years ago and willed all the horses on the place to Jim. You know Uncle Dan thought he owned most of the horses and a third of everything else. His name was never mentioned in the will and everything has changed hands. He says he is thankful to get a bite to eat. I told him Too bad. He says that is the way of the world.

He sleeps on an old worn out cot with his blankets without a pillow. Makes my head ache to think how he has been treated. One reason I send so few cards most of here are Tahoe scenery. I know you have them and they ask just as much or more for them than they are other places. I don't feel like buying them after the way Uncle Dan has been treated.

Hetty took very sick last Friday night with acute indigestion. She sleeps and Louise sleeps out of doors near our tent. In the night she came and called Rebecca. She went and called Alice. We did everything we knew how to do out there in the cold

– not much relief. We wanted to call the doctor – one in the camp. He came in the morning. He said we should never listen to her when she was so bad. Said he could have relieved her in a little while – wonder she lived at all. He went away Tuesday, he told me she is to stay in bed until next Sunday. Say- she is going to get up and dress pretty soon. I told her she had better mind the Dr. and if she got worse he couldn't blame her. The cook Mrs. Wood was sick and Hetty took her place in the kitchen. She had been working so hard and that extra work was too much for her. Saturday morning Mrs. Wood got up, got breakfast, and went back to bed – has been working ever since. All work is hard for their strength. You know a little what it is to get breakfast for such a large crowd. So many different dishes same as Vade did. They counted the other morning – one hundred ten for breakfast and that is the way it is here most of the time. Washing and ironing goes on most of the time from morn til night. I took Alice's place at the mangle. I like the work – easiest in camp. No tips though. A dining room girl got ten dollars for one the other morning. They all fare fine. Some of the dining room girls went out horseback riding last Wednesday. A dog frightened one horse, threw the girl onto the horn of the saddle, struck her in the stomach and then off. She is in bed yet. Dr. says it is not serious.

The reason I have time to write this letter is the engine is broken and will not start until this PM. Alice told me all about her Mother's sickness & death. Said she saw more flowers at her funeral than she had ever seen in her life. Took two trucks to carry them to the cemetery. Said when she first took sick that she would never get well. I sent you a folder of the beautiful Canadian scenery from Seattle. Did you receive it? The ones they have here are smaller and taken around Lake Tahoe. You never wrote you had received it, if not I am sorry – will bring the rest. Sent Rose one of the small ones here and put it in an envelope. I think the trip has helped Rebecca. I would hate to see her go back and work for Humphrey again. Mr. Wright was in an auto accident and had his leg broken below the knee last June.

Be sure and answer soon, will write when I can …. hustle and bustle.

Love to all,
Mother

Mary Phillips McConahy in California to her daughter Rebecca McConahy in Pennsylvania.

Dear Rebecca,

Received your welcome letter dated April 2 and contents noted.

Now that the Phillips & Bryson firm have dissolved partnership I cannot very well leave poor old Uncle Dan, and beside that I think as long as I have that land in Galt I had better improve it either for a home or so it can be sold and make something out of it. If there was a house on it Dan would go there this spring and commence improving. He says by the fall he will sow it with alfalfa and in two years the land shall have paid for itself.

I will tell you what I think you had better do. You and Bert's sister come west together, visit in Colorado. They are all lovely whole souled people. No need of being afraid of them. And then come and spend the summer at Rubicon Springs. The winter would do you both a world of good. Uncle Dan says he will furnish you with a tent and paraphernalia. Now that is quite an inducement. Can easily be brought over from Meeks Bay. Mr. Calwell offered me a place there to come and paint and make baskets to sell. I will give way for your and Elinor and teach you both how. You can tinsel postcards at 10c a piece and sell. You can make plenty of money there and in the fall Mr. Calwell can get you a half rate ticket for Santa Cruz. And I will rent a cottage from Mrs. Keoslin for you. I will go to Gilroy and pick fruit and put up plenty for winter and all spend the winter at Galt and live on the cream of the land. We will have our own cream and butter. By that time I think Willie and Myrtle will be ready to come, and next year the rest.

Write soon so I can reserve the nice little nook I have picked out at Rubicon.

Lovingly,
Mother

Alice Bryson Lyon in California to her aunt Mary Phillips McConahy and cousin Myrtle McConahy Keefer in Pennsylvania.

Vade, Calif.
Sept. 22, 1922

My Dear Aunt Mary and Myrtle,

I have been trying or intended to write you all summer but just never seemed to get around to it, so yesterday we were all speaking of you and delegated Alice Blair to write to you today and tell you all the Phillips news.

I was over to Carnelian Bay in July where Mrs. Woodruff is this summer and she said to give you her love when I wrote.

It's too bad you couldn't have been here this year as Dan has been so much better than he was in the mountians so you could have had more time to have visited with you.

Miss Wright was here again this year and asked all about you both.

I couldn't get Maggie Orelli's address as her folks were out of town and the rest of the people who know her didn't know her address. She and Mrs. Will Orelli were up to see me last winter and were asking all about you and were sorry not to have seen Aunt Mary last year.

I am enclosing two photographs of the youngsters and Dan, so I will close and let Alice Blair tell you all that has happened.

Much love to you all
Alice

Alice Blair, a friend of the Bryson's, to Mary Phillips McConahy in Pennsylvania.

Phillips
Sept 22, 1922

Dear Aunt Mary:

I have been thinking of writing you ever since I have been up here which has been nearly three weeks. I am enjoying myself fine. The weather is wonderful, the nights very pleasant. It has been very warm below in fact some of the warmest weather of the season. Everyone at Phillips are fine. Dan is as usual. All are working hard as usual. We speak of you often and hope that you are well. The children are very cute. Jane is running around now, don't talk much yet. Warren and Fanny were here this summer,

Warren had charge of the Store. Fanny did pantry work. Hetty is doing the cooking with the assistance of an Indian girl. The guests have all left, only transients now. The resorts haven't done nearly as well as usual this year.

I had company nearly all summer. My folks from Tonopah were with me for six weeks. I enjoyed their visit ever so much. My sister-in-law has two lovely children. My sister in law from Sac was with me a week. Dan wants to know when you are coming again. They surely would enjoy having you.

Before coming up here I was sure I had malaria but am feeling ever so much better now. This mountian air certainly is bracing. We all went on a picnic last week up to Echo Lake, rowed across the lake to little Echo, had our lunch on an island across the lake. We all enjoyed it ever so much. I was a little afraid to go out on the lake, but as it was nice and smooth, thought I would go anyway. It happened that it wasn't a bit rough.

I often think of our summer at Meek's Bay. Wasn't it beautiful there? I miss Vade so much. Poor woman, she certainly had a hard time of it.

I'll probably go home in a week or so. Remember me to Rebecka also Myrtle when you see her. With kindest regards to all I remain

Your sincerely,
Alice M. Blair

Letter written in rambling style – large letters rather incoherent. Not addressed to anyone. All in pencil. Mary McConahy's writing – Mrs. C. C. Phillips written in ink across letter. Josephine also written. All in Mary McConahy's writing.

May 5, 1926

My dear sister and all,

... the sad news of the passing of dear Joseph [Pollock]. So kind and good has gone to his reward. Soon it will be said of us. We too have passed. That "Bourne" from whence no traveler ever returns. May we so live as to be able to meet our loved ones on that happy shore.

For regard to that family tree it never materialized. All I have to go on is the family record. I did not have that at New Castle is the reason I did not write sooner.

Charles Carroll Phillips belongs the very pious Puritan stock. His grandfather Elisha Phillips was in the Revolutionary War – enlisted from Connecticut. His father Joseph Meachum Phillips was born in Conn. And served as a drummer boy in the War of 1812. His mother was born in Massachusetts.

And Charles Carroll Phillips was born up in the green hills of VT, Vershire Orange County in a large brick house. I saw the house. My Aunt Sylvia widow of Uncle Michael Phillips. She & her daughter Pricilla lived in a large brick house nearby. Her son Hazen & family liven in part of it and it was not all occupied. They said when Uncle sang in the choir that was all that was needed. His was such a melodious voice. What do you think of that for a Phillips?

If my eyes were better, I would like to tell you about my delightful visit among my sainted friends.

Alice Bryson Lyon in California to her Aunt Mary Phillips McConahy and her daughter Rebecca in Pennsylvania.

Phillips

June 20th 1928

Dearest Myrtle, Aunt Mary, and Rebecca,

I was more than ashamed when I received your letter today to think how long it has been since I last wrote you, not even answered your lovely Xmas gifts. We surely enjoyed and appreciated them all. Betty particularly felt like a million dollars with her silk bloomers. She is at the age where she likes to "doll up" all the time. Suppose Jane will be there next year, she is always a year behind Betty in habits. She's too independent to copy them at the same time but the big event in the family is an eightmonth's girl which we spoiled beyond all reason. Of course we wanted a boy but it doesn't make any difference. Betty and Jane are so crazy about her and Henry is the worst ever. If she opens her mouth they all call for me immediately so there I've put in the winter. Dan is just as bad as the rest and he adores her as he deems necessary he is terribly offended. Of course she was a lot of amusement for him this spring and he loves to take care of her.

Dan's general health is very good but his knees bother him a good deal. He looks a good deal older this spring, but just think he'll be 89 in another month and doesn't use a can and can hear as good as ever and reads all the papers. His mind is so clear, he can talk with anyone, and his judgment is always being sought after by the summer home people around here.

He just left the cabin and went to bed. It has turned quite cold up here so we all hug the fire as often as possible. Last week it was very warm. Dan came up Decoration Day and I came up

Saturday. I was up before but I had a lot of sewing to do and house cleaning so I went back.

Maggie Orelli is doing chamber work at the Ivy House yet. I don't know whether I told you or not that she is married again. Mrs. Hawley always sends us a box of candy at Xmas time but other than that we never hear from her. Alice is still single and she says happy. She lives all alone in the old home place. Charlie Leonardi lives in town, he works for the electric company, is married and has a son about 12 years old. His wife certainly rules the roost too and is a great lodge worker. I often see Fan. She lives just across the street and creek from me.

Henry is going to Del Monte in the morning to attend the DA's convention. Of course I'd like to go along but there is so much to do here before the 1st that I decided I had better stay home and then it would be hard to leave the baby.

Louise finished training this spring and has been on special cases in the hospital ever since but is to come home tomorrow for the summer. Babe has had one year at the University of California so she has quite a stretch before she will be out. Wells stayed home with Hetty winter and worked for a new lime company for a few months then came up here and painted, etc. for the summer. He has charge of the store.

Betty wants me to be sure and tell you that it snowed three inches here last Sunday (no it was a week ago). I sent them up as soon as school was out and it happened before I came. They are both in the 3rd grade too. Betty has a mania for writing letters so tell Mary not to be too surprised if she should fall heir to one some day. If she had ever met Mary she would be _____ with them.

I must do a dozen little things and get into bed. Be sure and write when you can as we always enjoy hearing from you and they mean so much to Dan. He is always asking me if I have written to you. Many, many thanks to you for all your lovely remembrances.

Much love,
Alice

Alice Bryson Lyon in California to Myrtle McConahy Keefer in Pennsylvania.

November 1928

Dearest Myrtle,

I was so glad to hear from you again and it always pleases Dan so much to hear of you all. He talks for days after we get a letter from you of all the spots he loved as a boy, where he skated, fished, picked berries, etc.

You evidently didn't get my last letter as I wrote you sometime in August so you missed the news that we have another baby girl in the family. Of course, being so much younger than the others, she is spoiled to death, to us she is perfect. She was thirteen months on the 5th so is at the cute age, just learning to walk and do tricks.

I came home about the middle of September and Dan came a week later. He has failed a great deal altho' I think he is better down here than he was in the mountains. Think it is getting to be too high up there for him. The Dr. says he hasn't a thing the matter with his heart, but it is naturally getting very weak. He had a touch of flu since he came home and I thought he had gone out one day but he came of it and seems better than he was before he had the flu. He can barely get around now but won't use a cane. Dr. said he will be surprised if he lasts thru the winter but he has fooled us more than once.

We bought a new radio which is very good and I think it has given Dan a new lease on life. He particularly enjoyed the political speeches as he doesn't read much anymore. Tonight there was a program given by Civil War veterans which he thought was great. He was so glad to hear Aunt Mary is better. Hetty went back on day at the sanitarium the 1st. She had a touch of the flu the week before so she had a poor start to go to work but she fells very well now. It seems everybody in town is having or has had the flu.

Tonight is the Armistice Dance and I surely hated to miss it but it was impossible to find someone to stay with Dan & the children. I guess I take after Grandmother & Mother because I love to dance, but when there are more babies than nurse girls – somebody has to stay home.

Louise finished her training last February and spent most of the summer in the mountains but Sis Richardson (Aunt Mary knows her) went to the Islands and as she and Wee are very chummy, she went with her. She is nursing there but guess she'll be home for Xmas. Says she likes Hawaii but not for good.

Babe and Wells are still at Phillips. They came down so Wells could vote but went right back up as he is surveying up there and Babe is keeping house for him. She is coming down soon to do some sewing before returning to U.C.

The state is building a new highway from here to the Lake. There will be no more steep grades & will be able to go to Phillips in about an hour and a half – and the first time I went up it took us three days. Suppose will have to have a landing field next.

Maggie Orelli is building a new home not very far from me. They have just started but think it is going to be very pretty. It's late & I'm cold so will continue later.

Much love to you all,
Alice

Alice Bryson Lyon in California to Rebecca McConahy in Pennsylvania.

November 5, 1932

Dear Rebecca,

It is terrible how the time has flown and I don't seem to get time to write. First I put it off because we did not tell Dan of Aunt Mary's death. We received the news about the time that three of our best friends died, and all suddenly, and it upset Dan so much we thought he would not live to go to the mountains. However he did not pick up as usual and we still have not told him. His mind is so bad now it would only confuse him and he never would get it right. When we bring up a new subject now it takes him a long time to forget it and it worries him so everybody thought, maybe it was best not to have him worry over Aunt Mary. If he picks up mentally I will of course tell him. He has failed so much since last winter we expect him to go out anytime. He can just get around and that is all. He talks very little and when he does everything is so jumbled & mixed one can't get anything out of it. Of course we never leave him alone anymore.

We were, of course, shocked by the news of Aunt Mary. She was such a dear. We always enjoyed her letters so and Dan always used to say if he didn't hear once in a while "Don't you think we ought to be getting a letter from the East?" I was so glad you sent his birthday card. It came the day before his birthday & he seemed pleased. About 50 of his friends up there got together and sang "old time songs" & then we had ice cream and cake. He enjoyed having so many around as he doesn't like to be alone not even in a different room. We always rather took it for granted Aunt Mary would outlive Dan but one never can tell. It was wonderful the things she did with her paints. We enjoy the painted glass pictures she sent so much.

I am ashamed to say how little I know about the Phillips family. I am sending the paper you sent on to John Doss as I don't know much about that family. Every once in awhile I meet a new one & in the last few years we have seen a good deal of John and his wife. However I think that he and his sisters are not so friendly so don't know how much information I can get but at least more than I know. When the family lived on the ranch it was all in the old family Bible (so mother told me) but of course that burned. I meant to get Hettie pinned down to it when she came but she went on duty immediately doing night duty so have seen precious little of her since as they have been busy. A lot of flu cases. I brought home a lot of old pictures from the office which I left there for safe keeping. Thought perhaps I can get some of the dates from them.

Ida May Phillips was the youngest girl. She had two children, Gertie and Johnny, and she married John B. Meloche.

Ester was the one that married John Doss and they had five children.

I noticed that you only had two girls (including Mother) so thought if you were advancing with the "tree" maybe you had better leave more space for the Meloche family. Gertie married a man by the name of Dan Hurlbut and they lived in Fresno. I'm sure she sent Hetty a Xmas card with her address on it so if

Hetty can find the card I'll write her about their side. She has no children and of course you knew Johnny was dead so there isn't much to learn about them.

Hetty knows a great deal more than I do as you know I'm about 30 years behind the cousins but I'll get together what I can as soon as possible. I was kind of a second addition.
Everyone is well now altho' Louise has been very bad with pneumonia. She is just out of bed now so will get along all right if she will be careful.

I'll promise to send the paper on as promptly as I get it back. Give my love to everyone.

Lovingly,
Alice.

Alice Bryson Lyon in California to Rebecca McConahy and family in Pennsylvania.

Placerville, California
February 8, 1933

Dear Rebecca and All:

Danny died last Thursday night at midnight. He had been in bed about two months, and although we knew he wouldn't be able to get up again, the end came a little sooner than we expected. He had hardening of the arteries, and it went to his kidneys too, but he lived three days after they quit functioning. Hetty was afraid he would go into convulsions, so she came up to stay the night with me so she could give him hypos, but we only gave him one about 9:00, which quieted him, although he did not go to sleep. About midnight we heard him take a long breath, and went in immediately (it was a terribly cold night and we had just put warm blankets around him and the electric pad) and come out to warm ourselves. He simply closed his eyes and that was all. I think he realized the end was near in the afternoon and tried so hard to tell me something, but he had gotten to mumbling so that I could not understand at all. Three bedsores were just about to come, as he had gotten so terribly thin and could not move himself. He never complained of any pain except a little rheumatism in his shoulder, and his heart was perfect and respiration normal, so had not uremic poisoning set in he probably would have lasted a long time. It is terribly lonely without him, and a dozen times a day I catch myself on the verge of going to see how he is. After he was laid away he was perfectly beautiful. One never would have imagined he was as old as he was. Not a wrinkle. He always kept his marvelous disposition and sense of humor. He used to say the funniest things after he went to bed, even, and his lovely pink cheeks never left him. We buried him in the last vacancy in the Phillips plot at the cemetery, and it seems nice to know the family can all be buried together. The girls couldn't come home for the funeral and we couldn't get Gertie (Aunt Ida's daughter) located, so there were only Hetty, Wells and his wife and Henry and myself at the funeral that belonged to him. Aunt Mary's picture is so lovely, and think Dan enjoyed it. We never did tell him of her passing.

Alice Bryson Lyon

Rebecca McConahy in Ellwood City, PA to her sister Myrtle in New Castle, PA. She has heart disease.

February 9, 1938

Dear Myrtle,

Am glad to hear that Mary is making progress in getting work, although it would be nice for her to be here and will be glad anytime she can come to have her do so. I have decided to stay pretty close to my bed until I can get an examination and a cardiogram reading of my heart. Am getting no place the way I have been doing. Am feeling better the last two or three days, but I get down in the "dumps" pretty well sometimes. But is going to be bed for me most of the time for some time to come. I have been having a good many callers since I have been in bed last time. When I was up and around no one seemed to bother. Yesterday Rita spent about two hours with me, then Edith Moon, then Mary ___ & Viv Shaner, & I can always count on Relief, but suppose when Grace gets home (they expect her to be home today) that she will not be around so much. Lyde is in quite frequently, also Mrs. Quigley. But everybody seems anxious to do something. Today so far have only had Mrs. Quigley. I nearly always have flowers. Just now have a nice bouquet sent by Mae Morrison. The Eastern Star sent me one of the bouquets from the tables. Yes, Lillie knows I have been sick and has been talking for some time of coming down, so yesterday (or the day before) Lillie, Vada & Maggie showed up and spent quite a while with me. Before they got out Lyde and Mrs. Bowater came. While they were all here Margaret Whittaker came in. That day Lydia did not get to work until about three o'clock. Company now does not seem to bother me but the week before I think it did. I feel much better than I did and would be glad to see you anytime. My aim now is to have no more spells, and the only way I can avoid it is by staying more close to my bed until I can find what is the matter. Want to get to work as quickly as possible. Had a letter from Dr. Pollock. He said his letter to you had been returned, so he thought he had better get his mailing list fixed up.

Lovingly,
Rebecca

Notes
Phillips Chronology
1920-1940

1920 Mary Norma Keefer was born (Myrtle McConahy Keefer's daughter).

1921 Vade died May 28.

Mehitable Jane (Hettie) Clark Sickles and Alice Elaine Bryson Lyon inherited Phillips Station.

Mehitable (Hettie) J. Clark Sickles appointed postmaster Sept. 24.

Jane Lyon was born (Alice Bryson Lyon's daughter).

Mary Phillips McConahy and daughter Rebecca visited her family in California.

D. D. Dowds died.

1927 Evelyn (Sally) Elaine Lyon was born (Alice Bryson Lyon's daughter).

1928 Elizabeth Lutton died in Denver Colorado.

1929 Phillips Station closed. Cottages were converted into housekeeping summer cabins.

1930 Rubicon Springs sold to Sierra Power Company.

1932 Mary Phillips McConahy died in Ellwood City, PA.

1933 Daniel Phillips died in Placerville, CA.

Myrtle McConahy Keefer corresponded with Vade's youngest daughter, Alice Bryson Lyon, until Myrtle's death in 1962.

1935 James Bryson died at Visalia, CA.

1939 Rebecca McConahy died.

Everything Up Our Way Has Changed

1941 - 1962

The years that followed continued to see many changes. Alice Bryson Lyon and Myrtle McConahy Keefer continued their correspondence, usually at Christmas time, until Myrtle died in 1962. This was quite remarkable considering that Alice was nine years old and my mother 20 when they first met in 1906. Alice and my mother had children at the same time -- my mother, who was older, had me late and Alice, who was younger, had her first child at twenty.

I have in my possession a copy of Robert Lewis Stevenson's *A Child's Garden of Verses* inscribed to Mary from Betty and Jane (Alice's children), Christmas, 1932. My family was also the recipient of many a box of California dried fruits and as a child I was less than thrilled by this. I remember mailing our gifts in

> *Everything up our way has changed –*
> *A new freeway will soon be*
> *built. Guess they will tunnel thru the*
> *mountain and although it*
> *isn't certain, they now plan to take*
> *all our cabins, so, we may be*
> *out of business before too long. We're getting*
> *past the age to keep*
> *on anyway and my grandchildren*
> *aren't old enough to take over,*
> *so, it's probably for the best.*
>
> —Alice Bryson Lyon,
> 1962

October so they would get way out to California in time for Christmas. This was before air mail.

In the 1940's my mother and her sisters, Lydia and Relief, renewed their acquaintance with Milton DeWitt Pollock of Decatur, Illinois. He visited them in Ellwood City and they visited him in Decatur.

Alice died in 1984. This ended a long association and a correspondence of almost a hundred years between the families of the oldest son and the youngest daughter of Joseph Meachem Phillips and Lydia Davis Phillips until Mary Jo and I arrived in Placerville, California in 1993 and met Sally.

The Letters

M. D. Pollock in Illinois to Myrtle McConahy Keefer in New Castle, Pennsylvania.

June 1950

Dear Cousin Myrtle,

Yours enclosing the program of the decoration of the graves of the unknown soldiers of the Castle View Burial Park where Mothers Phillips and Pollock families are at rest. All of which is very interesting.

I am answering this now as fast as I can so as not to forget. Not that I am so busy but I am unable to do very much due to "Old Father Time". I am hanging on to the 88th round that I have climbed to since my birth on April 20, 1863. It is likely that it may be the last round.

Since writing the preceding page I have gone to a show adjoining this hospital which we are presumed to attend as a group two o'clock p.m. twice weekly. I did not feel able to go but I did.

I do not remember if I ever told you that I am classified as Who's Who in the classified directory, Vo. 8, page 711 of Who's Who in Chicago and Illinois which is quite an honor as there are not many outside the city of Chicago so honored. I am an alumnus of Rush Medical College, Chicago, and of Chicago University.

Well, I did not expect to write this much when I began this letter.

Oh yes, I certainly did hear from you with good letters which I always enjoy, especially your trip to Washington.

I have had a dilated heart ever since influenza septicemia in 1937 and that is why I am here although I requested Decatur and Macon County Hospital, but finally landed here by a crooked judge who shifted me here. In replying through this office, best not to repeat.

We enjoyed our trip to Ellwood City and all the folks. The loss by the fire will surely be costly to replace.

I should explain that my eyes have gone so bad due to my very bad heart. I can scarcely see to write or read with a strong magnifying glass.

M.D.P.

Sept. 1950

Dear Myrtle,

When I received your letter from Canada yesterday, I though I would reply quickly as I did before. And behold I ran across this letter that I had written in haste, which is as stale as dirt but I cannot write another one in its place so here you are.

You may probably stop here on your way home although you did not state so.

When you reply confine your letter to news not related to this hospital. About the time I wrote the first letter, they, without previous notice, came and took all my belongings and took me to the visiting room where a social worker told me that she was taking me to her nursing home in Jacksonville, which I refused. She stated that she was to take me by force and left the room apparently for help – as she turned her back on me and walked out. I walked out unnoticed and back to my room here where the officers here also stated they would use force.

Briefly, I fought both groups off with a war of words daily for a week and I am still here for life I presume which may not be too long – I have to close so good by.

M.D.P.

Alice Bryson Lyon in California to her cousin Myrtle McConahy Keefer in Pennsylvania. This is the last letter in over 100 years of correspondence. Myrtle died March 21, 1962.

December 17, 1962

Dear Myrtle,

It's been a long time since I have heard from you and I've been thinking of you often lately. Wish you could come out to see me some summer. Hetty is very bad. Two more vertebrae collapsed this fall, her lungs are bad and about two months ago she fell and broke the pelvis bone. She can take about two steps now with help. So, my winter's cut out for me as I will have to go to Marin Co. most of the winter to help Louise with her. I just came down from the cabin Friday night. We have had a beautiful fall. It rained here last night, so suppose it snowed up there.

Did you ever meet my renters? They were going to call on you, but I never heard from them. Guess they owe me too much rent!

Everything up our way now has changed – A new freeway will soon be built. Guess they will tunnel thru the mountain and although it isn't certain, they now plan to take all our cabins, so, we may be out of business before too long. We're getting past the age to keep on anyway and my grand children aren't old enough to take over, so, it's probably for the best.

One grandson (Betty's boy) is in the Air Force and stationed in Turkey and Jane's son is in the Guard here in California. He will soon be out and expects to enter college in January.

Do hope you are well and enjoy the holiday season.

Love,
Alice

Notes

Phillips Chronology
1941 - 1998

1942	William Charles McConahy died.
1943	Lydia Mabel McConahy Brown Dowds died.

William Charles McConahy died.

1945	Relief McConahy Hartung died.
1950s	The Highway Department bought the 20 acres on the north side of Route 50 expecting to turn it into four lanes. This did not happen.
1952	Heavy snows collapsed the buildings at Phillips Station.
1953	Heavy snows collapsed the hotel at Rubicon Springs.
1961	Vade post office was closed.
1962	Myrtle McConahy Keefer died in New Castle, PA.
1983	Alice Elaine Bryson Lyon died at Echo Summit, CA.
1994	Evelyn "Sally" Elaine Lyon Myers' son Rodney Lumley died.

Louise Sickles Day died.

1996	Evelyn "Sally" Elaine Lyon Myers died.
1998	Jane Brunello died.

Epilogue
A 2012 Return to Tahoe

After all our work on these letters, Mary Jo and I felt a deep connection to our ancestors who contributed their labor and love to a growing nation. We wondered how we could share this connection with the rest of our family. Mary Jo decided to rent a house at Lake Tahoe in the summer of 2012 and invited our family to experience firsthand the beauty of this area and our family's history. In the Phillips' spirit of connecting the east and west, she also invited two cousins from California whom we had never met before. We all got along famously.

The trip was "all things Phillips". We drove to Echo Summit and then on to Phillips Station, the resort run by Phillips women until 1952 when heavy snows collapsed the buildings. We took the road up to the state-run ski resort now known as Sierra at Tahoe, formerly known as Pow Wow. At Phillips Station, we admired the meadow, the original structures, and the historic marker. Then we drove to Camp Richardson, known as the "Grove" in the Phillips' time. This is where the Phillips picked up supplies for their resorts from the steamboats. There we lunched on the shores of Lake Tahoe. We visited Taylor Creek, one of Great Uncle Dan's favorite fishing spots, and then took McKinney Road to the top of the mountain to the Rubicon Trailhead and saw the historic marker for Vade Bryson's resort.

We drove to Donner Lake, where the Phillips women spent a winter, and to Truckee. Before venturing out each day, we would read the appropriate letters and stories.

We returned to Pennsylvania with a deeper understanding of our ancestors, how they contributed to the history of Northern California, and how they weathered life's challenges. Learning about them gave us a better understanding of who we are and a sense of connection to the past. One can only hope that those strong Phillips genes have come down to us.

Even in this digital age, the earliest books about America's pioneers are being reprinted and new ones are being written. It is good to know that there is continued interest in the personal accounts of the westward expansion of the United States. It's satisfying to know that our family's letters contribute to the historical record. We hope you enjoyed this glimpse into the experience of the Phillips pioneers. Perhaps it will inspire you to delve into your family's history where you might discover common themes and unexpected truths in the unique voices of your forebearers.

Mary K. Sonntag
2013

Appendix

Brief Biographical
Information and
Obituaries

Stephen Phillips
(1779-1862)

As written by Rebecca McConahy

Stephen Phillips, son of Elisha Phillips and Mary Meachem Phillips was born Friday, November 26, 1779. He probably came to Western Pennsylvania in 1813 and settled in Phillipsburg, now Monaca, where he engaged in the boat building business. Later he moved across the river (Ohio) and continued in the boat building business. He was drowned off the steamer Poe on the Ohio River at Wheeling, West Virginia on his passage home from Portsmouth, Ohio, November 17, 1855. His body was never recovered. He was married to Rhoda Parsons, who was born Friday, October 25, 1782, and died at Freedom, PA, March 1, 1862.

Amoret Phillips Henry
(1819- 1889)

As written by Rebecca McConahy

Amoret Phillips Henry, only child of Joseph Meachem Phillips and Relief Childs Phillips, was born in Vershire, Orange County, Vermont, February 25, 1819, at two o'clock A.M.

She moved with her parents to Moravia, Pennsylvania, in the year 1836. On June 1, 1837, she was married to John Henry of Mount Jackson, Pennsylvania. John Henry and his family moved to Illinois, and settled near Arcola about 1895.

John Henry was born June 1, 1816 and died March 11, 1881.

The following children were born to Amoret Phillips Henry and John Henry:

William C. Henry
Joseph Phillips Henry
Cyrus Clarke Henry
Luella Jane Henry
James Henry
Thomas Logan Henry
Annie Mary Henry
Eliza Relief (Lida) Henry
Maude Henry

Joseph Wells Davis Phillips
(1827-1889)

From *The History of El Dorado County*, California *(1883)*

Joseph Wells Davis Phillips was born in Orange County, Vermont on the 9th of February 1827, and is the oldest son of Joseph M. and Lydia Phillips. When about 9 years old, his parents removed to Pennsylvania and settled in Lawrence County. In May 1846 he left home and went to Nauvoo, Hancock County, Illinois, where he engaged in clerking for four years. He then purchased the business and conducted it for several years. On the 20th day of December, 1852 he took passage on the steamship Northern Light for California and arrived at San Francisco January 16, 1853. He went to Nevada City and began hotel keeping in a house known as the Keystown. In June 1855 he went to Shasta County and there kept a hotel at Horsetown. In September 1857 he returned east leaving his family in California, they soon joined him, and removed to Coles County, Illinois, in March of 1858. In the fall, same year, they returned again to California and kept a boarding house in Tuolumne County, on the 22d day of June, 1860 he came to El Dorado County and located on a ranch between Hope and Lake valleys, here he spent the summer and the winter at Placerville. In 1862 he opened the Phillip Station on the stage road and made it his permanent abode till 1869.

In 1873 he located his present home on section 4, Township 11, Range 10 and began improving it. In 1874 he was the independent candidate for the Assembly and beaten by a very trifling majority. In 1879 he was again beaten for the same place by a very small vote. His brother Daniel is a partner in the ranch; they have about 40 acres under cultivation, all very productive land. Mr. Phillips is one of the enterprising and industrious men of El Dorado County, he has been engaged in many mining ventures that were not successful, but never gave up. He was wedded to Miss Mehitable J. Ball at Quincy, Illinois, on the 22d day of September 1851. They have two children: Sierra Nevada, born at Nevada City, California, July 28, 1854, now Mrs. A. W. Clark of Glenbrook, Nevada, and Ida M., born at Williamsfield, Ashtabula County, Ohio, on the 19th of May, 1858, now Mrs. J. B. Meloche, of Glenbrook, Nevada. Mr. Phillips was Superintendent of the United States Mining Company near Nevada City, the first one to erect pumps in that vicinity. In 1876 his property in the mountains was destroyed by fire.

"Another Pioneer Gone"

From the **Mountain Democrat**, *Saturday, January 19, 1889*
J. W. D. Phillips died suddenly on Sunday morning last at his home near Johnstown, this county of heart disease.

Saturday evening he sat up until about 10 o'clock chatting and joking with the family as usual and when he retired seemed to feel as well, apparently, as ever. Sunday morning his wife was awakened by a groan and said, "What is the matter?" To this there was no reply and thinking that something was wrong, she hurriedly struck a light calling to him and then shaking him, but all to no purpose, life being then extinct. He had never complained of this terrible disease.

The remains were brought to Placerville on Tuesday for burial and were conducted to the grave by Palmyra Lodge No. 151 F&AM of which deceased was one of the oldest members. The services were held in the Episcopal Church, the Rev. C. C. Pierce officiating. He delivered a very impressive address.

The floral tributes were appropriate and beautiful having been brought from San Francisco for the occasion. A large gathering of friends and neighbors were present to pay their last respects to this much loved and honored citizen.

Joseph W. D. Phillips was born in Orange City, Vermont on the 9th of February 1827 and was the oldest son of Joseph M. and Lydia Phillips. When about 9 years old his parents removed to Pennsylvania and settled in Lawrence County where he received a common school education, as good as could be given him in those days. When about 19 years old, feeling that he could take the responsibility of life on his shoulders, he ventured out for new territory and landed in Nauvoo, Hancock County, Illinois and engaged in mercantile business, first at salary, but with economy and industry, he soon became proprietor.

After conducting this business for a while, he concluded that single life was too lonesome, so was married to Miss Mehitable J. Ball of Quincy, Illinois in the early part of 1851. In December of the same year he and his wife sailed on the steamship Northern Light for the new gold fields of California, via Nicaragua route, crossed the Isthmus on New Year's Day and landed in San Francisco on January, 16, 1852. They proceeded directly to Nevada City, Nevada County starting the Hotel Keystone. Mrs. Phillips managed the business while he was engaged in mining.

In 1852 he removed to Shasta County where he lived about two years, engaged in the same business. In 1857 he returned to the East but being accustomed to our way of life here he was not contented and returned to this coast in the fall of 1858. He settled in Tuolome County near Shaw's Flat. It was while living there that he witnessed the depredation of the celebrated desperados, Joaquin Murietta, 3-fingered Jack and their gang, he himself having lost quite a lot of stock through them. In

1860 he removed to El Dorado County where he has resided ever since.

Mr. Phillips was gifted with more than common ability although in all his ventures luck seemed to be against him. He was one of our most industrious and energetic citizens and the community will miss him in the time to come. In politics, he was a Republican, although he ran for the Assembly in 1870 as an independent candidate, being beaten by a small majority.

He leaves a wife and two daughters, Mrs. J. W. Doss (Ester's daughter) of Sonoma County and Mrs. A. W. Clark (Vade) of this county. Also, many friends and neighbors to mourn his sudden departure.

Mehitable Jane Phillips
(1816-1906)

"A Venerable Lady Gone to Rest"

From the **Mountain Democrat**, *Saturday, February 10, 1906*

Mrs. Mehitable Jane Phillips, a sunny souled old mother in Israel died at the Courtland Hotel in Sparks, Nevada Saturday, February 3, 1906 at 7 o'clock in the morning.

She was a native of Newark, New Jersey and came thence to Tuolomne County in this state in 1860 and thence to Placerville.

When Page was elected to Congress, her husband J. W. D. Phillips bought his residence. He died several years ago but the family has lived or had interests in the county from that to the present time. Notable among those were and are their winter and summer ranges at Garden Valley and Phillips Station in the mountains, the latter place being named for the family.

Mrs. Phillips was a wonderfully bright and intelligent woman. She would have been 90 years of age the 22nd of March of this year. Her 89th birthday was celebrated last year when some of her friends gave her a party, and she was the liveliest one in the crowd.

She leaves one devoted daughter, Mrs. Sierra Nevada Bryson, wife of James Bryson of Reno and several grandchildren – two daughters having died several years ago. Her funeral was conducted at Winchell's Undertaking Parlors by Reverend C. E. Webb, pastor of the M. E. Church, and a quartet composed of Mrs. S. B. Wilson, Miss Reynolds, A.S. Fox and Sm. Blake rendered appropriate music. It was attended by a large number of old friends and acquaintances, who cherish the memory of a good woman.

Death of Mrs. Phillips

Mrs. Mehitable Phillips, the mother of Mrs. Nevada Bryson, died at the Courtland hotel at 7 o'clock Saturday morning. Mrs. Phillips had attained the ripe age of 90 years and was a California pioneer, having come to that State with her husband in 1850. She settled at Placerville and resided at that place until three months ago when she came to Sparks to make her home with her only child, Mrs. Bryson.

The McPhail undertaking period has charge-of-the-remains which will be shipped to Placerville for interment in the Masonic cemetery beside those of her husband who preceded her by 17 years.

Sierra Nevada "Vade" Phillips Bryson
(1854-1921)

From the **Mountain Democrat,** *Saturday, May 28, 1921*

The sorrow felt by the relatives and friends of Mrs. Vade Bryson, whose death occurred last Saturday after an illness of a few weeks, will be far-reaching; for, though she had not gathered to herself a great wealth of earthly possessions, she was rich in friends. As the owner and manager for years of Phillips Station, one of the most beautiful State highway resorts in California, people from many States in the Union, and from every walk in life had partaken of her open-handed hospitality, and felt her kindly influence. Much of interest could be written about this good woman whose family were among the stalwarts of early days. Born in Nevada City on July 28, 1854, she was named Sierra Nevada for the mountains that have always spelled "home" for her.

She went to Phillips when six years of age, and she had often recalled the fact that in those days of horse teams the road was kept open throughout the years and there was never a lull in the travel to and from Virginia City. For a number of years she lived with her little family at Kelsey where she was postmistress. She managed a resort at Rubicon Springs for several years, and after the Tahoe road became a State highway she came into possession of Phillips Station through the death of her mother. Through the strain and stress of her busy life she never complained, but met every one with a joke and sent them away with a smile. If she had a fault in the world it was an over-generous heart. Her funeral last Tuesday, which, at her request, was conducted by the members of Fallen Leaf Chapter No. 90, O. E. S., was a touching tribute of love and sympathy. She was a member of Mountain Fern Chapter of Georgetown, several members of which were present. The Worthy Matron, Mrs. Erla Blair, assisted by George Roleri, Worthy Patron, and the Star Officers gave the solemn burial service of the order in an impressive manner and Rev. J. E. Burkhart gave a brief address alluding to the life that had closed, as one of "service for others." The Placerville Quartette sang, "The Lord is My Shepherd," "Lead, Kindly Light" and "No Night There" and at the cemetery, after she had been laid in a veritable bed of flowers, they sang:

> Good night, it is morning now
> Good night, I am going home
> I have kept the Faith
> I have done my work
> And the Master bids me come.

She is survived by her husband, James Bryson, two devoted daughters, Mrs. Hettie Sickles and Mrs. Henry Lyon, and five grandchildren, Wells, Louise and Elinor Sickles, and Betty and Jane Lyon, her uncle Dan Phillips, and a niece, Mrs. Gertrude Hulbert.

Those present from elsewhere were John Meloche, her brother-in-law, and Clarice Makinney, both of San Francisco, Mr. and Mrs. D. Hurlburt and Mr. and Mrs. George Dohrman of Stockton, John Doss and George Dondero of Petaluma, J. Murphy and wife and their daughter and son-in-law, Mr. and Mrs. Kipp of Folson. Also several from Georgetown and Auburn.

Probate
Sierra Nevada Bryson

May 25, 1921
No. 1479

Estate includes real & personal property to a value of more than $10,000 including hotel or summer resort known as Phillips situated on Lake Tahoe Road at a distance of about 48 miles.

... lists husband James Bryson, age about 50, living in Williams, Colusa County, CA. ... lists daughters Mehitable J. Sickles, age 41 and Alice Lyon, age 21, both living in Placerville.

Descry. 320 acres of land together with hotel building, cottages, and other improvements, also furniture, bedding, tents and hotel furnishings and equipment, also 2 horses, wagons, harness and divers other personal property...

Includes inventory from Placerville Hardware for hotel – also numerous other billings from local stores and suppliers.

From El Dorado Republican, Friday, May 27, 1921 – page 1.
Sierra Nevada Bryson Estate – Mehitable E. Sickles has applied for letters of administration in the estate of her mother ...

James Bryson
(1876-1935)

From the **Mountain Democrat,** *January 3, 1935*
James Bryson, 59, father of Mrs. Henry S. Lyon and stepfather of Mrs. Hettie J. Sickles died Sunday at Visalia of

injuries received when the automobile in which he was riding skidded on wet pavement and overturned.

The funeral services were held on Wednesday morning from St. Patrick's Church in this city, the Rev. father T. J. Hayes officiating. Burial was in Union Cemetery.

Mr. Bryson had been for several years employed in a position of responsibility with the State Highway Department. Married a second time about a month ago, he was riding in a car with his wife and relatives at the time of the fatal crash. Mrs. Bryson and the others in the party were injured.

Born in Londonderry, Ireland, fifty-nine years ago, Mr. Bryson came to this country when but 15 years of age. As a young man he worked in various mines in this country and was later engaged in the operation of the resort known as Phillips Station. His wife, Mrs. Vade Clark Bryson passed away in May of 1921 and Mr. Bryson remarried only a month ago.

Mr. Bryson is survived by a daughter, Mrs. Alice Lyon, a step-daughter, Mrs. Hettie Sickles and 6 grandchildren; Betty, Jane & Evelyn Lyon and Louise Wells & Elinor Sickles in addition to his widow, Mrs. Belle Bryson.

Alice Elaine Lyon
(1899-1983)

From the Mountain Democrat

We had to sacrifice looks for strength at Phillips Station. There's nothing fancy or frilly here because everything was built to stay, even me I think sometimes.

—Alice Elanie Lyon,
1975

After living the entire 84 years of her life in El Dorado County, Alice Elaine Lyon is gone, but the history that she and her family brought to Echo Summit and the surrounding area lives on.

Mrs. Lyon died Friday of a heart attack. Funeral services will be held Tuesday at 2 p.m. in the Memory Chapel in Placerville.

Daughter of the late Sierra Nevada Phillips and wife of the late Henry Lyon, former El Dorado County District Attorney, Mrs. Lyon is survived by her daughters, Jane Brunello and Sally Lumley, both of Placerville; her grandchildren, Bonnie Caudillo of Santa Rosa, Richard Clark of Echo Summit, and Jim Brunelllo, Patti Bedient, Rod Lumley and Carol Pearson, all of Placerville; and seven great grandchildren.

"Alice was a very special person," said Del Laine, past president of the Lake Tahoe Historical Society, an organization in which Mrs. Lyon took an active part. "She was more than just a pioneer, she was the spirit of the area."

"People never thought of her in terms of years, she was ageless," Mrs. Laine said. "People thought of her in terms of presence. She was total openness that emulated what the mountains are all about."

"She touched us all in a good way and she will be missed very much," said June De Paepe, a friend of Mrs. Lyons's for more than 40 years. "She was the lady of the mountains."
Bobby Sprock, owner of Sierra Ski Ranch, said Mrs. Lyon was known for her friendliness.

"She liked to talk to everybody and tell tales of the early days here," Mrs. Sprock said. "She was a pioneer of the mountain, a true original. She was the type of person people in the mountains went to see. She was queen of it all here."

Mrs. Lyon's family owned the original Phillips Resort, built in 1863 by Mrs. Lyon's grandfather, J. W. D. Phillips. The 2 ½ story hotel was at first used mostly by people en route to the Comstock Lode in Virginia City, Nevada.

When traffic to the mines ebbed, the station was turned into a resort and operated during the summer. The second station burned in 1910 and heavy snows of the winter of 1951-52 resulted in the final collapse of the major structures.

Mrs. Lyon's mother also ran the Rubicon Mineral Springs Hotel and Resort on the west shore of Lake Tahoe. In 1908, the family returned to the summit and rebuilt the 50year-old station that had fallen into a state of disrepair.

Over the years, Phillips Station flourished and was known from coast to coast, catering to the likes of former U.S. Secretary of State Frank Jordan and former U.S. Defense Secretary Robert McNamara.

Phillips Station continued to operate until the Depression. It closed in 1929 and the operation was converted into housekeeping of summer cabins. The store was sold and the big winter of 1951-52 took care of the rest. In the late 1950's the cabins were sold to the state for the highway right-of-way.

Alice Elaine Lyon
(1899-1983)

From The Sacramento Bee, *Thursday, November 3, 1983*
Services for Alice Elaine Lyon, a native of Placerville who was considered an authority on early day life and times in the Sierra, have been held in Memory Chapel.

Mrs. Lyon, widow of former El Dorado County District Attorney Henry Lyon, died Friday at a South Lake Tahoe hospital. She was 84.

For the past several years, Mrs. Lyon had lived in a log cabin off Highway 50 near Echo Summit in an area that was homesteaded by her grandfather, J. D. Phillips, who had come to California in 1851.

She and her sister had operated Phillips Station, which, for more than 60 years, served as a summer resort hotel for scores of Sacramento area residents traveling to the Sierra area. The station was a portion of the land originally developed by Mrs. Lyon's grandfather.

Mrs. Lyon was a member of the Native Daughters of the Golden West, Placerville chapter, and a charter member of the Placerville Shakespeare Club.

She is survived by daughters, Sally Lumley and Jane Brunello, both of Placerville; six grandchildren and six great-grandchildren.

The family requests that any remembrances be sent to James Marshall Hospital in Placerville or the American Heart Association.

Alice E. Lyon

From the **El Dorado News,** *Monday, October 31, 1983*
Service for Alice Elaine Lyon, 84, of Placerville will be at 2 p.m. Tuesday at Memory Chapel. The Reverend Don Herman of the Lutheran Church will officiate. Burial will be in Placerville Union Cemetery.

Mrs. Lyon, the widow of former El Dorado County District Attorney Henry Lyon, died Oct. 28 at a South Lake Tahoe Hospital.

Born in Placerville, Mrs. Lyon lived most of her life there. For the last five years she lived near Echo Summit.

She was a member of the Native Daughter of the Golden West Parlor No. 9 of Placerville and a charter member of the Placerville Shakespeare Club.

Mrs. Lyon is survived by daughters Sally Lumley and Jane Brunello, both of Placerville; a niece Louise Day of Marin County; six grandchildren; and six great-grandchildren.

Evelyn 'Sally' Elaine Meyers (1927 – 1996)

From the Logbook

Evelyn "Sally" Elaine Meyers, 66, died December 31 at her home in Placerville. She was a native of Placerville, coming from a pioneer family. Her father, Henry S. Lyon, was born in Smith Flat and was district attorney of El Dorado County for more than 25 years. Her mother, Alice Lyon was born in Placerville and her great-uncle founded Philips Resort on Highway 50 in 1856. The property still remains with the family.

Mrs. Meyers worked as a legal secretary all her life, working first with her father, then with Daryl McKinstry when he was county counsel. Eventually she went to work in private practice. She was a charter member of the Legal Secretaries Association, a member of the Episcopal Church and Daughters of the Nile. Her hobbies were her garden, her cabin and her family and friends.

Mrs. Meyers is survived by her husband, Wallace Meyers; daughter Carol Pearson; sister Jane Brunello; stepsons Steve Shortes and Daryl Meyers; two nieces and one nephew; and six grandchildren. She was preceded in death by her first husband, Ray Lumley and son, Rodney Lumley.

Services for Mrs. Meyers will be held at 1 p.m. Saturday, January 6 at the Episcopal Church of Our Savior, followed by a gathering at the home of her daughter, Carol Pearson. Arrangements are being made by Chapel of the Pines Funeral Home.

Charles Carroll Phillips
(1829 – 1899)

As written by Rebecca McConahy

Charles Carroll Phillips was born Thursday morning, July 30, 1829, at 11 o'clock, in Orange County, Vermont. He moved with his parents to Western Pennsylvania, in 1836, and settled on a farm in Taylor Township, then Beaver County, but now Lawrence County, near Moravia, at "Hardscrabble Dam," so named because the canal boats had difficulty getting over the riffle in the river at that place.

During the gold excitement in California, he was out in that state at two different times. He was married to Elizabeth Lutton, a daughter of Jacob Lutton and Ruth Hennon Lutton, of Shenango Township, Lawrence County, Pennsylvania, May 16, 1854. About 1867, he and his family went to Illinois, where he remained until he fall of 1874, when he left Illinois for Kansas, and located in the neighborhood of Wichita, and later went to Colorado, where he engaged in the mining business prior to his death, which occurred at Victor, Colorado, April 1, 1899.

"Charles Phillips was a famous debater, a natural orator, and well versed in literature and science. People came for miles when it was known that Phillips was to debate with someone worthy of his steel, during the days of the East Moravia Literary Society in 1866 and 1867."

From the New Castle News

Elizabeth Lutton Phillips, wife of Charles Carroll Phillips, was born in Shenango Township, Lawrence County, Pennsylvania, February 20, 1834, and died at Denver, Colorado, March 24, 1928.

The following children were born to Charles Carroll Phillips and Elizabeth Lutton Phillips: Relief, Joseph, Audley, William, Bessie, Mary, Charley, George, Evra

Charles Carroll Phillips
Dead in the West a Talented Former Resident of Taylor Township Passes Away*

*[Ed. note: source unknown]

Word has been received by friends in this county of the death of Charles C. Phillips, a former resident of this county, at Victor Colorado, on April 1st, 1899. Mr. Phillips was born and raised on the old Phillips farm at Hardscrabble Dame in Taylor Township, this county and was a man of marked ability in many respects.

During the gold excitement in California, he was out in that state at two different times for several years. In 1869 he left Moravia for Illinois and has resided in Illinois and other western states from that until the time of his death. In 1867-68 he was a leading member in the old East Moravia Literary society, which comprised among its members, Henry Edwards, Thomas Burton, Jennie Burton Joseph Morrehead, lately deceased, Joseph H. McConahy, J. Wylie Forbes, Stephen Robinson and John G. McConahy of this city.

Mr. Phillips was a famous debater, a natural orator and well versed in literature and science. John Q. Stewart and Thomas M. Steward occasionally appeared in this society as debaters and others from different parts of the county who were noted at this time as debaters, took part in the exercises of this old literary society.

People came for miles when it was known that Phillips was on for debate with some persons worthy of his steel, to hear him speak. He was married to a daughter of Jacob Lutton, who was a brother of the late Wm. B. Lutton, and brother of Mrs. Mary McConahy of Ellwood City and a brother-in-law of the late Cyrus P. Fields, of Little Beaver Township. He was an enthusiastic member of the Methodist Church and his little speeches in the old Methodist church at Moravia, giving his experience while prospecting in the mountains of California wherein he would picture the glory of the Creator were a masterpiece of eloquence.

His old friends in Lawrence County will hear the news of his death with sadness. He was of a restless disposition, not content to stay long in one place, and away from friends and the home of his childhood, his remains will be laid to rest, but his memory will long be cherished by those who knew him best.

"'Tis said it matters but little
When earth again mingles with earth;
We can die in the land of the stranger
As well as the land of our birth."

Former Citizen Charles C. Phillips
Died at His Home in Colorado Recently*

*[Ed. note: source unknown]

Word has been received in this city announcing the death of Mr. Charles C. Phillips at Victor, Colorado on last Saturday. Mr. Phillips was born and reared near Moravia, this county, and will be remembered by the speakers in this part of the country. He belonged to a Literary organization which met at Moravia, just after the close of the war and of which such men as John G. McConahy, Thomas Stewart, Hon. John Q. A. Stewart, Thomas Burton, John Wiley Forbes, Steven Robinson and Hon. Henry Edwards were members. When it was known that Mr. Phillips was to debate people came for miles to hear him. During the early gold excitement in California he went to Colorado and has lived there ever since. He was married to a daughter of Jacob Lutton, and he was a brother of Mrs. Mary McConahy, of Ellwood City. Mr. Phillips was a man of wonderful natural talent and a most forceful speaker. He was 70 years of age.

Lydia Maria Phillips Pollock
(1831 – 1903)

As written by Rebecca McConahy

Lydia Maria Phillips, daughter of Joseph M. Phillips and Lydia Davis Phillips, was born at Vershire, Orange County, Vermont, Saturday, June 28, 1831. In the autumn of 1836, she came to Western Pennsylvania, and settled on a farm that her parents purchased near East Moravia (now West Pittsburgh). She lived there until her marriage October 31, 1850, to James Harvey Pollock. After her marriage she lived at Enon Valley where her husband conducted a general store. In 1863 the family moved to Illinois, and finally located at Foosland, where the Pollocks were the parents of seven sons and one daughter, the youngest being the daughter. Two of the boys, Robert and Milton, were doctors and Samuel was a dentist. Robert practiced medicine in Rocky Ford, Colorado and Milton in Decatur, Illinois, and Samuel, the dentist, practiced in Rocky Ford, Colorado.

The following children were born to Lydia and James Pollock:

David Wells Pollack
Joseph Phillips Pollack
Samuel Pollack
Robert Martin Pollack
Charles Pollack
Milton DeWitt Pollack
Grant Pollack
Emma Pollack

Mrs. Lydia Maria Pollock Passes Away at Advanced Age*

*[Ed. note: source unknown]

Mrs. Lydia Maria Pollock, a former resident of Lawrence County, is dead at Foosland, Illinois at the residence of her son, D. W. Pollock. She was 72 years of age. Many people in New Castle and Lawrence County will be grieved to learn of her demise.

Mrs. Pollock was the daughter of Joseph and Lydia Phillips. She was born in Vershire, VT on June 25, 1831. In the autumn of 1849 the family removed to Moravia, this city. There the daughter met and married James H. Pollock, a member of one of the county's oldest families. Mr. and Mrs. Pollock lived for 18 years at Enon Valley, where the husband conducted a store. Thirty five years ago Mrs. Pollock went west, and had ever since resided there. Her death was caused by heart failure.

The departed lady is survived by eight children – seven sons and a daughter.[Ed. note: For an accurate listing of the children's names, see p. 416.] The sons are Dr. R. W. Pollock, Dr. Samuel Pollock and Joseph of Rocky Ford, Colorado. Col. D. W. Pollock of Decatur, Illinois and M. W. and G. Pollock of Foosland. Mrs. Pollock is survived by a sister and by a brother – Mrs. Mary McConahy of Ellwood City, and D. D. Phillips of Tahoe City, CA.

Mrs. Pollock was a lady of beautiful Christian character, her life being a showing forth of the virtues of her religion. She was an earnest and faithful member of the Methodist Church and will be remembered for her many acts of kindness.

Relief Phillips Fields
(1833 – 1881)

As written by Rebecca McConahy

Relief was born in Orange County, Vermont in 1833 and married Cyrus P. Fields. She died near Enon Valley PA January 21, 1881.

Relief and Cyrus had the following children:

Ira Phillips Fields
Mary Louisa Fields
Joseph Cyrus Fields

[Ed. note: For an accurate listing of the children's names, see p. 37.]

Died at her home near Enon, PA Jan. 21, 1881. Mrs. Relief, beloved wife of Cyrus P. Fields, Esq., in the 48th year of her age.

This beloved sister in Christ was called away from earth very suddenly. On Sabbath, Jan. 16th, she was at the Lord's table, although even then suffering from the first approaches of the disease which so swiftly carried her out of life. She was exceedingly faithful in the discharge of all her duties as wife and mother and as a member of the church, specially loved. A grief-stricken neighborhood and church fully attested their appreciation of her modest and genuine worth by the intense and tearful sympathy shown on the day of her burial. A sorely bereaved husband, in whose home she was, in a very empathic sense, the central column, is left to mourn the great loss which came upon him so unexpectedly with the dawn of that dark day of sadness. When he suddenly became convinced she was about to depart …….he was enabled to pray most feverently, "Jesus, take her spirit," and we doubted not that prayer had been answered when we saw the smile that yet lighted up the countenance of that white-faced sleeper, as though the soul yet lingered for a little to light up the palace it had so long inhabited. A sweet little girl of twelve Summers, with much of her mother's spirit, trying now to make a desolate home seem brighter, will have the blessing of her mother's god to rest upon her and the dear boys, bereft of a mother's love just at the time when they most needed its restraining and controlling and moulding influence, will, we earnestly hope, live worthy of such a mother and such a love.

Henry Phillips
(1835-1836)

As written by Rebecca McConahy

Henry Phillips was born April 1, 1835, on Tuesday, p.m. at two o'clock. He died March 26, 1836, on Saturday, aged eleven months, twenty-six days.

Alden Church Phillips
(1837-1869)

As written by Rebecca McConahy

Alden Church Phillips was born August 26, 1837, at East Moravia, Pennsylvania (now West Pittsburgh). When he was a young man he went to California, where his brother, Wells, was living. On May 5, 1869, he was thrown from a horse and injured, and died from the effects of the injury September 15, 1869, aged 32 years. He was buried on a knoll where there were a dozen other graves, about 200 yards from Lake Tahoe, CA near the hotel known as "Lake House."

Daniel Davis Phillips
(1839 – 1933)

As written by Rebecca McConahy

Daniel Davis Phillips was born in East Moravia (now West Pittsburgh, Lawrence County), Pennsylvania, July 25, 1839, where he resided until about the year 1868, at which time he went to Illinois, and later joined his brother, Wells in California, where he resided until his death February 2, 1933. The following clipping was taken from one of the papers at Placerville, California.

Phillips Obsequies Are Held on Sunday
Early-Day Resort Operator
Called to Final Rest Thursday Night

From the **Mountain News,** *Placerville, Cal.**

"Funeral services were held Sunday afternoon from the Federated Church for Daniel Phillips, 93, who died last Thursday night at the home of District Attorney and Mrs. Henry S. Lyon, with whom he had made his home for many years."

"The funeral services were conducted by the Rev. Charles W. Null, and burial was in the family plot in Union Cemetery."

"Mr. Phillips had been associated with his brother in the resort business at Rubicon, Glenbrook, and at Phillips Station. This last named place founded by the brother of Daniel Phillips, but since Daniel outlived his brother, and continued to spend his summers at the resort, the popular impression got about that Daniel Phillips was the founder of the resort."

"A native of Pennsylvania, Mr. Phillips was born July 25, 1839, on the site of what is now West Pittsburgh. He came to California forty years later, and had lived in this county continuously since that time, except for a period of about a year, which he spent in Oregon in the early 1880's."

"Until about fifteen years ago, he lived at Garden Valley, spending the winter there mining and ranching and going to the mountains each succeeding summer to assist in the resort business."

"For many years past, owing to infirmities brought about by advancing age, Mr. Phillips had retired from active life. He had made his home during the winter with Mr. and Mrs. Lyon, and each summer had moved to Phillips Station, where he was affectionately known to a large number of summer visitors as "Uncle Dan.""

"During his last years, "Uncle Dan" had been cared for by his two grand nieces, Mrs. Lyon and Mrs. Mehitable Sickles, each of whom endeavored to leave nothing undone to insure his comfort and well-being."

"He is survived by four nieces and one nephew living in the east, a grand niece, Mrs. Dan Hurlburt, of Fresno; and Mrs. Sickles and Mrs. Lyons, and five great grand-nieces and one great-grand nephew."

Mary Phillips McConahy
(1846 – 1932)

As written by Rebecca McConahy

Mary Phillips, youngest child of Joseph Meachem Phillips and Lydia Davis Phillips, was born February 13, 1846, on Friday, at the home of her parents near East Moravia, (now West Pittsburgh, Lawrence County) Pennsylvania. She spent all her young life on this farm, which was located along the Beaver River, near what was then called "Hard Scrabble," so called because the canal boats had so much trouble in getting over the riffle in the Beaver River at that place. She obtained her education in the public schools near her home, part of the time going to the "Conner" school, and sometimes attending the "Pleasant Hill" school, which was quite a distance from her home. She was the youngest of a large family, her parents coming to Western Pennsylvania, from Orange County, Vermont, in 1836. Her brother just older, Daniel Davis Phillips, was seven years her senior.

About 1868 the home farm was sold, and she and her mother and brother Daniel, went to Illinois, and settled near Ashkum, Illinois, where they lived until 1870, when they were forced to return to Pennsylvania on account of her mother's health. This was a new country and many people suffered from ague, and her mother was not able to overcome the effects of it. Other members of the family preceded them to Illinois, being C.C. Phillips and Lydia Maria Phillips Pollock and family. After returning to Pennsylvania, Mary's mother, Lydia, died at the home of her daughter, Mrs. Relief Fields, on September 1, 1870, near Enon Valley. Lydia was buried on the old home farm at the side of her husband, Joseph M. Phillips.

After the death of her mother, Mary Phillips, resided with her sister, Mrs. Relief Fields, until January 1872, when she took a trip to Vermont to visit her relatives there. Mary remained in Vermont until May 1872 when she returned to Moravia, Pennsylvania and married Joseph Hennon McConahy, on June 11, 1872. A double wedding ceremony was performed at the McConahy home, as a sister of Joseph H. McConahy, Belle McConahy, was married to Martin Ritchie at the same time.

After her marriage in 1872, she resided at Moravia, on the East side of the river, where she remained until about 1880, when she and her family moved to the old "McConahy" homestead on the West side of the river where she lived until about 1885. Then she moved to the village of Moravia, where her husband, Joseph H. McConahy, conducted a general store and was postmaster. Most of her married life she lived in and about Moravia until 1894, when she moved with her family to Ellwood City, where she resided until her death, May 7, 1932. Her husband, Joseph Hennon McConahy, died November 21, 1895. After moving to Ellwood City, Mary Phillips McConahy made several trips to California to visit her brother and other friends living there.

The following children were born to Mary Phillips McConahy and Joseph Hennon McConahy:

Lydia Mable McConahy (b) April 2, 1873, (d) May 4, 1943

Rebecca McConahy (b) January 29, 1874, (d) September 8, 1939

William Charles McConahy (b) October 11, 1876, (d) March 13, 1943

Relief McConahy (b) June 23, 1879, (d) May 8, 1945

Wells Phillips McConahy (b) July 1, 1883, disappeared in California 1900. He was never found.

Mary Myrtle McConahy (b) June 25, 1886, (d) March 24, 1962

Joseph H. McConahy*
(1834–1895)
(Mary Phillips McConahy's husband)

*[Ed. note: source unknown]

Joseph H. McConahy, the well-known court attaché, was severely injured by a horse in charge of a careless driver on Pittsburgh Street Wednesday evening of last week. Mr. McConahy was crossing the street near the Union Station when he was knocked down by the animal, which had become frightened at a railroad train. The infuriated beast after knocking the man down dashed over his prostrate body, leaving him with several severe cuts and bruises. Mr. McConahy was picked up and carried into the Pierce House where his wounds were examined and dressed by a physician. They consisted of a large gash over the eye and several bruises on his body. The injured man, although very sore, is able to get about again.

WILL LIKELY DIE

Tipstave Mr. Joseph McConahy's Condition Very Serious
The Effects of the Accident He Met with in New Castle
Will Likely Kill Him –
Was Unconscious Sunday morning*

*[Ed. note: source unknown]

Readers of the "Courant" will remember that a week ago last Wednesday Tip-Stave Joseph McConahy, while coming across from the courthouse in the evening met with a serious accident. He was crossing the street to go to the Hotel Pierce, when a runaway horse attached to a buggy ran into him, and he was knocked down. The shaft struck him on the side and his head came in contact with the pavement. He was picked up and taken into the hotel and in a day or two was taken to his home in Ellwood. He was getting along nicely until Sunday morning when he became unable to speak and since then he has become unconscious. A New Castle physician called to see him Sunday afternoon. It is feared that the inner lining of the brain is fractured and unless he shows marked improvement within a few hours, it will be necessary to trepan the skull to relieve the pressure on the brain. His condition is very serious and it is feared that he cannot recover. Mr. McConahy is well known all over Lawrence County. He was a graduate of the Washington-Jefferson College and has been in attendance at all the Democratic conventions for years. His friends earnestly hope that he will pull through, but the case is considered extremely serious.

Joseph H. McConahy, a tipstaff at our courts and a well known and prominent resident of the county, died at his home in Ellwood City about 2 o'clock Thursday afternoon. He was the son of the late William McConahy and was born on the homestead farm just across the river from Newport. Mr. McConahy, about a month ago, was knocked down by a team of horses on Pittsburgh Street and was seriously injured by the horse's hoofs and the vehicle attached to them. For a few days it was thought that he would recover and he was taken to his home. A short time after his arrival at home he grew worse and became unconscious. He remained in this condition until death came. Deceased was member of the Moravia Presbyterian Church and was among the foremost workers in the congregation. All his ways in life were honorable and just and he died respected by all his large number of acquaintances. He was united in marriage with Miss Mary Phillips, who still survives, as do their six children. The latter are: Lydia, Relief, Rebecca, Myrtle, Wells, and William, who all reside with their parents in Ellwood. They have the sincerest sympathy of the whole community. Deceased was a brother of Mrs. S. W. Smith of this city and a cousin of Albert and Thomas McConahy of Wayne Township and John G. McConahy, Esquire of this city. The funeral services were held Sunday and were largely attended. Interment was made in the cemetery at Slippery Rock Church.

As was stated briefly in the "Courant" of Thursday, Joseph H. McConahy died at his home in Ellwood City, this county, that afternoon at 2 o'clock.

It will be remembered by the readers of the "Courant" that about four weeks ago while on his way from the court house in this city to the Hotel Pierce, he was struck by a runaway horse and thrown to the ground, sustaining injuries which at first were not considered of a very serious nature, but which developed into alarming symptoms. He became unconscious about two weeks after the incident and gradually sank until death came to his relief. It is now thought that the inner lining of the brain was broken and this was the cause of death. He was unconscious the greater part of the time for the last two weeks and it was seen that he could not get well. Mr. McConahy was born at what is known as Hard Scrabble in Taylor Township and at the time of his death was 61 years of age. When a young man, he graduated with high honors from the Washington and Jefferson College in Washington, this state, and for some time followed the profession of schoolteacher. He was twice a teacher in California and had seen much of the United States when he was a young man. When the war broke out, he was teaching in a Lexington, Kentucky academy, but his strong love of the union and the north, made him bitter enemies in that southern state and he was obliged like many other northern people to leave the state. The last few years of his life, he was a merchant and had a general store at Moravia, and was at one time the postmaster of that place. A year or two ago he was appointed a court tip staff and held that position until the time of his death. He was an honest, good citizen and had many friends all over the county. He was a lifelong Democrat, and several times was nominated by that party for high county offices, but owing to the great majority of the opposition did not succeed in the election. In 1872 he was united in marriage to Mary Phillips, and she with four daughters and two sons are left to mourn the kindest of husbands and the best of fathers. He was a member of the Moravia Presbyterian Church and as such he did all that he could in the work of the church. He was conscientious, kind, courteous and gentlemanly and although he never did any great thing in this world, still he did the best he could. He was the son of William McConahy, long since deceased, and had an immense connection all over the county. Few men were better known than the deceased, for there were few Democratic conventions or gatherings in that county that he was not present.

His funeral took place on Saturday afternoon, and in spite of the inclement weather, was largely attended. Rev. J. C. Gourley conducted services at the residence and at the Presbyterian church, of which the deceased was a member. Interment at Slippery Rock Cemetery. The immediate survivors of the deceased are his wife, two sons and four daughters.

Relief McConahy Hartung*
(1879 – 1945)

*[Ed. note: source unknown]

Wedding Bells Ring
Wily Cupid Invades the Sanctum of the Eagle and Motor
and Makes Captive the Senior Member of the Firm*

Yesterday at high noon, at the residence of the bride's mother, Miss Relief Vivian McConahy became the bride of S. Albert Hartung, the Rev. W. H. Leslie performing the ceremony in the presence of the immediate families of the contracting parties and a few invited friends.

Immediately at the close of the ceremony the party sat down to a bountiful wedding dinner, to which ample justice was done by all.

Mr. and Mrs. Hartung left on the 5:09 train for Cleveland, Niagara Falls and other eastern points, and will be absent about two weeks. The bride and groom were accompanied to the train by a merry party of friends who started them upon their way with showers of rice and the traditional old shoes.

The guests present were the mother and sisters of the bride; Mr. and Mrs. Hartung, father and mother of the groom; also a brother and sister and a niece from Beaver Falls; Misses Matilda and Margaret Morrow, of Moravia; Mrs. Martin Ritchie, of New Castle; Mr. and Mrs. Fred Cowden, of Mt. Ayr; Mr. and Mrs. John Hogue and children; Miss Florence Martin; Miss Bessie Poister and Mr. and Mrs. M. D. McMahan.

Lydia McConahy Brown*
(1873 –1943)

*[Ed. note: source unknown]

Mr. Ralph Brown, a young mail carrier, of Swissvale, near Pittsburgh, and Miss Lydia McConahy, of Ellwood City, will be united in marriage Wednesday evening at 9o'clock at the home of the bride's mother, on Fountain Avenue, Ellwood, by Rev. Bell, of the Slippery Rock Presbyterian Church. It will be a quiet home affair, only a few friends and the families being present. Miss McConahy for the past five years has been at the Bell telephone central at Ellwood City, and previous to that time was connected with the postal department of that place as clerk. The couple will reside at Swissvale.

MARRIED*
McConahy – Brown

*[Ed. note: source unknown]

A quiet home wedding united the lives of Miss Lydia McConahy, of this cit-, and Mr. Ralph Brown, of Swissvale, at the home of the bride on Wednesday evening at eight o'clock. Rev. Charles Bell, of the Slippery Rock Presbyterian Church officiated.

Only the relatives and a few invited guests witnessed the ceremony after which an inviting wedding supper was partaken of.

The bride is a daughter of Mrs. Mary P. McConahy and has been employed as day operator at the Bell Telephone office for the past four years in which capacity she made many friends. The groom is a son of Mr. and Mrs. J. M. Brown, of this city, and is employed as mail carrier at Swissvale, Pa.

Mr. and Mrs. Brown will reside in Swissvale.

Their many friends extend congratulations.

Ralph Brown
(?- 1914)

Former Local Man Dies in California
Ellwood City, March 14, 1914*

*[Ed. note: source unknown]

Ralph Brown, for many years a resident of this place where he was employed at the Baker Forge company, and later a letter carrier at Frisco, died at his home in Bakersfield, Cal., Tuesday from hemorrhage. Death came after an illness of several years and it was partly because of the illness that Brown moved to California. He is survived by his wife and son Cecil, aged 8 years. His father, J. F. Brown of California also survives him as does the following brothers and sisters: Nellie of Mercer, Joseph Brown of Mt. Pleasant, Arthur Brown and Hazel DeWitt Brown of Florida.

Funeral services were held yesterday and interment was made in Bakersfield. Mrs. Brown is also well known here having been Miss Lydia McConahy of this city before her marriage.

Bibliography

The Saga of Lake Tahoe
E. B. Scott
Sierra-Tahoe Publishing Co.
2525 West 10th Street
Antioch, CA 94509
Copyright 1957, renewed March 1985
Reprinted 2000

*Along the Georgetown Divide: A Collection of Stories and
Reminiscences about the Famed Georgetown Divide*
Georgia Gardner
Published privately by Georgia Gardner
1993

Jeepers Jamboree, The First Years...
Compiled & Arranged by Bud & Peg Presba
Rubicon River Enterprises, Inc.
First Edition, 1983

Women of the Sierra
Anne Seagraves
Wesanne Publications (July 1990)

About the Authors

Mary K. Sonntag was born in New Castle, PA and currently lives in Lansdale, PA. She met her husband, Tom, on a blind date and they were married for 51 years. She has four children and five grandchildren. Aside from her interest in family history, she enjoys reading, needlework, and the out-of-doors. She is an avid Pittsburgh Steelers fan.

Throughout her life, Mary has stayed connected to her family and friends though letters. So, it's no surprise that her family's letters were of great interest to her. Compiling these letters, conducting the research, and writing this book was a 15-year labor of love. Her friends always told her she should write a book and lo and behold she has!

Mary Jo Sonntag was born to wander just like her ancestors. Her spirit of adventure was ignited when she was 16 and spent the summer studying French in Switzerland. Since then, she has traveled the world. An avid storyteller, Mary Jo delights friends and family with stories of her adventures. She also enjoys hiking, biking, gardening and cooking.

Mary Jo lives in Pittsburgh, PA and holds degrees from Seton Hill University and The Pennsylvania State University. In her professional life, she coaches leaders worldwide to successfully execute their roles and achieve their potential.

WA